T. S. BAYER (1694-1738)

Scandinavian Institute of Asian Studies
Monograph Series

China:

No. 16 Trygve Lötveit: Chinese Communism, 1931-1934
        Sources for the understanding of contemporary China

No. 21 Robert Tung: Proscribed Chinese Writing
        A textbook for students of the modern Chinese language

No. 38 Hans J. Hinrup: An Index to *Chinese Literature* 1951-1976
        Alphabetical and subject indexes to this Chinese Journal

No. 42 N.H. Leon: Character Indexes of Modern Chinese
        Reflecting recent developments of the Chinese language

No. 43 Göran Aijmer: Economic Man in Sha Tin
        Chinese immigrant gardeners in a Hong Kong valley

No. 45 Christoph Harbsmeier: Aspects of Classical Chinese Syntax
        The basic problems of classical Chinese grammar

No. 50 S.A.M. Adshead: Province and Politics in late Imperial China
        Viceregal government in Szechwan, 1898-1911

No. 52 Donald B. Wagner: Dabieshan
        Traditional Chinese iron-production techniques

SCANDINAVIAN INSTITUTE OF ASIAN STUDIES
MONOGRAPH SERIES   NO. 54

T. S. Bayer (1694-1738)

Pioneer Sinologist

Knud Lundbæk

聖

Curzon Press

Scandinavian Institute of Asian Studies
Kejsergade 2, DK-1155 Copenhagen K

First published 1986

Curzon Press Ltd : London and Malmö

© Knud Lundbæk 1986

ISBN 0 7007 0189 3
ISSN 0069 1712

Printed by Narayana Press, Gylling, DK-8300 Odder, Denmark

To
TUA

Published with the support of the
Danish Research Council for the Humanities

CONTENTS

Acknowledgements	x
Abbreviations	xi
Foreword	xii
Three Words about the Chinese Characters	xiii

1. INTRODUCTION	1
Jesuit Sinology	2
The Orientalists	3
The Primordial or Perfect Language	4
T. S. Bayer, Pioneer Sinologist	4
Bayer's Latin Style	6

PART I
BAYER'S LIFE

2. PRUSSIAN YEARS	11
The Setting	11
Königsberg	12
The Young Bayer	12
3. RUSSIAN YEARS	16
The Setting	16
St Petersburg	16
The Academy of Sciences	16
Bayer the Academician	18

PART II
FIRST CHINESE STUDIES

4. *DE ECLIPSI SINICA*	31
5. *MUSEUM SINICUM*	39
The Preface	39
Bayer's History of Sinology	39
Last Part of the Preface	97
6. THE CHINESE LANGUAGE	102
Sources of Inspiration	102
The Materials	109
The Origin of the Chinese Script	111
The Nature of the Chinese Characters	115
The Dictionary	118
The Grammar	126
On the Chin Ceu (Zhangzhou) Dialect	129

The Chrestomathy	130
The Life of Confucius	131
The Great Learning	132
Xiao Er Lun	134
Addendum on Time, Weights and Measures	140

PART III
AFTER THE *MUSEUM SINICUM*

Preliminary	151
7. CORRESPONDENCE WITH THE PEKING JESUITS	154
8. *DE HORIS SINICIS*	171
9. ARTICLES IN THE *COMMENTARII* OF THE ST PETERSBURG ACADEMY	174
'On the Zi Hui Dictionary'	174
'On the Spring and Autumn Annals'	179
10. SMALLER ARTICLES IN THE *MISCELLANEA BEROLINENSIA*	185
11. THE BIG CHINESE DICTIONARY	188
The Big Dictionary in Bayer's Letters	189
The Big Dictionary in Leningrad	197
12. FINALE	204
Last Words	204
Last Days	207
Epilogue	217
Appendix	219
Bibliography	221
Glossary of Chinese Terms	231
Index	236

ILLUSTRATIONS

1	T. S. Bayer's *Ex Libris*	22
2	*Prospect of Königsburg*	23
3	*Monumentum Sinicum.* The inscription on the Nestorian Stele, from Athanasius Kircher's *China . . . illustrata,* 1667	24
4	Christian Mentzel (1622-1701), physician and sinologist	25
5	Joseph Nicolas Delisle (1688-1768), French astronomer	26
6	Domnique Parrenin (1665-1741), French Jesuit missionary in Peking	27
7	The nine elementary characters, from Bayer's *Museum Sinicum,* 1730	116
8	a-b. First pages of the dictionary in Bayer's *Museum Sinicum,* 1730	122-3
9	The St Petersburg Academy of Sciences and the Kunstkammer	141
10	The Library of the St Petersburg Academy	142
11	Page 1 of the Dedication to Empress Anne, from the *Commentarii Academiae Scientarum Imperialis Petropolitanae,* Vol. III, 1732	143
12	The origin of the Chinese characters according to Martino Martini	144
13	Mentzel's *Xiao Er Lun,* the first of two plates	145
14	Count Biron's Chinese sundial	146
15	Title page of Bayer's copy of the *Zi Hui* dictionary	211
16	The Dalai Lama's seal	212
17	Parrenin's poem in seal- and standard characters	213
18	Title page of Bayer's big dictionary	214
19	First page of Bayer's big dictionary	215
20	Page from Bayer's big dictionary, the last volume	216

Nos. 1 and 15-18 are reproduced with the permission of Glasgow University Library, Special Collections. Nos. 5, 9 and 18-20 are reproduced with the permission of the Archives of the Akademia Nauk, Leningrad.

ACKNOWLEDGEMENTS

While working with T. S. Bayer and his Chinese studies I have received help and advice from several individuals and institutions. I am grateful to Professor David E. Mungello, Coe College, Cedar Rapids, Iowa, USA, who took it upon him to read the manuscript and gave me his expert advice on it. I want to thank Mr. Peter Terkelsen, M.A., Aarhus, for patiently checking my translation of the Preface to the *Museum Sinicum* and several other parts of Bayer's works. My thanks go also to Mrs. Else Glahn, Anne Wedell-Wedellsborg and Mr. Chen Xianchun, lecturers at the Aarhus University of East Asian Studies, as well as to Professor Søren Egerod and Mr. Leif Littrup, lecturer, Institute of East Asian Studies, University of Copenhagen, for their help with several Chinese language problems. Father Joseph Dehergne, S. J., archivist, 'Les Fontaines', Chantilly, has helped me in many ways in the course of the years – for that I want to thank him here.

I have benefited greatly from the kind and efficient help of librarians and curators in the Aarhus State Library, the Royal Library and the University Library in Copenhagen, the Bibliothèque nationale in Paris, the Library of 'Les Fontaines', Chantilly, the Staatsbibliothek Preussischer Kulturbesitz, Berlin DBR, the Deutsche Staatsbibliothek, Berlin DDR, the Biblioteca Apostolica Vaticana, Rome, and the Archives of the Academy of Sciences in Leningrad. It is my privilege and pleasure to extend my gratitude to all of them.

I owe a special debt to Mr. David J. Weston, Assistant Librarian in the Special Collection, Glasgow University Library, who guided my steps through the Glasgow Bayeriana, carefully catalogued by him.

ABBREVIATIONS

Benzelius Correspondence: *Letters to Erik Benzelius from learned Foreigners*, I-II. Ed. A. Erikson. Göteborg 1979

Bibliotheca Sinica: Henri Cordier: *Bibliotheca Sinica. Dictionnaire bibliographique des ouvrages relatifs à l'empire chinois.* Deuxième edition. Paris 1904-22

Hunter Books: Mungo Ferguson: *The printed Books in the Library of the Hunterian Museum in the University of Glasgow.* Glasgow 1930. The last page, p. 396, lists 79 'Miscellaneous Books and Papers in Chinese and Manchu Language', with very short English 'titles'

Hunter MS: John Young and P. Henderson Aitken: *A Catalogue of the Manuscripts in the Library of the Hunterian Museum in the University of Glasgow.* Glasgow 1908

Lacroze Correspondence: *Thesauri Epistolici Lacroziani, Tomus I-III.* Ed. I. L. Uhl. Leipzig 1742-6

Materiali: Gerhard Friedrich Müller: *Materiali dlja Istorii Imperatorskoi Akademia Nauk, Vol. 6 (1725-43).* St Petersburg 1890

Pfister: Louis Pfister: *Notices biographiques et bibliographiques sur les Jésuites de l'ancienne mission de Chine, 1552-1773.* Chang-Hai 1932

Sylloge: *Sylloge Nova Epistolarum varii Argumenti,* I-V. Ed. I. L. Uhl. Nuremberg 1760-9

Wolff Correspondence: See Appendix: Bibliographies – Manuscripts – Letters

FOREWORD

The intention of the present work is to contribute to our knowledge about the birth-pangs and the early years of European sinology in the last years of the seventeenth and the first years of the eighteenth century, especially in Central and Eastern Europe.

It deals with the Chinese studies of Theophilus (Gottlieb) Siegfried Bayer (1694-1738), a young Prussian classical scholar who worked for the first part of his short life in Königsberg, an old centre of academic culture in East Prussia and for the last twelve years at the newly-founded Academy of Sciences in St Petersburg.

During Bayer's lifetime the philosophers' sinophilia and enthusiasm for all kinds of *chinoiserie* among all social classes were still prevalent in Europe. Critical voices were heard against the China Jesuits' image of the Celestial Empire as presented in their many publications, but in reality against the powerful Society of Jesus in general. The turn of the tide, the transition from China admiration to China contempt, occurred only around the middle of the eighteenth century and did not culminate till the last years of it.

Bayer, however, was never a sinophile – his last work may even have contributed to the decline and fall of European sinophilia. His starting point was an early interest in the history of the Christian churches in Asia before the opening of the sea route to India and beyond. A devout Christian and, by training, a fine classicist he became interested in the languages in which the gospel and the Christian dogma had been spread far and wide in the South and the East, especially in Syriac and Ethiopian.

How it came to pass and by which various impulses he was led into a lifelong study of the Chinese language and literature will be discussed in the present book, based upon a presentation of his printed works as well as manuscripts and letters.

The only one of Bayer's Chinese studies that is known today – and at that hardly more than by the title – is his book *Museum Sinicum*. His later sinological works are probably known to very few readers, among other things because most of them were printed in the annual of the St Petersburg Academy, the *Commentarii Academiae Scientiarum Imperialis Petropolitanae*.

The first 100 pages of the long Preface to the *Museum Sinicum* is Bayer's 'History of Sinology', from the earliest times, but mostly dealing with what he knew or thought he knew about Chinese studies in the seventeenth century, ending with a kind of sinological autobiography. These pages are brought in translation here because of their vivid presentation of the state of 'sinology' at this early period when China was more an object of desire than one of gratification.

THREE WORDS ABOUT THE CHINESE CHARACTERS

On the pages of the present book certain simple sinological terms and concepts appear again and again. The brief information contained in the following lines is for the benefit of readers who are not acquainted with the Chinese language.

It is a well-known fact that Chinese is not written with letters of an alphabet or with syllabic symbols but with characters consisting of certain combinations of lines or strokes of the writing brush. Most of the characters are said to consist of two different kinds of elements: one usually called the radical, which often, but far from always, indicates or suggests the meaning of the character, and another element, called the phonetic because in many cases it gives an idea, however approximately, of its pronunciation.

The number of elements regarded as radicals has varied in the course of time, but from the seventeenth century until recently a certain system of 214 radicals has been accepted and used in dictionaries commonly used in China. In these dictionaries the individual character is assigned to a radical which forms part of it. There is, however, a certain arbitrariness in this, as many characters contain more than one element that is a radical in the system. The characters traditionally regarded as 'belonging to' this or that radical, are listed under it in the dictionaries according to the number of extra lines or strokes, from one to more than twenty.

The first Chinese-European dictionary printed in Europe – the *Dictionnaire chinois, français et latin,* published in Paris in 1813 – was arranged in the same way. Since then most dictionaries used by students of Chinese have been arranged alphabetically according to the pronunciation of the Chinese word. They all, however, include a Radical Index where the characters are given according to the above-mentioned 214 radical system. This is necessary for finding the meaning of a character when the sound of the word is not known.

In the present book we are going to hear much about Chinese characters, radicals, and phonetics, and especially about Chinese dictionaries. Throughout his life T.S. Bayer regarded the arrangement of the characters in dictionaries as the most important part of sinology. For reasons we are going to explain he never came to understand the structure of the individual characters or the 'meaning' of the arrangement of them in the dictionaries. He was convinced that there was a *system* underlying the apparent confusion of the Chinese characters. He felt that something had gone wrong in China in the course of history – the Chinese had forgotten the system. It was for European philologists – himself included – to rediscover it.

As for the pronunciation of Chinese words it suffices here to say that spoken Chinese, especially in its older forms, is a monosyllabic language, in principle at least. The number of syllables is restricted, but each of them is pronounced in formal speech with one of four so-called tones, a change of tone producing a change of meaning. Bayer never got the opportunity to study the tonal system of the Chinese language.

1
INTRODUCTION

At the gate of European academic sinology two towering figures appear, Theophilus (Gottlieb) Siegfried Bayer (1694-1738) of the St Petersburg Academy of Sciences, and Étienne Fourmont (1683-1745) of the Académie des inscriptions et belles-lettres in Paris. Bayer's *Museum Sinicum*, the first book about the Chinese language to be printed in Europe, was published in St Petersburg in 1730. A few years later Fourmont published his *Meditationes sinicae* ... and his *Linguae sinarum mandarinicae hieroglyphicae grammatica duplex* ... in Paris (1737, 1742).

The personality of these two men was as different as can be imagined: here was pious and timid Bayer, there was arrogant and virulent Fourmont. Their situations were also very different: Bayer in a newly-founded Academy in the small, new, modern-style capital of Peter the Great's Russia, Fourmont in one of the famous old academies in Paris, the mental capital of Europe and the capital of France, *'mère des arts, des armes et des lois'*. As to their facilities for indulging in Chinese studies, as a young man Bayer had sat for less than a year in the Royal Library in Berlin, copying from a missionary vocabulary and from old Jesuit manuscripts and letters. When he came to St Petersburg in 1726 he found no Chinese books there and no works by China missionaries. In his last years he had the benefit of being advised by the learned Jesuits in Peking, but it usually took a year or more before a letter from St Petersburg was received in Peking and the same time before a reply arrived. Fourmont had the large Chinese collections of the Bibliothèque royale at his disposal and for some years he had a young French-speaking Chinese to help him.

Étienne Fourmont and his sinological works have been discussed several times, e.g. by Abel Rémusat in his *Élémens de la grammaire chinoise* (1822) and his *Nouveaux mélanges asiatiques* (1829), as well as by Henri Cordier in his long article in the *Centenaire de l'Ecole des langues orientales vivantes* (1895). However, most of it deals with his moral qualities, his work being dismissed as quaint and incomprehensible. An analysis of Fourmont's two large books and a serious estimate of his ideas has yet to be made.

To my knowledge – except for a few pages in Franz Babinger's inaugural thesis *Gottlieb Siegfried Bayer* (1915) – there is no study of Bayer's sinological works.

Before giving a sketch of T.S. Bayer's place in the early history of sinology a few general remarks about the three roots of European sinology – the studies of the China Jesuits, the orientalists in Europe, and the search for a universal, philosophical language – may not be amiss.

JESUIT SINOLOGY

Sinology, in the widest sense of the word, the serious study of one or more aspects of the Chinese civilization, started with missionary studies in the seventeenth and eighteenth centuries. The Jesuits were the first who gained a foothold in China, in the first years of the seventeenth century already penetrating influential circles in Peking. In their publications, many of which became best-sellers, translated into many languages, they revealed to the European reader the geography and the natural riches of this vast empire, as well as the organization of the Chinese state, ruled by a benevolent monarch taking advice from highly-educated and impeccable counsellors. They explained the philosophy and the religious sects in China and described the customs and elaborate ceremonies of the Chinese.

This splendid picture of a high culture at the other end of the world obviously derived from sincere admiration on the part of many of the Jesuits, but already from the middle of the seventeenth century several reasons – first of all rivalry and jealousy between the Jesuits and the other missionary groups that had arrived on the scene – led to a certain degree of mistrust in the Jesuit image of China.

However, the Jesuit publications, aiming at a broad audience of educated people, created the intense sinophilia of that century. The French and English philosophers vied with each other in praising the model state with its honest citizens, and the appearance on the European market of the inimitable porcelain and of lacquer wares swelled the wave of admiration.

There was one kind of Europeans, however, who were not satisfied: the learned linguists, especially the orientalists who complained because the Jesuits, the only Europeans who had an opportunity to learn Chinese, dealt so sparingly with the Chinese language in their published works. And they had reason to complain, for actually the information about that language – if we omit lyrical passages – contained in the many China books, all the way up to the end of the eighteenth century – can be printed on less than ten pages.

The Jesuits themselves did not need printed grammars or dictionaries, the newcomers being taught by the old hands in China, but apart from that it is hard to escape the impression of their positively guarding the mysteries of the Chinese language, for fear of other people reading their hands. In the course of time, however, a few Jesuits visiting Europe came to give away some bits of the secret, and two or three copies of handwritten missionaries' dictionaries had found their way into great libraries. It was only with the publication of the *Museum Sinicum* that an attempt was made to give the reading public in Europe a Chinese grammar and dictionary.

Bayer put them together from scraps: Jesuit books and letters, tiny printed works of earlier German enthusiasts, and from a Chinese-Spanish dictionary kept in the Royal Library in Berlin.

THE ORIENTALISTS

When Bayer started on his academic career at the beginning of the eighteenth century, 'oriental languages', i.e. the languages of the Near East, had been studied intensively and competently for more than a century in many European universities – Hebrew and the related languages and dialects, Arabic and Ethiopean, but also Coptic, Armenian and Persian.

The oriental language studies of the seventeenth century were to a great extent determined by the work with polyglot Bibles, produced during years of labour by teams of orientalists, e.g. the *Paris Polyglot* (1645) and the *London Polyglot* (1657). In these works each page of the Old Testament shows the masoretic Hebrew text, followed side by side in narrow columns, by the text of the Septuagint and old translations into other oriental languages, extracted from libraries and archives. The *Paris Polyglot,* besides Hebrew, includes Aramaic (called at the time Chaldeic), Samaritan, Syriac and Arabic. In the *London Polyglot* there is also Ethiopic and Persian.

Of course these magnificent tomes were showpieces of linguistic erudition, but they were meant as aids to the understanding of the Bible. Studying difficult and perhaps corrupt passages in the Hebrew texts, a comparison with old translations that might have been made from a better text was often thought to be useful. However, it is clear that they also furnished an apparatus for the beginning of independent studies of oriental languages, as it can be seen from the simultaneous publications of multilanguage dictionaries by some of the team workers. Studies of oriental languages thus little by little became unrelated to biblical exegesis and were more and more seen as adjuncts to the understanding of history, just like geography and numismatics. The point of view was usually not what we would call a purely linguistic one; it was not comparative linguistics as that term was to be used in the nineteenth century, but the idea of comparison was there all the same. The term used was 'harmonic studies', often in conjunction with 'etymological studies', e.g. as in the title of one influential book, Johann Heinrich Hottinger's *Etymologicum orientale sive lexicon harmonicum heptaglotton* ... (1661).

In the Preface to Bayer's *Museum Sinicum* we are going to meet several of the famous orientalists of the seventeenth century and of his own day. Most of them were involved – in one way or another – in the search for an understanding of the mysteries of the strange 'hieroglyphic' script of the Chinese.

Bayer himself was an orientalist besides being, or rather becoming, a sinologist. Many pages in his printed works include passages in Arabic, Persion and Syriac and a number of articles from his later years deal with Central Asian languages – Mongolian, Tibetan and Manchu. His vast correspondence with many European scholars and with the Jesuits in Peking is filled with enthusiasm for these strange subjects.

However, these endeavours will not be discussed in the present book.

THE PRIMORDIAL OR PERFECT LANGUAGE

Besides missionary zeal and orientalist labour, speculations about a primordial or perfect language was a driving force in emerging sinology.

In the Preface to his *Museum Sinicum* we will find Bayer discussing the various hypotheses about the 'Adamitic' language – Hebrew, of course, for most people, but there had been other proposals, e.g. Gothic – and Chinese!

None of the known languages seemed to be ideal languages, hence the speculations about constructing an artificial one that should be a perfect system of communication. Bishop Wilkins spent many years on such a project and published a huge book about it that was admired, but not more. Leibniz dreamed all his life of the possibility of producing a kind of universal language, and Bülffinger argued that it *could* be done – we shall hear more about his arguments later on.

Bayer had heard that Étienne Fourmont in Paris had discovered that the Chinese language, as manifested in the character script, was a logical and rational system. Bayer maintained, and that perhaps was his most original idea, that the Chinese had forgotten or distorted it, especially in the arrangement of their dictionaries. He, however, would restore it and reveal the beauty of its structure.

Part of the drama of Bayer's life – for drama there was – is related to this idea that permeated his whole scholarly life. But at the very end of it things happened to him that made him despair of ever being able to demonstrate that the Chinese language was a philosophical language.

T.S. BAYER

Bayer was born, so to speak, into sinology. At his baptism one of his godfathers was a certain Gottfried Bartsch, an engraver, who had come to Königsberg and had become a friend of the Bayer family. Bartsch had worked for some time with the fabulous Andreas Müller, the Berlin provost who had dazed the learned world by declaring that he had invented a *Clavis sinica,* a key to the Chinese language, with the help of which any child could learn to read Chinese in the course of a few days. However, in his old age he burnt all his papers, including the famous *Clavis sinica.* As a child Bayer may have been listening to Bartsch telling the family about the Chinese studies of that strange personality, and when he reached the age of nineteen years he was smitten by the Chinese fever.

After graduating from the university he stayed for some months in Berlin, probably occupied most of the time with Chinese studies. Back in Königsberg in 1718 he published his first sinological work, a small book which contained a sketch of a Chinese grammar. It was when he came to St Petersburg in 1726 that he began seriously to consider writing a book about the Chinese language and Chinese literature.

Later on we shall see how and to what extent the book he produced, the *Museum Sinicum,* can qualify as a textbook of the Chinese language. But here already there are two things that need to be said: it was not possible to learn to speak or read Chinese from Bayer's book; secondly, Bayer was perfectly and painfully aware of that fact and states it many times in the book.

Why then publish it? Bayer felt, and he was supported in this feeling by his old friend the great Lacroze in Berlin, as well as by his new friend Theophanes, the learned Archbishop of Novgorod, that it was his duty to do so. There were no books about the Chinese language on the market. He had had access to information about that language because he had happened to study in the Royal Library in Berlin, where some handwritten material about the Chinese language was kept. It was not very much and in spite of all his endeavours, Bayer certainly did not come to 'know Chinese'. But he felt that he simply had to arrange the information he had gathered together, to collect his thoughts and sit down and write a text that could be printed and published, thus making it possible for others to go on with his work.

On one of the first pages of his *Museum Sinicum,* and in many of his letters, Bayer quotes from Theocritus' *Bucolics:* 'The Greeks got into Troy by trying, everything is done by trying!'

However, soon after the publication of the *Museum Sinicum* – for various reasons which we are going to discuss later – Bayer decided to go on with Chinese studies. For the rest of his life he worked hard in this difficult field and produced a number of sinological works. In trying to place T. S. Bayer in the history of sinology, a consideration of these works is at least as important as an estimate of his *Museum Sinicum.*

Bayer cultivated several other fields of learning besides sinology and we shall note them briefly in the following. Here it may be in order to mention what he did *not* engage in. He was an antiquarian, an historian, a philologist and a linguist, but he always kept out of theology and philosophy. He was interested in the history of the church, not in dogma. His remarks about Christianity are commonplaces or emotional utterances. As for philosophy, he became involved in speculations about the old science of *Ars combinatoria* in relation to his studies of the Chinese script, but it is significant that in the numerous asides strewn over his pages he refrains from commenting seriously on the great issues in Chinese philosophy which occupied the minds of many of his contemporaries. Late in his life he read the volume of Leibniz' letters which came out in 1735, containing highly explosive matter, written by China missionaries about the metaphysics of the ancient and modern Chinese philosophers. He refers to this volume in his last published work, but he does not mention Leibniz' important comments on these problems, printed there.

BAYER'S LATIN STYLE

Nearly all of Bayer's works are in Latin, and all his Chinese studies are. This was normal at the time, of course, although there were tendencies already towards writing in the national languages. We will hear about Bishop Wilkins in the seventeenth century writing his great book about a philosophical language in English, and about Christian Mentzel publishing his Chinese chronology in German. In the eighteenth century the French Peking Jesuits made a point of writing in French, but they had to write to Bayer in Latin. Anyhow, publishing one's work in Latin was a way of popularizing it: in this language it was available to all European scholars. On the other hand, beyond Latin many of them had great difficulty in reading any other language than their mother tongue.

Most of Bayer's works, but especially those of his young days, are composed in a very personal style; the arrangement and presentation of his findings and thoughts are often elusive and capricious, with digressions and jumps, sometimes lacking new paragraphs where one would have expected them. This way of writing was not uncommon, of course, at Bayer's time, but in his case the problem is increased by his immoderate use of quotations from Greek and Latin classical authors. Usually he does not indicate whom he is quoting, and very often the citations are built into the text as mere allusions, some of them slightly inappropriate to the matter under discussions. Moreover, he had the troublesome habit of giving the titles of other scholars' works in an abbreviated form within his sentences, without marking them as titles. Obviously he is writing for a small group of readers who are supposed to know what he is referring to.

Bayer was proud of his Latin style and in his letters he often complains of the barbarisms of his contemporaries, but Johann Christoph Wolff, the great Hamburg orientalist, and a correspondent of his, had this to say about it in a letter to Lacroze written in 1721: 'This refined man aims too much at a polished Latin style, resulting, it seems to me, in unnecessary obscurity. He imitates the ancients by his habit of quoting from literature' (Lacroze Correspondence, Vol. II, p. 167).

This letter was published shortly after Bayer's death, but many years after, in 1770, Christian Adolph Klotz came to his defence in the preface to his edition of Bayer's smaller works, the *Theophili Sigefridi Bayeri Opuscula ...*, Halle, 1770. It is true, he says, that Bayer often inserted quotations from the great poets, with whose work he was so familiar. There are readers who cannot follow him on his subtle ways, but his style is the delight of those who are knowledgeable about the Latin language. Wolff was wrong, he says, citing the depreciatory remark in the letter to Lacroze.

However, Bayer himself was aware of his uninhibited verbosity. He ends a letter to Bishop Benzelius, dated 30 April 1731, with the following words: 'I am not a talkative person but when I write I simply cannot contain myself' (Benzelius Correspondence, II, p. 338).

PART I
BAYER'S LIFE

2
PRUSSIAN YEARS

THE SETTING

The Margravate and Electorate of Brandenburg, a state in the Holy Roman Empire, was ruled from 1640 to 1688 by Friedrich Wilhelm, called the Great Elector, who was also Duke of Prussia. This province, making up one-third of the territories of the Brandenburg-Prussia state, lay outside the Empire. On his accession to the throne in 1640 the country was still ravaged by the armies of the Thirty Years War, especially by the Swedes. After the treaty of Westphalia (1648), which officially put an end to the war, the Great Elector employed his great talents in repairing the terrible damage caused by the war, rebuilding his territories into a well-organized and powerful state.

His son, Friedrich III, joined the Great Alliance against Louis XIV and fought against the French armies (1688-97). In 1701, with the sanction of the Emperor in Vienna, he secured a regal title for himself, crowning himself King Friedrich I *in* Prussia. This extravagant prince, fond of pomp and trying to emulate the court in Paris, adorned Berlin with sumptuous public buildings and also supported the sciences by founding the Berlin Academy – the *Societas Regia Scientarum* – and the university of Halle.

In 1713 he was succeeded by his son, Friedrich Wilhelm I, who ruled the country till his death in 1740. He is said to have been the opposite of his father in nearly every respect, leading a frugal life and insisting on the necessity of rigorous economy, not only in the royal household, but also in the whole state administration. He hated the Jesuits, did nothing for the universities but a great deal for elementary education, making it obligatory for parents in every town and village to send their children to school.

In the Preface to Bayer's *Museum Sinicum* we shall meet with the Great Elector as the protector of Andreas Müller and Christian Mentzel, the villain and one of the heroes of his play. We get a glimpse – a critical one – of the court life of King Friedrich I in connection with the author's childhood acquaintance with the painter-engraver Gottfried Bartsch. Friedrich Wilhelm I does not appear, but Bayer's decision to accept employment in Peter the Great's Academy in St Petersburg may perhaps be related to this king's indifference to scholarly studies.

Königsberg

Königsberg – Bayer's native town – had been founded by the Knights of the Teutonic Order in 1255. It was the *Haupt- und Residenz Stadt* of the Duchy of Prussia, acquired by the Elector of Brandenburg in 1618. During the Thirty Years War it had opted for neutrality and was thus spared the devastations of the war.

Friedrich III, Elector of Brandenburg, had lent lustre to it in 1701 by choosing it as the place for his coronation as King Friedrich I *in* Prussia. It was a Protestant stronghold, but a Catholic minority was tolerated, and from 1650 to 1780 a few Jesuits were allowed to keep a school there.

It had a fine academic tradition, the university having been founded in 1544 (on the model of the University of Copenhagen). There were two important libraries, the Wallenrodt Library and the Municipal Library (Altstädtische Bibliothek), where Bayer was librarian from 1718 to 1725. However, in Bayer's day the university was degenerating, perhaps because of the riots of the fewer and fewer students, perhaps because '*die Professor nits taugen*', as King Friedrich Wilhelm said of them.

The Young Bayer

Gottlieb Siegfried Bayer came from a German Protestant family, settled in Hungary in the 16th century.[1] His paternal grandfather, Johannes Bayer (1635-74) was an educated man who served as assistant headmaster at the *Gymnasium* in the town called Eperjes. His father, Johann Friedrich Bayer (1670- after 1738) moved to East Prussia; first to Dantzig and then to Königsberg, where he lived the rest of his life as a poor and pious painter married to a painter's daughter, Anna Kathrina, born Porrath.

---

1 *Gottlieb Siegfried Bayer (1694-1738). Ein Beitrag zur Geschichte der morgenländischen Studien im 18. Jahrhundert* (1915) – the inaugural dissertation of Franz Babinger. It is an impressive work, especially when we consider that the author was only 22 years old when he submitted it to the Königliche Bayerische Ludwig-Maximilians-Universität in Munich. I have used it freely, especially for the biographical information, most of which he took from an article about Bayer's life and works published in the *Bibliothèquie Germanique* in 1741. The editor of this journal writes in a footnote that it is based on an autobiography composed by the late Mr. Bayer. It appears from a letter from the editor to Bayer in 1737 that Bayer had sent it to him on 30 august of that year (see p. 219). – Babinger also used G.F. Müller's work on the early history of the St Petersburg Academy of Sciences (see Note 12). – Babinger's book covers all the works of Bayer, only six of its 85 pages dealing (with some misunderstandings) with his Chinese studies. – In his publications and in his correspondence Bayer always used the latinised form of his first name, Theophilus. He always abbreviated Theophilus to 'T.', not to 'Th.'. I have followed him in that.

Gottlieb Siegfried was born in 1694. At school he showed great aptitude for study, learning Latin and Greek without difficulty and immatriculating in the University of Königsberg at the age of sixteen. There he studied theology and philosophy and read Hebrew with Abraham Wolff (1680-1731). As he relates so vividly in the Preface to his *Museum Sinicum,* it was at the age of nineteen that he suddenly conceived of the idea of studying Chinese. After a period of illness, during which he stayed with his grand-uncle Johannes Sartorius, who was professor of Rhetoric in Dantzig, he returned to Königsberg and defended his doctoral thesis there in 1716.[2] Endowed with a scholarship from the Königsberg city council he went on a study tour to other German university towns. He stayed for several months in Berlin where he met many important scholars.

By far the most important one for Bayer was Lacroze (Mathurin Veyssière de la Croze), member of the Berlin Academy and librarian at the Royal Library. This extraordinary man had shown his talents and his independent and stubborn spirit already as a boy, leaving school at 14, having learnt Latin to perfection, to pass to Guadeloupe, where he learned Spanish, Portuguese and English. Aged 21 he entered a Benedectine monastery in France, but fled from it and went to Basel where he was converted to the Reformed Church. In Berlin, from 1697 onwards, he occupied himself at the Royal Library with studies of oriental languages, compiling Syriac, Armenian and Coptic dictionaries. He was outspokenly anti-Catholic and especially venomous against the Jesuits.[3] Lacroze was 55 when Bayer, aged 22, met him in Berlin. A warm friendship sprang up between these two men, based on mutual admiration, which lasted for the next ten years.

It was at the Royal Library, and with Lacroze's help, that Bayer got the opportunity to study and to copy many texts from among the papers left by Christian Mentzel (1622-1701), the court physician and – late in life – enthusiastic 'sinologist'. There he also saw Chinese dictionaries and a Chinese-Spanish missionary's vocabulary as well as short missionary grammars from which he took copious excerpts. He also saw a large Chinese historical work, one that was called at the time the 'Chinese Annals' (see Part II, chapter 1).

Leaving Berlin he passed through Frankfurt-on-the-Oder, Halle, Leipzig

---

2 *Vindiciae Verborum Christi* . . .(1716). It deals with Christ's last words on the cross: 'Eli, Eli, lama sabaktini' – at the very moment when darkness descended over Golgatha. We are going to hear much about that darkness in the following.
3 One of his orientalist books, the *Histoire du Christianisme des Indes,* was published in Bayer's lifetime (1724). The Coptic dictionary, revised, abbreviated and supplemented by several hands, was published many years after his death (*Lexicon Aegyptiaco-Latinum,* 1775), His Armenian dictionary, on which he is said to have worked for twelve years, and his Syriac dictionary were never printed. His *Vindiciae veterum Scriptorum contra Harduinum* (1708) was a polemic work against this Jesuit.

and other German university towns, where he met many scholars working in various fields of oriental languages and the history of the Eastern Church, before finally returning to his native Königsberg late in 1717. In Halle he had met a pupil of the great Ethiopean scholar Hiob Ludolff (1624-1702), who is remembered in the Preface to the *Museum Sinicum*. In Leipzig the editor of the *Acta Eruditorum* commissioned him to write for his famous journal. On his travels he had received an offer from his home town of a bursary to finance a study tour to Holland and England, but he refused it on grounds of ill health.

Back in Königsberg in 1718 Bayer was made a librarian in the Municipal Library. In the same year he published his first sinological work, the *De Eclipsi Sinica*. Some years later he became assistant headmaster, and then headmaster of the *Gymnasium*. He worked there and also taught Greek literature – especially poetry – as *Privatdozent* at the university until towards the end of 1725. During these eight years, besides a number of small articles in various journals, he published four books on Greek and Roman antiquities, one on the history of the Congregatio de Propaganda Fide, and an essay about the treasures of his own Municipal Library.[4] While thus busily engaged in his studies, he carried on a voluminous correspondence with scholars – with Lacroze, but also with others – in other parts of Germany and abroad.

It may seem as if during these years, after 1718, he had decided that his *De Eclipsi Sinica* should be both his first and his last excursion into that strange field, but that was not so. In the Lacroze correspondence there is a small letter dated 7 April 1719, from a certain Henricus Bartsch in Königsberg, asking Lacroze if he could have on loan, with the security of the Senate, Diaz' Vocabulary and Mentzel's papers. This man who could ask for a loan of manuscripts from the Royal Library in Berlin, offering municipal security, was probably Heinrich Bartsch, the son of a mayor of Königsberg Altstadt, a rich book collector who had donated over 500 Bibles and many manuscripts to the Stadtbibliothek and who had been responsible for its being opened to the public in 1714.[5]

In the same correspondence there is a letter from Lacroze to Bayer, dated 30 April the same year, containing the following words: 'I shall grant Mr. Bartsch's request about the things he asked for in your name. I am telling him so in the letter (enclosed) which I want you personally to give to him. Be assured that in the future I shall act similarly, attending as much as I can to

---

4 *Programma quo Bibliothecam Senatus Paleopolitani . . . apertum iri . . .* (1718).
5 Lacroze Correspondence, I, pp. 1-2. – Heinrich Bartsch jun. (1667-1728), municipal secretary and archivist in Königsberg, book collector. He carried on an extensive correspondence with many scholars. See F. Gause: *Die Geschichte der Stadt Königsberg*, Vol. I, p. 430 and Vol. II, p. 66 and 75.

your cause'.⁶

The letter from Königsberg, written by an important person, and the guarded words in Lacroze's letter to Bayer, may suggest a transaction that was perhaps not quite regular. Bayer never mentions having had this material in Königsberg, either in his printed works or in the letters I have seen, but it may perhaps be assumed that he had it for a period. He could hardly have copied the more than two thousand characters we find in his *Museum Sinicum* during his stay in Berlin in 1716, and, as far as we know, he never returned there. It seems reasonable to conclude that, after the publication of the *De Eclipsi Sinica*, he decided to go on, and for that purpose turned for help to his old friend in the Royal Library in Berlin. The Eclipse book itself points in that direction. There is one sentence that promises further sinological research (see Part II, chapter 1). Anyhow, *if* the Diaz Vocabulary and Mentzel's papers went to Königsberg they came back safely to Berlin!⁷

Many other letters in the Lacroze correspondence show Bayer's continued interest in Chinese matters. Among other things he asked Lacroze to look up certain characters in the Diaz Vocabulary for him, and Lacroze did so.

It must have been clear to Lacroze that his young friend was becoming more and more absorbed in Chinese. In his letters he seems to try to divert Bayer's attention to other Asian languages, Mongolian and Tibetan. But above all Lacroze wanted Bayer to concentrate on his own speciality, the Coptic language! There is only one person besides myself, he says, who understands this language, namely Jablonski.⁸ If only Bayer would devote himself to Coptic, this would 'open up for him the whole field of sacred and profane antiquities' – but his appeal was to no avail.⁹

In 1726 Bayer moved to St Petersburg with his beloved wife, daughter of a Königsberg merchant, whom he had married in 1720. He was to stay in this city for the rest of his short life, spending a large part of his time on Chinese studies.

6. Lacroze Correspondence, III, pp. 47-9.
7 However, there is one difficulty. In 1722 (?) Bayer asked Lacroze to copy out for him the first part of the *Great Learning* 'from the Mentzel Codex' in the Royal Library in Berlin. Lacroze did so and sent it to him in a letter dated 30 April 1723. Had Bayer forgotten to copy this text (properly?), or did he only get the Diaz Vocabulary? – Lacroze Correspondence, III, pp. 57-9 and II, p. 277. Bayer's letter is dated 22 August but has no year.
8 Supposedly Paul Ernst Jablonsky (1693-1757), Professor of Theology in Berlin. He does not seem to have published anything about the Coptic language, but he was interested in the Nestorians, as was Lacroze.
9 The Lacroze Correspondence contains 43 letters from Bayer written between 1716 and 1728 and one from 1736, as well as 31 of Lacroze's letters written during the years 1716 to 1724. The last of them was not written in 1731, as stated, but in 1722 or 1723. These long, uninhibited and friendly letters demonstrate the inexhaustible learned curiosity of their writers and contain much important information about Bayer's studies of Chinese and other Asian languages.

3
RUSSIAN YEARS

THE SETTING

St Petersburg

St Petersburg was Peter the Great's work, and a central element in his passionate and relentless endeavour to transform the old Muscovy into a modern and powerful European state. It was to provide a maritime outlet to the Baltic, to be a fortress, to be the administrative centre of the Russian Empire, and to be a beautiful Western-style city.

The construction of the city in the unhealthy swamps along the Neva River started with the Peter and Paul Fortress in 1703. The city grew at the cost of hundreds of thousands of lives among the conscripted labourers, till on Peter's death in 1725 it had 70,000 inhabitants, most of whom had been forced to build houses and palaces in accordance with the Czar's orders.

At the time when Bayer lived there, St Petersburg consisted of three parts, the old Petersburg behind and to each side of the Peter and Paul Fortress on the right bank of the Neva, the Admiralty, a shipbuilding wharf on the left bank, and Vasilevski Island, between the arms of the dividing river, with its commercial harbour at the tip of the Strelka, the Exchange, the Kunstkammer and the 'Twelve Colleges'.

According to Peter's plans Vasilevski Island should have been the centre of the city. However, upstream from the Admiralty were palaces of the nobility, and here, in the 1730s and 1740s, arose the Winter Palace, shifting, in the course of the years, the centre of the city to that side of the river.

The Kunstkammer, and the neighbouring buildings facing the Admiralty on the other side of the river, were the site of the Academy from 1727 onwards. The Kunstkammer, with its central tower containing the astronomical observatory, a beautiful library hall and the Anatomical Theatre in the basement, was one of the most impressive buildings in St Petersburg.

The Academy of Sciences

The St Petersburg Academy, the Academia Scientiarum Imperialis Petropolitana, was conceived by Peter the Great, who corresponded about it with Leibniz and the philosopher Christian Wolff in Halle. Peter the Great had his physician, Lorenz Blumentrost, draw up a charter for it, modelled partly on that of the Royal Society in London and the Académie des sciences in Paris, but with the difference that the academicians should also be professors, charged with giving regular public lectures. One of them should also supervise a grammar school for children of the Russian nobility attached to the Academy. In 1723-4 suitable candidates from the sciences and the humanities were sought through personal contacts in the German states and in France, as well as through an advertisement in the *Leipziger Gelehrte Zeitung*.

Peter the Great did not live to see his Academy work, as he died in February 1725, but his widow and successor to the throne, Catherine, confirmed the charter. The recruiting went on and the first assembly was held on 13 November 1725. In the course of the years 1725-6 a total of fifteen academicians had arrived, some of them bringing with them one or two 'pupils' who were soon after to be called *adjuncti*. Among them was the young historian, Gerhard Friedrich Müller, from Leipzig, who later became professor of history.

The first academicians included persons who had already made a name for themselves in the learned world, such as the Basel mathematician, Jacob Hermann, the Tübingen philosopher, Georg Bernhard Bülffinger (Bilfinger), the brothers Bernoulli, sons of the great Basel mathematician, Johannes Bernoulli, and the French astronomer, Joseph Nicolas Delisle, who was a member of the Académie des sciences in Paris, professor at the Collège des Quatre Nations and had the title of Royal Councillor. Hermann was 48 years old, but most of the others were hardly thirty, or in their early thirties.

(In 1727 they were joined by another Basel scholar, the twenty-year-old Leonhard Euler, the genial mathematician who was to illumine the St Petersburg Academy more than any other of its members.)

Bayer had witnessed the flocking of scholars from his post in Königsberg. On 12 May 1725 he wrote to Bishop Benzelius in Gothenburg:

> Over the last few days I have had talks with the famous mathematician Jacob Hermann and with Bülffinger, the philosopher, who are here . . . on their way to St Petersburg. The Bernoulli brothers . . . and Delisle, the excellent astronomer will be here soon. Christian Goldbach . . . passed through recently, also *en route* to St Petersburg . . .[10]

In February 1726 Bayer joined them, having accepted an invitation to the chair of Greek and Roman antiquities, arranged by his fellow-townsman Christian Goldbach.[11]

10 Benzelius Correspondence, No. 245.
11 Christian Goldbach (1690-1764), German mathematician and fine Latinist, born in Königsberg. He did not want a chair in the Academy but accepted the post of secretary. He

The president of the Academy was the court physician, Lorenz Blumentrost (1692-1755), but usually he left its administration in the hands of his friend, Johann Daniel Schumacher (1690-1761), an Alsatian with a dubious academic education, who had come to St Petersburg already in 1714 as a secretary for foreign correspondence in the Medical Chancellery and as a librarian at the Imperial Library. Still with no more official a title than that of a librarian, he ruled the Academy till his death – for 35 years.

The indignation of the academicians who had to submit to the arbitrary decisions of this man created a virulent atmosphere which, together with incessant in-fights about rank and precedence and a rude and aggressive style of *disputatio* at the assemblies, made the Academy a rather unpleasant workplace for a man like Bayer.

In its first years the Academy held its meetings in a palace in the old Petersburg quarter, but in 1727-8 it moved to the new Kunstkammer on Vasilevski Island. Ordinary meetings were held twice a week, public assemblies thrice a year. Public lectures were given in the morning every day, but nobody came to them except a few of the other academicians and most of the *adjuncti*.

From 1728 onwards the Academy published its *Commentarii Academiae Scientiarum Imperialis Petropolitanae*.

Bayer the Academician

Most of what we know about Bayer in his St Petersburg years is contained in G. F. Müller's *Materials for a History of the Imperial Academy of Science*.[12]

Müller came to know Bayer well in his first years at the Academy. He admired him greatly for his industry and vast erudition, calling him *'der grosse Bayer'*, and deploring his untimely death as a great loss to the Academy and to the learned world in general. He insisted that his eight volumes of correspondence left to the Academy ought to be published, offering to arrange for an edition of them. He says about Bayer that 'in spite of his absorption in his

---

published a number of mathematical articles in the St Petersburg *Commentarii* between 1728 and 1739. From 1742 in the service of the Ministry of Foreign Affairs in Moscow. He was one of Bayer's most intimate friends. In the *Museum Sinicum* he quoted from one of Goldbach's Latin poems. His life and works are described in Ju. Ch. Kopelevič and A. P. Juškevič's *Christian Goldbach*, Moskow, 1983.

12 Gerhard Friedrich Müller (1705-83), German historian and geographer, member of the St Petersburg Academy from 1726 to 1765, director of the archives of the Ministry of Foreign Affairs from 1765 to his death. – His *Materiali dlja Istorii Imperatorskoi Akademii Nauk*, Vol. 6 (1725-43), St Petersburg, 1890, was written in the 1760s at the request of the Academy, which wanted to publish a 50 years' Jubilee volume. It took more than a hundred years before it came out as a 600-page work in German but with a Russian title page and a Russian Index.

studies and the school dust that clung to him, he was a pleasant personality'. As a matter of fact, Müller wrote with more sympathy and warmth about Bayer than about any of the other St Petersburg academicians.

When the Bayer family arrived in St Petersburg, early in 1726, they were put up in a house, in the neighbourhood of the old Academy, half of which was occupied by another newly-arrived academician, Joseph Nicolas Delisle, the French astronomer who became Bayer's intimate friend and remained so to the very end.[13]

The academicians' annual salary was between 600 and 1,800 roubles per year. Bayer's starting salary was 600 roubles, hardly enough to support a family, but it was raised to 800 roubles a few months after his arrival, when he became supervisor of the grammar school attached to the Academy. Most of the others got between 800 and 1,000 roubles; Delisle got 1,800, but that was because he was already a member of the Académie des sciences in Paris and had the title of Royal Councillor, when he came to Russia.

Bayer seems to have always kept out of the quarrels and fights between the various members of the Academy, disliking the general atmosphere of 'pride, pigheadedness, hatred, jealousy and envy' – this is how Müller characterizes the Imperial Academy. Like most of the others, however, he could not avoid coming into conflict with the despotical Schumacher. We do not need to relate here the many instances when Schumacher's intrigues and dirty tricks made life uncomfortable for Bayer. Bayer detested and despised him, and Schumacher reciprocated his feelings. The fact that Bayer had been a librarian at the old and rich Municipal Library at Königsberg and had even published a book about its treasures did not endear him to the librarian of the newly-founded Imperial Library of St Petersburg.

Bayer had a five-year contract with the possibility of prolongation, as did most of the others at the Academy. Suffering from home-sickness, and constantly worried about the problems with Schumacher, he formed plans about returning to his native Königsberg already after a few years in St Petersburg. In 1733 – after seven years in the Academy – he did actually tender his resignation. However, the new president, Baron Keyserling, who knew him from Königsberg, persuaded him to stay on, offering to raise his salary to 1,000 roubles. In 1737 he again wanted to retire and this time he was in real earnest.[14]

13 Joseph Nicolas Delisle (1688-1768), French astronomer and geographer, member of the Académie des Sciences of Paris. He came to the St Petersburg Academy of Sciences in 1725 where he inaugurated the Institute of Astronomy. He worked there until 1747 when he returned to Paris and continued his astronomical studies there. Undoubtedly Bayer had much of the astronomical information in his works from Delisle.
14 In a letter to Johann Christoph Wolff, dated 8 April 1733, Bayer writes that he hopes to return to Germany by the end of the year. (Wolff Correspondence, Sup.Ep., Bl. 134-5).

His ever-increasing involvement in Chinese studies after 1730 had resulted in a change in his situation in the Academy. In 1735 it was decided that a young German classicist by the name of Johann Georg Lotter (1702-37) should take over his chair of Greek and Roman Antiquities, while Bayer became professor of Oriental Antiquities.

Bayer worked very hard during these years. He began to present papers to the Academy shortly after he arrived and continued to do so till his death. His industriousness is testified by the *Commentarii* of the Academy: alone to represent the Humanities, he had three or four often long articles printed in each of the first eight volumes, and one or two in the following three, published several years after his death. Most of them are about the ancient Scythians and about early Russian history. He also wrote two books, the *Historia Osrhoëna et Edessena, ex nummis illustrata* ... 1734, and the *Historia Regni Graecorum Bactriani* ... published in the year of his death, in 1738. These works fall outside our subject and will not be discussed in the present book which deals only with T.S. Bayer as a pioneer sinologist.

Before coming to St Petersburg, Bayer had already published his first Chinese study, the small book called *De Eclipsi Sinica* (1718). In St Petersburg, he published his *Museum Sinicum* (1730), a two volume 'Textbook of Chinese', a very primitive one indeed, but it *was* the first book about the Chinese language to be printed in Europe. There are no indications that at the time he intended to go on with Chinese studies, but it so happened that a few months after the publication of the book – it came off the press in the first months of the year 1731 – he got the opportunity to use a large Chinese-Latin dictionary.

Sawa Raguzinskij-Vladislavich, the leader of the Russian embassy who had negotiated the treaty between Russia and China in Peking in 1726-7, had just arrived in Moscow, bringing with him this dictionary, a gift from its author, Dominique Parrenin, one of the Peking Jesuits who had assisted at the conference and acted as Chinese and Manchu interpreter. When Count Ostermann, the most powerful person at the Russian court, heard about the dictionary he persuaded Raguzinskij-Vladislavich to lend it to the young academician who had just published a book about the Chinese language.[15] At about the same time Bayer received one or two Chinese lexica from Peking.

This unexpected stroke of good luck may have been felt by Bayer as some kind of sign from above that he had to pursue his Chinese studies: he immedi-

---

15 Count Ostermann: Andrei Ivanovich Ostermann (1686-1747), the all-powerful minister of Foreign Affairs and Commerce under Peter the Great, Cathrine I, Peter II and Anne. After the *coup d'état* in 1741 which made Elizabeth empress of Russia he was banished to Siberia where he died six years later. – Parrenin: see Note 8 to 'After the *Museum Sinicum*' – Sawa Raguzinskij-Vladislavich (approx. 1670-1738), Russian government figure and diplomat. From 1725-8 he headed the Russian mission to China and signed the Kiakhta Treaty in 1727. In Bayer's correspondance with the Peking Jesuits he is always called Sawa Vladislavich.

ately copied the large dictionary and sent a copy of his *Museum Sinicum* to the Jesuit Fathers in Peking, asking for help and advice. And before he could receive their answers he started on a huge project: a big multi-volume Chinese-Latin dictionary to be published by the Imperial Academy. From then on Chinese studies were to become his main occupation, and when the friendly answers arrived from Peking he must have felt sure that he was destined to inaugurate the study of Chinese language and literature in the West – in competition with the great Fourmont in Paris.

The main result of these studies were his book *De Horis Sinicis,* published in 1735, and two lengthy articles, the first of them printed in the year of his death, in 1738, the second one two years later, in 1740.

The rest of the present book will discuss Bayer's sinological works in chronological order, starting with the work he published many years before he came to St Petersburg, the *De Eclipsi Sinica.* This is followed by an exposition of his *Museum Sinicum,* beginning with a translation of the first part of its Preface, which is Bayer's 'History of Sinology'. The last part of the book is devoted to Bayer's studies after he had established contacts with the learned Jesuits in Peking, starting with a presentation of his correspondence with them.[16]

---

16 We have very little information about Bayer's private life in St Petersburg. His marriage is said to have been a very happy one, and his wife bore him eight children, four of whom, however, died at a tender age. We hear that the Delisles and the Bayers visited each other, but Bayer only refers to learned conversations – probably in Latin, for Bayer did not understand spoken French, and Delisle did not understand German – neither of them learned Russian. The Bayers probably also met socially with their fellow-townsman Christian Goldbach who was about their own age. Bayer and Goldbach had known each other for many years and Goldbach shared Bayer's taste for refined Latin prose and poetry. Perhaps they also frequented the company of the old Leutmann, but there is no direct evidence of it (see Note 53 to 'After the *Museum Sinicum*'). – We do know, however, one important thing about Bayer as a private person: we know who was his favourite among the authors of his time! It was Barthold Heinrich Brockes (1680-1747), the Hamburg poet, beloved in Germany for his *Irdische Vergnügen in Gott* (1721-48), mostly nature poetry with precise descriptions in the style of contemporary English poets, whom he admired and translated. Tolerant, optimistic and free of dogmatism he praises God, who created this beautiful world for the benefit of human beings. Several of his arias and cantatas were set to music by Telemann, Händel and other composers. In five letters to Johann Christoph Wolff in Hamburg, filled with exuberant praise and unbounded admiration, he sent his warm greetings to Brockes, his Orpheus, who refreshes him when he feels low and excites in him a nearly divine frenzy. (Wolff Correspondence, Sup.Ep. 114 and 122). Bayer seems also to have corresponded with Brockes, two letters to him have been preserved. Cf. Geoffrey Howard Sutton's 'Neun Briefe von Barthold Heinrich Brockes an unbekannte Empfänger', in (Ed.) Hans Dieter Loose: *Barthold Heinrich Brockes (1680-1747) – Dichter und Ratsherr in Hamburg.* (1980), pp. 105-35.

Fig. 1. T.S. Bayer's *Ex libris:* a sceptre on top of a palm tree, standing on a mountain, i.e. the orientalist from Königsberg. Found by Mr. David J. Weston, Glasgow University Library, Special Collections, under a Hunterian Bookplate in Didacus Cogllaclus: *Dictionarium sive Thesauri linguae Iaponicae compendium.* Rome 1632.

Fig. 2. Prospect of Königsberg. From Georg Braun: *Urbium praecipuarum totius Mundi, Tomus III* (Cologne 1581).

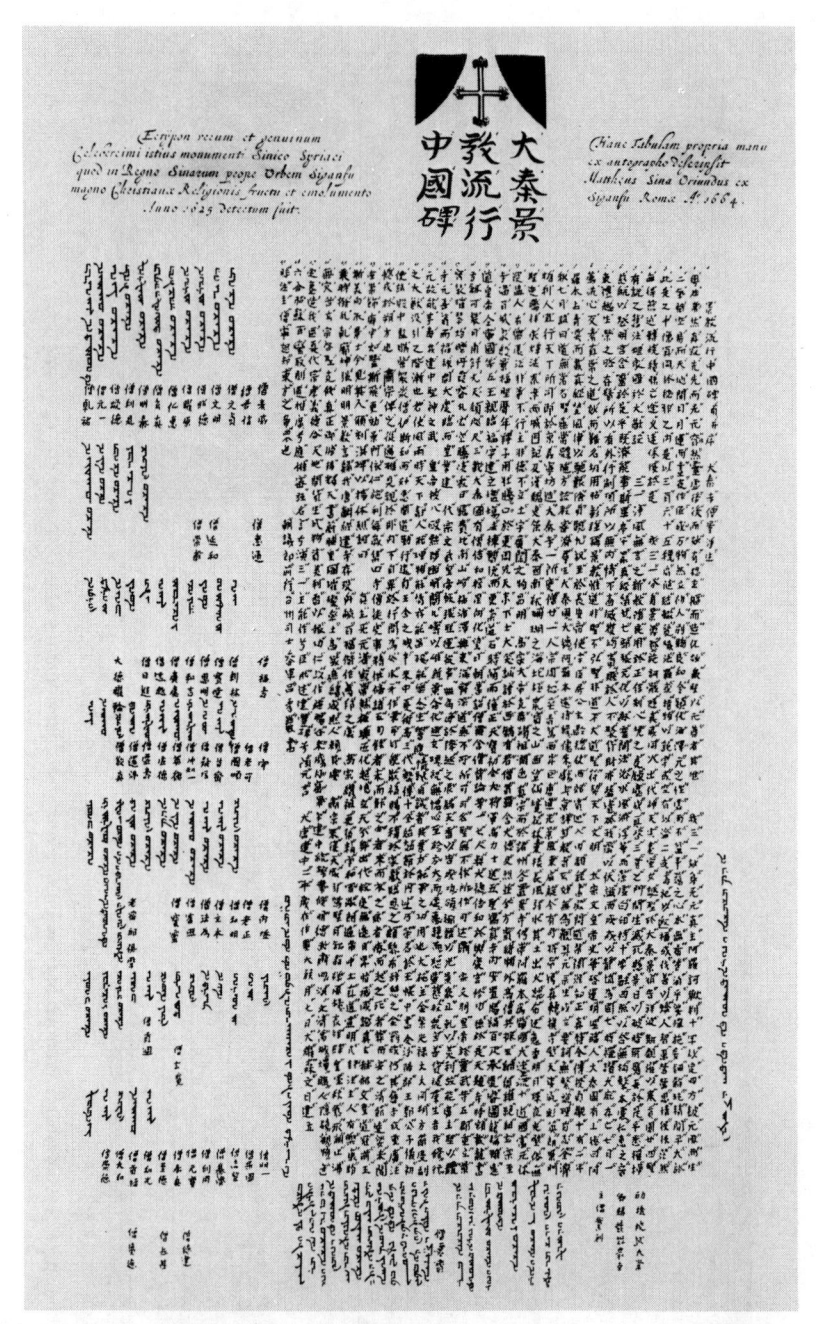

Fig. 3. *Momentum Sinicum*. The inscription on the Nestorian Stele, from Athanasius Kircher: *China . . . Illustrata*, 1667.

Fig. 4. Christian Mentzel (1622-1701), physician and sinologist.

Fig. 5. Joseph Nicolas Delisle (1688-1768), French astronomer, Bayer's great friend in St Petersburg.

Fig. 6. Dominique Parrenin (1665-1741), French Jesuit missionary in Peking, Bayer's 'teacher'.

PART II
FIRST CHINESE STUDIES

4
DE ECLIPSI SINICA

Bayer's first Chinese study, a small book entitled *De Eclipsi Sinica ...*, was published in Königsberg in 1718. It contains a 42-page article dealing with a much discussed problem: that of the solar eclipse reported to have been observed in China in A.D. 31 and its relationship to the 'darkening of the sky over Golgatha', described in the New Testament. This is followed by a nine-page Appendix on the Chinese language, introduced by a long dedicatory letter to his old friend Lacroze, the librarian in the Royal Library in Berlin. There is one engraved plate with Chinese characters, among others those from the 'Chinese Annals' where the eclipse is mentioned. There are no characters corresponding to the words and phrases in the Language Appendix. The characters of this plate are by no means finely drawn, but it is interesting that they are rather better than those we are to meet when we come to the *Museum Sinicum*.[1]

The problem which Bayer chose to deal with in his first publication about Chinese matters, the nature of the 'darkness over Golgatha', sometimes called the Paschal Eclipse, had always been debated among theologians, historians and astronomers. In Luke 23, 44-45 it is described as follows: 'And it was about the sixth hour, and there was darkness all over the earth until the ninth hour. And the sun was darkened ...'

From the earliest Church fathers onwards, this phenomenon had been understood either as a solar eclipse, or as a local thunderstorm, or as a supernatural cosmic miracle. When the China Jesuits of the seventeenth century began to study the Chinese history books, they found in them apparently precise indications about solar eclipses all the way back to before 2,000 B.C. One of these eclipses attracted the attention of the missionaries. In the 'Chinese Annals', as they were called, i.e. Sima Guang's *Zizhi Tongjian*, the 'Universal Mirror for Government', they found an entry about a solar eclipse occurring during the reign of the Eastern Han emperor, Guang Wu, followed by a sentence about forbidding the use of the word *sheng* (holy).[2]

---

1 With a letter to the orientalist Johann Christoph Wolff in Hamburg, dated 15 May 1719, Bayer sent him a number of copies of his *De Eclipsi Sinica*, 200 of which had been printed at his own expense. He asks Wolff if he could persuade a bookseller to buy them at a price of 'eight of your Groschen'. From a letter written a few months later it appears that the bookseller has accepted the offer, and now Bayer suggests that he take over the rest of the edition, one hundred copies, at a price of seven Groschen! (Wolff Correspondence, Supp. Ep. 114).

2 Sima Guang (1019-86), famous Song dynasty historian and statesman. His History of China, the *Zizhi Tongjian*, or Universal Mirror for Government, was completed in 1084. In more than 300 juan it covers the period from 425 B.C. to A.D. 959. The existence of this work was well known in the seventeenth century in Europe, where it was always spoken of as the 'Annales Sinici'. It should not be confused with the abbreviation of it, produced by the philosopher Zhu Xi and his pupils in 1172, the *Tongjian Gangmu*. This work was translated

Comparing Chinese with European chronology, they calculated that this eclipse had occurred in the spring of A.D. 33. Speculations arose immediately as to whether this was the darkness over Golgatha. If so, the missionaries, talking to the Chinese, could point to a statement in their own ancient books related to the gospel they were bringing to them.

The event had been noted by the China Jesuit Philippe Couplet, in the *Chronology* printed in the great *Confucius Sinarum Philosophus* which he edited in Paris in 1687. He had added the cautious remark: 'Whether this eclipse was that which occurred when Christ died is for the astronomers to decide'. However, there were still people who identified the 'darkness over Golgatha' with the eclipse mentioned in the old Chinese work. In Europe this eclipse was often referred to simply as the 'Chinese Eclipse', and this is the meaning of the title that Bayer gave to his book.

Bayer must have started to write his book shortly after his arrival in Königsberg. In a letter to Lacroze, written in July 1718, he tells him that he is publishing a small book about the eclipse 'thought to have occurred while Christ was on his cross. I deny that it was an eclipse and also that the Chinese knew anything about such a phenomenon.'[3]

Bayer may have had several reasons for writing his *De Eclipsi Sinica*. His first book, the dissertation of 1716, mentioned above, had been about Christ's last words on the cross. A text on the darkness over Golgatha seemed a natural sequence to that. He was full of the new insights into Chinese matters he had just acquired by studying Christian Mentzel's papers on the Chinese language and examining the Diaz Vocabulary in the Royal Library in Berlin. His relationship to his Berlin patron, Lacroze, the great linguist and church historian, must have made him wish to repay the help and kindness he had received from that man by promptly publishing a work on this problem and in which he could insert a dedicatory letter expressing his gratitude. A dozen or so letters each way, long, learned and very amiable ones, had already passed between them during the months when Bayer was working in other German universities, before he came back to Königsberg. Bayer's affectionate admiration for Lacroze was unbounded, and Lacroze saw in this young scholar a coming luminary, repeating again and again his wish to help him on. Finally, of course, Bayer may have felt the urge to present himself as quickly as possible to the reading public as a Chinese scholar, because another young German scholar, Polycarp Leyser, had just published a work on the Chinese language (see below).

---

into French by J.A.M. de Moyriac de Mailla, S.J. and published in Paris in 1777-85 – 11 volumes in 4° – under the title of *Histoire Générale de la Chine*. – De Mailla had sent it to Paris already in the 1730s, as we are going to see in the chapter on Bayer's correspondence with the Peking Jesuits.

3 Lacroze Correspondence, I, p. 41.

In selecting the eclipse problem he knew that he would be performing against an interesting backdrop. The last publication of Andreas Müller, the mysterious Berlin provost-sinologist, dealt with the 'Chinese Eclipse'. What could be more natural for Bayer than to try to emulate and criticize that man, whose reputation as the secret inventor of a *Clavis Sinica* was still *sub judice*?

The text of the *De Eclipsi Sinica* is a loosely-woven structure of thoughts and findings, plus a great deal of reading, aiming at a definite conclusion but deviating into digressions and digressions from digressions. If one traces the arguments as they appear here and there in the meanders of the text, they turn out to be quite simple:

1. The eclipse described in Sima Guang's history book is one among many others. It is described like any other eclipse, it is a *bona fide* eclipse, there is nothing extraordinary about it.

2. The 'three hours of darkness over the earth' cannot have been caused by an eclipse, for an eclipse is not seen everywhere on the planet, and eclipses do not last for three hours.

3. The crucifixion took place at, or about, full moon (the Paschal Full Moon). Eclipses do not occur at full moon.

Therefore the popular idea about a connection between the Chinese eclipse and the 'darkness' described in the Bible is unwarranted.

Bayer's many digressions in the text itself, and also in his letter to Lacroze, contain many things that the reader would find him taking up again in the *Museum Sinicum*, and which we will meet in later chapters. Here it suffices to mention one point where the two texts differ, namely in the author's attitude towards the Jesuits.

In one place we find a kind of criticism that is absent from the *Museum Sinicum* and his later works. Why is it, he asks, that the Jesuits – or some of them at least – restrict their teaching of the Christian religion to something that looks so very much as if it were Greek or Roman philosophy – or even Chinese? Bayer mentions especially Ricci, in whose works, according to his information, the death of Christ is passed over in silence. He knows this, he says, from Navarrete's book, i.e. the famous *Tratados historicos ... de la Monarchia de China,* published in Madrid in 1676 by Domingo Navarrete, the anti-Jesuit Dominican. He quotes a sentence from it in Spanish and notes the page on which it is found.[4] This book had been a shock to Bayer, both as far

---

4 Father Mathew Riccius suppress'd the Passion and Death of Christ, which he did to impose upon the people'. Bayer probably had it from Lacroze. In a letter dated 23 January 1717 Lacroze tells him that he has just received a copy of it from a friend in Lisbon (Lacroze Correspondence, III, pp. 19-20). This letter contains a long quotation from the book, but not the one that Bayer cites, nor is it found anywhere else in the printed Lacroze correspondence. Bayer knew that Navarrete took it from Yang Guangxian's pamphlet *Pi Sie Lun (Pie Xie Lun)*, printed in 1659, but he does not mention Navarrete's comment on it: 'It is plain that the

as Navarrete's own vitriolic attacks were concerned and because of the enclosed highly controversial text, written by Niccolo Longobardi, Ricci's successor as superior of the China mission. He had rejected Ricci's 'accomodation technique', i.e. the acceptance of the ancestor cult of the Chinese and their veneration of Confucius as innocent civil ceremonies. Bayer never recovered from this shock, and even in his letters to his Jesuit friends in Peking, so many years later, he still insisted upon the importance of elucidating the difference in opinion of the two first superiors of the Jesuit China mission (see Part III, 1).

Bayer also touched upon another closely related *cause célèbre*, from the late seventeenth century, the book called *Innocentia Victrix*, an apology in Latin and Chinese which the Jesuits had sent to the Kang Xi emperor in 1669, defending themselves against accusations from Yang Guangxian, an official campaigning against the missionaries. Bayer wrote, correctly, about its ultra-short 'definition' of the Christian faith, adding that this is only what Confucius said: 'Adore Heaven, love your neighbour and know yourself' – no reason is given as to why we believe in the Christian God![5]

All this looks as if it had been written to please his anti-Jesuit patron, Lacroze, although Bayer is careful to mention Chinese works published by China Jesuits which were impeccable, also adding, 'I know that much of the writings against the China Jesuits are produced by people who see their own interest in denigrating them.'

great man had no such design'. (Book VI, chapter XV. These quotes are taken from the fine English translation, published in London in 1704, p. 286). – For Yang Guangxian see the long article by Fang Chao-ying in A.W. Hummel (Ed.): *Eminent Chinese of the Ch'ing Period*, Washington, 1943. – For Navarrete see Note 31 to the preface to the *Museum Sinicum*. – The book in which Ricci (see Note 26 to Preface) was said to have passed over the death of Christ in silence is his famous 'catechism', the *Tianzhu Shiyi*, published in Peking in 1603. It contains eight chapters in two volumes, mostly scholastic analyses of the attributes of God and polemics against the Buddhists and the Neo-Confucians of the Song period. It is true that all there is about the death of Christ is two small sentences towards the end of the work, one stating that at the age of 33 years he ascended into Heaven, the other that shortly before he had announced the day when it would happen before the eyes of many of his disciples. We know now that Ricci himself regarded it as the 'first part of a Chinese catechism', but a second one never appeared. This is clear from the Introduction to the Latin translation of the Preface and the summaries of the chapters of the book which he sent to Rome in 1604 (Bibliotheca Casanatense, Rome, No. 2136). For an extended discussion of the *Tianzhu Shiye* see d'Elia's *Fonte Ricciani*, mentioned in Note 13 to 'After the *Museum Sinicum*', Volume II, pp. 292-301. Ricci's book was not translated into a European language till late in the eighteenth century. Bayer obtained a copy of the Chinese edition from Peking later on (see p. 162).

5 Bayer must have got his information about the *Innocentia Victrix* from the magnificient *Commentariorum de Augustissimae Bibliotheca Caesarea Vindobonensi Liber primus, etc.*, published in Vienna, 1665-79 by Peter Lambeck (1628-80). In Vol. V, Appendix XIII, pp. 418-19, Lambeck announces that this year (1672) the Imperial Library received several things from Prosper Intorcetta, S.J. (see Note 33 to 'Preface to the *Museum Sinicum*'), e.g. the

There are also some deprecatory remarks about Couplet, the editor of the *Confucius Sinarum Philosophus*. Bayer knew from this Jesuit's letters to Christian Mentzel, which he had studied in Berlin, that he had no great training in Chinese; Couplet admitted to it himself. So how could he have translated the huge 'Chinese Annals', and made the summary of them that is printed under his name at the end of the *Confucius Sinarum Philosophus*?[6]

However, it was not only the Jesuits who met with his criticism – all Chinese philosophy is also attacked: 'The publication of the *Confucius Sinarum Philosophus* removed a gross error from the mind of the Europeans. Before that time it was believed that deep wisdom lay hidden in the works of Confucius, but once we gained access to them this opinion evaporated'.

With these words, however, Bayer did not mean to deny the fine moral qualities of the old Chinese philosopher. As a proof of his integrity he inserted two small pieces from the *Great Learning,* one of the Four Books, a translation of which had been printed in the *Confucius Sinarum Philosophus*. One of them deals with our duty to renew ourselves each day, the other one points to the importance of remaining on the right way, once we have found it. Bayer took the Chinese characters and the transliterations from Mentzel's papers in Berlin.[7]

And now about Bayer's translation of the eclipse text in Sima Guang's *Zizhi Tongjian*. He knew this text from a small book called *De Eclipsi Passionali Disquisitio*, published in Berlin in 1685. It had been written by Andreas Müller, the Berlin orientalist about whom we are going to hear a great deal in the following. Müller had found the much-discussed text in the 'Chinese Annals' in the Royal Library in Berlin. In his *De Eclipsi Passionali Disquisitio* he printed it – 30 characters in all – together with his own attempt

---

Scientia Sinica Politico-Moralis and the *Innocentia Vitrix,* written by Buglio, Magelhães and Verbiest, the three Jesuits who remained at the court in Peking during the Canton exile in 1669. In Vol. VII, Additamentum II, pp. 348-98, he printed these two texts, but only the Latin part of them. – The great problem of the right way to preach the Gospel in China – the Rites Controversy – will not be discussed in the present book. Bayer had no access to its intricacies. For recent important works on that subject see Jacques Gernet: *Chine et christianisme – Action et réaction*, Paris 1982, and David E. Mungello: *Curious Land*, Stuttgart 1985.

6 Hunter MS No. 299.

7 For the *Great Learning* in Mentzel's papers, see Note 40 to the '*Museum Sinicum:* The Chinese Language'. – In the Lacroze Correspondence we find the plates with the Chinese characters of the two pieces which occur in Chapter II and III of the *Great Learning*, written out by Lacroze. But they are placed just before other plates with the characters of chapter I of this work, and inserted with a letter of 30 April 1723, where he writes: 'I am sending you here what you wanted, the first period of the Confucian book.' The first pages, with the small pieces which Bayer had asked for in 1718 and which he incorporated in his Eclipse book, have been misplaced by the editor of the Correspondence (Lacroze Correspondence, I, p. 42, II, p. 277, III, p. 56).

at a translation.

Sima Guang's text runs as follows:

In the seventh year of the Emperor Guang Wu's reign, on the last day (*hui*), called *gui hai*, of the third month of spring there was a solar eclipse. The emperor summoned each of the officials to bring a secret report (adding that) those of them who did so should not use the word *sheng* (holy).

In Berlin in 1716 Bayer had found his way to this paragraph in Sima Guang's work by following the precise indications given by Müller in his *De Eclipsi Passionali Disquisitio:* 'Volume 42, fol. 12'. Müller had been unable to translate the word *hui* – the last day of the month – and *gui hai*, two cyclical characters giving the name of the day. Bayer found the correct meaning of the word *hui*, but he thought that *gui hai* meant 'at noon'. Müller, in his translation of the last part of the phrase, the one about the Emperor's reaction to the eclipse, had committed errors but he did understand that in using the term *sheng*, the Emperor was referring to his own title. Bayer chose to read the text as if the Emperor had said that it was the officials who were not to be called *sheng*. He defended his reading in a discussion of the various meanings of this word:

Sheng means excellent, just, learned, etc. It is used about emperors, kings, heroes, high dignitaries and about ancient sages: Confucius was a *Sheng,* of course, and Navarrete says that Ricci himself was called a *Sheng!* So Müller's interpretation implying the humility of the Emperor facing a portent, is quite unjustified.

There is no reason to discuss further the respective merits of young Bayer's speculations and those of Andreas Müller, who had been forced in his old age to publish his translation of these lines as a proof of his ability to read Chinese.

The last nine pages of the *De Eclipsi Sinica* contain Bayer's instructions – *praeceptiones* – about the Chinese language. They read like a summary of the main parts of the grammar he was going to publish in his *Museum Sinicum* in 1730. They need not detain us here, therefore, except for a few notes to indicate the way Bayer presented his insights in 1718.

At the beginning he states clearly from where he has his information about the Chinese language: 'I have taken some instructions from Martini, Couplet, Picques and Mentzel'. In the Preface to the *Museum Sinicum* we will find him explaining these sources more precisely.

Bayer includes the same list of syllables as in the *Museum Sinicum,* writing them in the Spanish way, in contrast to the home-made German one he uses for the Eclipse text.

There is a brief statement about certain tones that are of importance for the understanding of Chinese words. Then follow small sections on substantives, pronouns, verbs, prepositions, adverbs, conjunctions, etc., again similar to although much shorter than in the *Museum Sinicum,* and finally two pages about Chinese dictionaries. They are arranged, Bayer says, in a certain manner according to the strokes: the 'root', usually consisting of several simple lines, is followed by other elements composed of the same kind of strokes or of others. The left part of the composed characters is regarded as the 'radical' and the whole dictionary is arranged according to them – 'but this is not always so'.

Bayer mentions Christian Mentzel's great Chinese-Latin dictionary, 'which he had written to Tentzel's *Monatliche Unterrredungen* about'.[8] We are going to hear more about it in the Preface to the *Museum Sinicum.* Speaking of the handwritten Chinese-Latin dictionaries by the missionaries in China, he remarks that they are arranged in such a way that makes them of little use for Europeans – 'we should return to the old system of the Chinese lexicographers'. By this he is probably only referring to the alphabetical arrangements of the Chinese words in the Diaz Vocabulary he had seen in Berlin.

The great difference between Bayer's presentation of the Chinese language here and in the *Museum Sinicum* is that in the latter work he included all the words in Chinese characters. He refers to the problem in a short section, with examples of measure words. He refrains from giving more of them, 'because I cannot include the characters'.

As to possible future studies of Chinese matters he says in one place that he would like to say more about the language in an article about the origin of the Chinese people, 'if other scholars would approve of such an enterprise.' There is nothing about plans to produce a Chinese dictionary. On the contrary, he wants someone else to do that. In the dedicatory letter to Lacroze he speaks about the plans of a certain Polycarp Leyser:

> I have received through friends (a copy of) the *Clavis Sinica* that Leyser has. It is composed by Mentzel, as appears from his inability to write Chinese characters properly, you know that as well as I do, and Leyser is right when he criticizes it. It is not a key to the entire language nor to all dictionaries, but only to one of them, which Mentzel wanted to edit, and which is in your Royal Library. However, this dictionary is not arranged well enough by the Chinese. It could and it should be arranged in a better way by somebody in Europe for the use of our scholars. Therefore I am urging Leyser to take up that problem so that we may get a dictionary that is more extensive and more accurately composed and arranged. If he does so, it could be further enriched afterwards.'

---

8 *Monatliche Unterredungen,* 1690, pp. 900-1. See Note 83 to the 'Preface to the *Museum Sinicum*'.

This man by the name of Polycarp Leyser, whom Bayer introduces here as if he were known to everyone of his readers, was a young German scholar, only four years older than Bayer. In 1717, the year before the appearance of the *De Eclipsi Sinica*, he had published a small book called *Apparatus literarius*, including an article about the Chinese language. Here he says that he has a great Chinese-Latin dictionary ready to print. However nothing came of it, and Leyser died two years before Bayer published his next sinological work, the *Museum Sinicum*.[9] As mentioned in the Foreword, the first 100 pages of the Preface to that work is Bayer's 'History of Sinology', ending with a kind of sinological autobiography. In what follows here this part of his Preface is brought in translation, uninterrupted except for the numbers referring to the notes.

---

9 Bayer returns to Polycarp Leyser (1690-1728) and Mentzel's lexicon – meaning his *Clavis Sinica* – in the 'Preface to the *Museum Sinicum*' (see p. 85).

5
MUSEUM SINICUM

THE PREFACE

Bayer's History of Sinology

It took a long time before European scholars began to study Chinese language and literature, and still today such study is not cultivated as it ought to be, considering the value and practical usefulness of Chinese.

For how much is there in the works of Marcianus of Heraclea[1] and Cosmas Indicopleustes the Egyptian,[2] writing much later, about the Chinese people? Certainly nobody said a word about their language, their literature, or their philosophy, before the time when the Mongols under Prince Ogdai had conquered the Chinese in the southern provinces in 1238, and some years later had invaded Persia, as described in the literature.[3] In 1253, Hulagu was sent to Persia by his elder brother Mangu Khan. He had with him some Chinese scholars, among them one Fu Muen Gi, called Gin Xim, i.e. Holy and Learned in all Sciences.[4] This man expounded Chinese astronomy and chronology in accordance with the tradition of their ancient scientists, to Nasir al-din, who at the time was working on the Tables of the Ilkhan.[5]

---

1 Marcianus, fifth century Greek geographer, born in Heraclea in Pontus, author of the *Periplus of the Outer Sea,* based mainly on Ptolemy. It contains a few words about a country in the Far East: 'The nations of the Sinae lie at the extremity of the habitable world and adjoins the eastern Terra incognita . . . the city called Thinae is the capital' (Henry Yule: *Cathay and the Way thither,* New Edition, London, 1913-16).
2 Cosmas, called Indicopleustes (the India traveller), sixth-century Byzantine merchant and traveller who visited Ethiopia and Ceylon. Later in life, as a monk, he wrote his famous *Christian Topograpy.* In the eleventh book of this work we find the following words: 'The country of silk is the remotest of all the Indies . . . Tzinitza is the name of this country . . . further than Tzinitza there is neither navigation nor inhabited country' (ibid.).
3 *The Mongols:* a synopsis and dates of the Mongol rulers mentioned by Bayer. On the death of Genghis Khan (1162-1227) the Mongol Empire stretched from the north China Sea to the banks of the Dnieper. Ogdai, one of his sons, was Great Khan (Khakhan) from 1229 to 1241. Mangu, a grandson of Ogdai, was Great Khan 1252-9. It was during his reign that the monk Rubrouck visited his capital Karakorum. His brother was the famous Kublai, who became Great Khan in 1260, founded the Yuan (Mongol) dynasty of China in 1280 and ruled it till his death in 1294. Another of Mangu's brothers was Hulagu who governed Persia as provincial Khan (Ilkhan) from 1256 to 1295. He was followed by his son Abagha (1265-81), by another son, Nicudar Ahmed, who was murdered in 1284 and then by Abagha's son Arghun (1284-91). Arghun's son Ghazan Mahmud ruled Persia from 1295 to 1304, followed by his brother Uljaitu, who reigned 1304-16.
4 Fu Muen Gi (see Note 7).
5 Nasir al-din al-Tusi (1201-74), Persian scientist, one of the greatest in Islam, working for Hulagu after his conquest of Persia. He wrote a great number of books on theology, philoso-

After his greatgrandfather, Hulagu, his grandfather, Abaga, and his father, Argun, Ghazan became governor of Persia under Kublai Khan, the Emperor (1295). At the time when he ordered Rashid al-din to write the Ghazan Annals, *he had two Chinese philosophers at his court in order to learn from them not only about the astronomy and the chronology of the Chinese, but also about their medical sciences and history in accordance with their tradition.*[6] *All this would have been forgotten were it not for Al-Baidawi, who – exactly 456 years ago – began to study Chinese history, relying on these authors: he mentions that he has seen Chinese books, praising their incredibly elegant script, and explaining the typographical procedure. However, the information he gives is very meagre.*[7]

At that time William of Rubrouck was sent to the Tartars as ambassador for Louis IX, the French king (1253). There he learned that, when they write, the Chinese use brushes in the manner of painters, forming each letter with several strokes.[8]

Marco Polo, the Venetian, who came after him, worked for seventeen years either at Kublai Khan's court or in public service as a royal governor in the provinces (1275). Living among them he became versed in the four languages of these peoples, conversing freely with them and also understanding their philosophy and literature.[9] *However, from his extant writings it is difficult to judge how much Chinese he knew.*

   phy, mathematics, astronomy, astrology, geography and medicine. The *Tables of the Ilkhan (Al-zij al-ilkhani)*, deals with Chinese, Greek, Arabic and Persian chronology and with astronomy, partly based on his own observations in the famous observatory he built in Maragha. Parts of a later elaboration of these tables were published in London in 1650 by John Greaves (see Note 48).
6 Rashid al-din (1247-1318), famous Persian statesman, physician and historian who served under successive Ilkhans from Hulagu to after Ghazan's time. He wrote a great *Universal History*, including not only the history of the Mongols but also information about European states, India and China. The first part of this work was called the *Annals of Ghazan*.
7 Al-Baidawi. Bayer took the story about 'Fu Muen Gi' (see Note 4) and the following information from Andreas Müller's *Abdallae Baidavaei Historia Sinensis,* printed in Berlin, 1679. It is now known that this book is not by Al-Baidawi, a Persian theologian and historian who died in 1286, but part of another *Universal History* written by Al-Banakati, a contemporary of Rashid al-din and like him working at Ghazan's court. Al-Banakati took his information about Chinese books and script from Rashid al-din's work (George Sarton: *Introduction to the History of Science* (1927-48), Vol. III, Part I, pp. 969-77).
8 William of Rubrouck (Rubruquis), c. 1215-70. Flemish Franciscan friar. In the years 1253-5, under orders of King Louis IX, he visited the camp of Manghu Khan close to Karakorum in the present Mongolian Peoples Republic. He wrote a lively and interesting description of his voyage, which was used extensively by Roger Bacon. It was published in several collections in the sixteenth and seventeenth centuries. Rubrouck was particularly interested in languages. The passage about the Chinese script runs as follows in his 'dog-Latin': 'Faciunt in una figura plures literas comprehendentes unam dictionem'.
9 Marco Polo, c. 1254-1324, a young Venetian traveller and explorer, the most famous of all the

From him in particular, but also from Johannes Plano Carpini,[10] *who travelled to these parts of the world as envoy of Pope Innocent IV before Rubrouck's time, Vincent de Beauvais, Antonino of Florence, and other Italians, Germans and Frenchmen learned about the Tartars.*[11,12] *Still, however, they obtained no information about Chinese literature.*

Hayton the Armenian, who was about the same age as Marco Polo, learned about the Chinese script from the Tartars he frequented.[13] *(United by a pact with the Armenian king, a relative of Hayton, they were causing trouble in Asia.) I suspect that he did not know more than what he told Nicolo Falconi, who told it again to Pope Clement V — nothing else, namely, other than that their letters were very beautiful. As to their culture and philosophy, however, he understood that they regarded other peoples as blind and unable to distinguish light from darkness — the Europeans being, at most, one-eyed. They themselves alone had dispersed the ugly mist from their minds and looked at the world with both eyes.*

At that time our holy Christian religion was brought to the Far East and to the court of the emperors by Nestorian missionaries.[14] *This we know not only from the evidence of the Nestorian Stele — unjustly suspected, in my opinion, by*

  early travellers to the East and the first to give a description of China. He worked in the administration of Kublai Khan's court in Khanbalik (now Peking) and in the provinces from 1275 to 1291-2. He returned to Venice by the sea route, on the way escorting a Chinese bride to Arghun, the Persian Ilkhan. In 1298-9 he dictated a narrative of his travels and experiences to a French man of letters. This wonderful book circulated in innumerable handwritten copies and has been printed again and again in many languages ever since the fifteenth century. Regarded for centuries as containing less facts than fancy it is now known to be surprisingly correct in nearly all its information. – The four languages: The text has 'four scripts', – perhaps Uighur, Tibetan, Arabic and Chinese? (Sarton, ibid. Vol. II, Part II, p. 1057).
10 Johannes Plano Carpini (Giovanni del Pian del Carpine), c. 1182-1252. Italian Franciscan. In the years 1245-7 he visited Karakorum as diplomatic envoy of the Pope. Extracts of his narrative, the *Liber Tartarum,* were published in English and French in the sixteenth and seventeenth centuries.
11 Vincent de Beauvais, d. 1264. French Dominican, librarian and tutor to King Louis IX, author of the immense encyclopedia called *Speculum Majus,* a compilation of extracts from all kinds of texts. The historical part of the *Speculum* contains an abridgement of Plano Carpini's book about the Tartars.
12 Antonin of Florence, Antonino Pierozzi, 1389-1459, Saint, Archbishop of Florence. Among his works is a *Summa historialis.*
13 Hayton the Armenian, called Hayton the Monk, died c. 1314. Armenian historian, cousin of the King Hayton II, who reigned from 1289-97. In 1307, during a visit to France, Hayton dictated a geography and history of Asia to Nicolas Falcon (sometimes called Salcon, as here in Bayer's text). This man wrote it out for Pope Clemens V and the work circulated under the title *Flos historiarum partium Orientis.* There are numerous editions in many languages. The statement about the Chinese script runs as follows: 'The Cathayans have letters that in their beauty resemble somehow the Latin letters'. (H. Yule, see Note 1, gives the original French text and the Latin translation on pp. 259-61 of Volume I, part 9.)
14 The Nestorians, a Syriac sect considered heterodox, successfully carried out missionary work

some persons – but also from Gregorius Barhebraeus of Melitene and other Syrian and Arabic authors.[15] Later, however, the situation in Asia changed, obliterating the memory of Christianity among the Chinese and closing the overland route to China for us – at that time the Portuguese sea route to the East had not yet been opened. For after the death of Kublai Khan, who had subdued the whole of China and with difficulty sustained the weight of all Asia on his shoulders, disagreement between the princes and factional interests resulted in the Mongol Empire being divided up into four great separate states. These tumultuous events, going on for many years, prevented our further access to China.

Moreover, a certain sudden change of heart produced disastrous results, not only for our commerce and our curiosity about foreign things, but also for our holy religion, inflicting upon it, as it were, an incurable and deadly wound. Before, the situation in Asia had been such that the whole house of Genghis Khan strongly favoured the Christian church, many of the princes being baptized and having Christian wives. And even after Hulagu's son, Nicudar, became interested in the Muhammadan faith, assumed the name of Ahmad, and finally converted to Muhammadanism, these vacillations did not hurt our cause but led to his own ruin and that of his whole family. For they aroused an incredible hatred for him among the other princes, who regarded his conversion as disgusting and unworthy.

However, shortly afterwards the same thing happened to Uljaitu, a brother of the above mentioned Ghazan. He ruled the largest part of the empire after it had been divided at Kublai Khan's death. This prince, in spite of the fact that he had been piously brought up by his Christian mother, nonetheless went over to the Muhammadan faith and took the name of Gaiatheddin Muhammad Codabenda. That was the end of Christianity in the Far East. The Christian churches that had been flourishing in northern Asia were either crushed in the storm or else fell to pieces and sank into ruins.

During this violent conflagration and because of the strong anti-Christian climate, Europeans regarded it as dangerous – and indeed it was – to travel to the Persian provinces, not to mention to proceed from there to the more eastern regions disrupted by the rivalry of contending princes. Finally, after the Tartars had been chased completely out of China (1370), these people, the neighbours and once the rulers of China, ceased to harbour much information about this

in Near and Central Asia in the fifth to thirteenth centuries. Established in China in the year 635, during the Tang dynasty. It was suppressed there in 845 but re-emerged during the Pax Mongolica in the 13-14th centuries. Rubrouck, Marco Polo and other travellers and missionaries reported about Nestorians in China at that time. – For the Nestorian Stele, see Note 55.

15 Gregorius Barhebraeus (Abu-l-Faraj), 1226-86, the Syriac historian and philosopher, prolific writer and translator of scientific works, 'the Vincent de Beauvais of the Syriac world'.

country, which was now closed to them.[16]

So little communication was there between Europe and China that once it was unveiled to us again it appeared as a new world, inhabited by a people that cultivated politeness, refined manners and elegance according to the teaching and the principles of their ancestors, thus vying for this kind of glory with the European nations, but separated from them by wild tribes of vast barbarous regions. The ancient authors, before the time of Cosmas the Egyptian who visited Indian ports at the time of Justinian, hardly knew that there was such a people – not the Seres, as they thought, but the Chinese – that lived in such a state, having such manners and obeying such laws. Before the time of the Mongol empire China had never been praised for its wisdom or its literature, and after its fall, for more than 140 years this country seemed more and more to fade away, to disappear as a star declining in the skies.

Everybody knows how the sea route to the East was opened. For many years the Chinese did not allow foreigners to enter their country, excluding not only profitable trade, but also thwarting the desire of learned Europeans for exact information about China.

Xavier came to India in search of the people most worthy of receiving our holy religion.[17] *When he understood that the Chinese were regarded as the most learned, the most industrious, in short the most admirable people in the world, he could not rest till he had reached their country and had obtained for himself the honour of having started missionary work among them – were it even to be at the risk of his life.*

At that time there were clever Portuguese, in Malacca, who had found out how to travel to China, and even some Chinese merchants. Stimulated by these encounters, Xavier wanted to join Diego Pereira, who had been sent to that country by King Johannes III of Portugal, carrying rich presents and commissioned to negotiate a treaty, including the release of Portuguese persons imprisoned in China. Pereira being forbidden to enter China, Xavier sailed to Japan. Here it became clear to him that his missionary work was hampered by the

---

16 The time of the last Mongol Emperor was one of incessant peasants' revolts. Finally, in 1368, a former Buddhist monk, turned soldier, succeeded in overturning the Mongol dynasty, proclaiming himself the Hong Wu emperor of a new dynasty, the Ming dynasty (1368-1644).

17 Francisco Xavier, born in 1506 in the kingdom of Navarra (to Spain 1512), co-founder with Ignatius Loyola of the Society of Jesus, the 'Apostle of the Indies'. In India and Malacca 1542-9, Japan 1549-51. Returned to Goa in India 1552, making plans for an embassy to China under Diego Pereira, a Portuguese sea captain. Because the governor of Malacca would not allow Pereira to sail to China, Xavier went alone, arriving at a small island off the coast of Guangdong, a port and rendezvous for Europeans not then admitted to the mainland of China, but he could not persuade anybody to take him to Canton. He died a few months later on the island (1552). Bayer's account of these events is not quite clear, it is the language problems that occupy his mind. (See Donald F. Lach: *Asia in the Making of Europe*, I, pp. 281-5 (1965).

admiration of the Japanese for the Chinese, whom they regarded as the wisest in the world. The fact that this nation was not Christian was decisive for the Japanese, for whom the opinion of the Chinese was authoritative. This strengthened his resolution but he had to wait for more than two years before he got an opportunity to carry it into effect.

Now it often happened that Chinese merchants visited him and expressed admiration for European religious books, and Xavier in turn had them explain to him the principles of the Chinese language and its script. He saw Japanese children studying Chinese and noted that they were taught the meaning, not the Chinese sound, of the characters, reciting the Chinese text in their own language. Apparently the Chinese characters were pictures, and Xavier decided to commit himself to this kind of mute learning as much as he could. He composed a book about the origin of the world and the life of Jesus Christ in Japanese and had it written out in Chinese characters, hoping to use it when he had reached the land of his desire, until he had learned the language and the script. But he died before he could reap the fruit of his well-planned endeavour; the sea captains and the interpreters refused – even when he offered to pay for it – to help him to undertake his sacred missionary expedition. He then returned to India, but after that he came by ship to a certain island close to a Chinese port, and there he met his death (1552).

Twelve years after Xavier's death, Luis de Velasco, the viceroy of Mexico, sent a fleet under the command of Miguel López Legazpi who occupied the islands which came to be known as the Philippines. Martin de Rada of Pomplona went over to these islands with other Augustinians to administer this region for his order. At that time the Chinese were fighting the terrible pirate, Li Feng. The Spanish attacked him and thus a certain seed of friendship was sown between the two nations with the result that de Rada and a Mexican friar, by name Jeronimo Marin, came to visit China, accepting the courteous invitation of the Chinese admiral (1575). They were followed by Pietro d'Alfaro and Martin Ignatius de Loyola, two Franciscans, about the time when the Augustinian Juan Gonzalez Mendoça arrived in China as the envoy of the Spanish king (1580).[18]

It was from the Philippines that the first Chinese books – perhaps acquired in Manilla – were sent to the Vatican and to the Escorial Monastery near Madrid. When de Rada brought about one hundred Chinese books back with him to the

---

18 Martin de Rada, learned Spanish Augustinian, died 1578. – Jeronimo Marin, Augustinian. – Pietro d'Alfaro and Martin Ignatio de Loyola, Franciscans. The Augustinians were in Fukien for two months in 1575, the Fransciscans in 1579. – Juan Gonzales de Mendoça, (1545-1614), Spanish Augustinian, living in Mexico. His book *Historia de las cosas mas notables, ritos y costumbres del gran reyno de la China*, Rome, 1585, was the first of the great China books (after Marco Polo's). It became a bestseller, being printed in 46 editions between 1585 and 1600, in seven languages. Gonzales de Mendoça was never in China.

Philippines, where there were people who could read them, Mendoça conceived the idea of writing a book elucidating the condition and the extent of the power of the Chinese empire. He travelled back to Rome, and, in Spanish, to Pope Sixtus V he described his voyage and that of the above-mentioned friars.[19] In the printed edition he added this narrative to the commentaries derived from the Chinese books. How slight and how insignificant, however, the information he brings about the Chinese language and the Chinese script! He does show three Chinese characters – the first to be printed in Europe – but they are so horribly distorted that it is very hard indeed to see what they are.[20] They looked even worse in the German edition, and in the Latin one which Marcus Henning made for European readers from Francesco Avanzo's Italian version. You need a mirror to approach the truth![21] The book also contains some words described such as the author had heard them in the provinces. Later on, the grand old Joseph Justus Scaliger incorporated these phonetic monsters in his immortal De Emendatione Temporum.[22] That was all, and who would believe that Mendoça knew more? While in Rome, he was visited by Angelo Rocca from Camerino, an Augustinian himself and a very cautious scholar.[23] This man published his Bibliotheca Apostolica Vaticana, in which he develops a far-fetched and abstruse theory about all the languages of the world. As a matter of fact, however, he simply copied the text of Konrad von Gesner's Mithridates, *published 30 years before, adding and subtracting a few things of no importance.*[24] The few things he had to say about the Chinese language he had from Michele Ruggieri, not from Mendoça.

19 The text says that Mendoça described the voyage to Pope Sixtus IV, a misprint for Pope Sixtus V (1585-90). Actually, however, Mendoça had told his story to his predecessor Gregory XIII (1572-85), who ordained him to publish it, as it appears from the privilege of Sixtus V to Avanzi's Italian translation, *Dell' Historia delle China . . .*, Rome, 1586.
20 These three characters were reproduced in general works about languages, e.g. in Claude Duret's *Thresor de l'histoire des langues de cest univers . . .*, Coligny, 1613.
21 The Latin translation by Marcus Henning, Augustinian friar, was printed in Frankfurt-on-Main in 1589. A German translation appearing in the same year and also in Frankfurt-on-Main gives no translator's name.
22 Joseph Justus Scaliger, 1540-1609. A towering figure in the world of erudition of the sixteenth century, Protestant and hated by the Jesuits. His *Opus Novum De Emendatione Temporum* (1583), compares and accommodates the chronology of the ancient Greek and Romans with that of the Jews, the Persians, Babylonians and Egyptians.
23 Angelo Roccha (Ròcca), 1545-1620, librarian and director of the Typographia Vaticana, book collector. The *Bibliotheca apostolica Vaticana* (1691) is a luxuriously produced but quite fantastic work about various kinds of scripts 'invented' by Adam, Seth and Moses, by Isis, Mercurius and Thot of Egypt, and by a number of Greek kings. The Lord's Prayer is shown in many languages, including Chinese (in transliteration), which he says he has from Michele Ruggieri, S.J. (See Note 25.) As Bayer states, he does not mention Gonzalez de Mendoça.
24 Konrad von Gesner, 1516-65, German-Swiss physician and polyhistor. His *Mithridates de Differentiis Linguis*, (1555), describes about 130 languages and presents the Lord's Prayer in 22 of them.

Ruggieri,[25] the first Jesuit to enter China (1581), returned to Italy some years later, leaving Matteo Ricci in the southern provinces of the Chinese empire.[26] Ruggieri was the first European who applied himself seriously to the study of the Chinese language in order to study the literature, employing for that purpose a Chinese painter. Today it is easy to see how hard these first industrious missionaries had to work, and what they had to suffer, labouring in this mysterious field, especially as they were living among people who were exceedingly suspicious and hated foreigners. Such genius would have seemed a miracle even in antiquity! Had it not been for the greediness of the Chinese, who succumbed to the temptation of accepting money for helping them, it would not have been possible. Ricci became so well versed in the language, that the Chinese praised him to the skies for it, and many later missionaries mastered it so perfectly that they were envied by the most learned among them.

I, however, do not envy these men their reputation and certainly do not want to detract from it, although it is not the place to enlarge upon that matter here. But I do want to acknowledge what I have learned from them and to emphasize the advance in the understanding of Chinese which we owe to their labour.

It often happened that specially skilled and authoritative Jesuits were sent back to Rome to settle the affairs of the Society, or theological matters. Many of these men were pressed by friends to publish something about China. But really, how much did these works contribute to the development of Chinese studies? In my opinion the Portuguese Alvaro Semedo was the first to bring important information.[27] Much material that was sent to some secret Jesuit

---

25 Michele Ruggieri (1543-1607), of Naples, the first Jesuit missionary to China. He arrived in Macao in 1579 and started a missionary station in nearby Shaoxing in 1582. He was sent back to Italy already in 1588, where he remained for the rest of his life. Bayer did not know his translation of the beginning of one of the Confucian Classics, the *Great Learning*, printed in Antonio Possevino's *Bibliotheca Selecta* . . . , Book IX (1593, 1603, 1607). There the name of that work is not given; it is just called 'A Chinese Book', but Bayer would have recognized it for he knew the *Great Learning*, translations from which are printed in his *De Eclipsi Sinici* and in Volume II of the *Museum Sinicum*. (See Knud Lundbæk: 'The first translation from a Confucian Classic in Europe', *China Mission Studies (1550-1800) Bulletin*, I, 1-11, 1979.)

26 Matteo Ricci (1552-1610), the second Jesuit missionary in China. Worked with Ruggieri from 1583 to 1588 in the Canton province. From 1601 established in Peking, where he won the friendship of several influential literati, some of whom became Christians. He wrote a number of mathematical and astronomical books in Chinese. For his 'catechism', the *Tianzhu Shiye*, see Note 4 to '*De Eclipsi Sinica*'. His 'diary' was published in Europe shortly after his death by Trigault (see note 29).

27 Alvaro Semedo (1586-1658), Portuguese Jesuit missionary in various parts of China, 1613-58. In Rome as procurator for the Chinese vice-province 1640-2, bringing with him the manuscript which was published in Madrid in 1642 under the title of *Imperio de la China* . . . Several editions in French, Italian and English were printed in the following years. Five simple Chinese characters were presented in this book. (See Note 74.)

archive to be considered by the General shows that he was a serious and excellent person (I obtained it together with other Jesuit notes from Rostgaard's library.) [28]

He wrote about the difference between the language of the court and that of the provinces, about the nature of the court language, and about the nature and the theory of the script, better, perhaps, than anybody else, but still quite briefly and in an obscure manner as if he was speaking about miraculous things. However, the characters he had incorporated were left out in the printed text, either by ignorance or to keep down the price of the book.

Nothing was added to Semedo's description of the Chinese language in the writings of Trigault or Magalhães, nor even in those of Martini, nor in those of Gabiani, Couplet, Rougemont, Grelon, Le Gobien or anybody else in the field. [29] *They were occupied with quite other matters, not the ones we are dealing with here; such things were of no importance for their purpose. Louis Le Comte did, however, write something of interest that added to what we knew from Semedo.* [30]

28 Frederik Rostgaard (1671-1745), high official at the Danish court. After his disgrace in 1725 his rich collections of books and manuscripts were sold at an auction in Copenhagen in 1726. The printed catalogue does not mention Jesuit manuscripts.
29 All these were Jesuits and all except Le Gobien were China missionaries. Nicolas Trigault (1577-1628), Flemish Jesuit. Came to China in 1610, the year of Matteo Ricci's death. In Europe 1614-18, bringing with him Ricci's 'diary' or 'commentaries' which he published in Augsburg in 1615 under the title of *De Christiana Expeditione apud Sinas suscepta ab Societate Jesu. Ex P. Matthaei Riccii ejusdem commentariis.* This was the next great China book after that of Gonzalez de Mendoça, and the first one to present a wealth of information based on personal experiences in the provinces and in Peking, written by a completely sinicized European. It did deal with the Chinese language, but only in a very general way. This book appeared in many editions and translations in the following years. There are two modern editions: L. Gallagher: *China in the Sixteenth Century – The Journal of Matteo Ricci* (1953) and Ricci (M.), Trigault (N.): *Histoire de l'expédition chrétienne au royaume de la Chine* (1978). – Gabriel Magalhães (1610-77), Portuguese Jesuit, in the China mission 1640-77. Engineer and constructor of automatic machines at the Imperial court of Peking from 1648, and enthusiastic admirer of the Chinese language. He wrote what was to become another great China book in 1668, calling it *The Twelve Wonders of China*. It was edited twenty years later in Paris as the *Nouvelle relation de la Chine* by Gabriel de Magaillans (1688). Actually this book contains much new information about the Chinese language – presumably Bayer had never seen it. Had he done so he would also have mentioned the little translation from the *Great Learning* printed in it with eight fine Chinese characters. – Martino Martini, see Note 44. His ideas about the origin of the Chinese script were rejected by Bayer. – Giandominico Gabiani (1623-94), Italian Jesuit in the China mission 1656-94). – Philippe Couplet, see Note 36. – François de Rougemont (1624-76), Belgian Jesuit, in China 1658 till his death. He was one of the four authors of the *Confucius Sinarum Philosophus* (see Note 36). – Adrien Grelon (1618-96), French Jesuit in the Canadian mission, later in China (1656-96). – Charles Le Gobien (1653-1708), procurator for the China mission in Paris.
30 Louis Le Comte (1655-1728), French Jesuit, in China only for four years (1687-91). After returning to France he served for some years as confessor to the young Duchess of Bour-

In the following years there were many who devoted themselves more to contentious exercises because of the conflict between the Jesuits and the other orders, the controversy over the terms and ceremonies greatly inflaming their minds. Thus the benefit we had expected from their publications was consumed in the flames of this fight.

Domingo Navarrete, sometime superior of the Dominican mission to China, was a past master in that field. He was a very intelligent, judicious and learned person, but also very harsh and violent, entertaining when he satirized over his adversaries, and coarse when he attacked them.[31] It is well known that Navarrete's work was the source of some small anti-Jesuit books that appeared in Belgium and France. I have heard from my elders that they were written by the famous Antoine Arnauld of Sorbonne.[32] This is why the first volume of Navarrete's book is hard to find in Spain. The second one was simply suppressed.

These quarrels arose mainly over the philosophy of Confucius, which, according to the Jesuits, contained much enlightenment and truth, while others deplored such improper evaluations. Therefore I take the opportunity to speak here about the works of this philosopher which the Jesuits published. The first one was printed in Latin and Chinese, partly in Canton, partly in Goa in India, and was edited by the Sicilian Jesuit, Prosper Intorcetta.[33] It contained an

gogne. His book, *Nouveaux mémoires sur l'état présent de la Chine* (1696, with numerous re-editions and translations) was condemned – together with that of Le Gobien – as erroneous and dangerous by the Sorbonne theologians in 1700.

31 Domingo Navarrete (1618-86), learned Spanish Dominican missionary, in China 1658-70. Archbishop of San Domingo from 1677 till his death. He disliked the Jesuits – in China and elsewhere – and regarded the accommodation method of Matteo Ricci as wrong and disastrous for spreading the Gospel in China. His *Tratados historicos, politicos, ethicos y religiosos de la monarchia de China* (1676) was full of venomous attacks on the Jesuits and contained a translation of Niccolo Longobardi's 'Brevis relatio . . .', written in the 1620s against Ricci's accommodation method (see Note 13 to After the *Museum Sinicum*). Navarrete wrote an even harsher continuation to the *Tratados* . . ., called the *Controversias antiguas y modernos de la mision de la gran China*. It was only partly printed and only very few copies of the parts printed came out. (See J.S. Cummings: *The travels and controversies of Friar Domingo Navarrete* (1962).

32 Antoine Arnauld (1612-94), 'le grand Arnauld' famous and redoubtable Jansenist controversialist. Persecuted in France he spent the last sixteen years of his life in Brussels. He had a copy of Navarrete's *Controversias* (see previous Note) and made heavy use of it in the sixth volume of his *Morale pratique des Jésuites* (Tome 34 of the *Oeuvres de Messire Antoine Arnauld* (1780). Bayer mentioned Navarrete and Arnauld already in his *De Eclipsi Sinica*.

33 Prospero Intorcetta (1625-96), Sicilian Jesuit, in China 1659-96. In Rome as procurator of the Society, 1671-4. He brought with him copies of two very important works: 1. *Sapientia Sinica*, containing the Chinese text with a Latin translation by Inacio a Costa and himself of the *Great Learning* and the first part of the *Analects*, two of the *Four Books* which were the cornerstones of the Confucian tradition, and a *Life of Confucius* (1662), and 2. *Sinarum Scientia Politico-Moralis*, the Chinese text with his translation of the *Doctrine of the Mean*, another of the *Four Books*, and a new *Life of Confucius* (1667, 1669). The first of them was printed in Jianchang in the Jiangxi province, the second one in Canton and Goa. These two works with

approbation signed by the following Jesuits: Inácio de Costa, Jacques Le Faure, Matias da Maia, Feliciano Pacheco, António de Gouvea, Pietro Canevari, Francesco Brancati, Giovanni Francesco De Ferreriis, Humbert Augery, Adrien Grelon, Jacques Motel, Giandominico Gabiani, Manuel Jorge, Philippe Couplet, François Rougemont and Christian Herdtrich.[34]

When Intorcetta came to Rome he sent a copy of this book to the Imperial Library in Vienna. He also encouraged Kircher to publish his translation of Confucius' works with his commentaries,[35] *but the European reader had to wait until 1687 before he could read the* Confucius Sinarum Philosophus, *published in Paris in that year. The editors of this book, as is well known, were Intorcetta, Herdtrich, Rougemont and Couplet.*[36]

This edition does not differ from that which had been published in China and Goa, except for the fact that in the Life of Confucius *a few phrases about the nobility of Confucius' family and about the Confucian cult and about the honours which the Yongle emperor bestowed upon him had been omitted,*

their Chinese characters and the word-for-word translation into Latin, printed in the Chinese way from wooden plates, were of the greatest interest to European orientalists, but very few copies seem to have been available in Europe. Bayer never mentions the first of them. – Philippe Couplet in a letter to an unknown person, written from his Canton exile in 1666, says that Intorcetta has been chosen as procurator and will bring with him his translation of the 'Moral Philosophy of Confucius'. He should be encouraged to get it printed in Belgium, the best place for such an endeavour – he has worked so hard at it that it may justly be called his work. (C.F. Waldeck: 'Le Père Philippe Couplet, Malinois, S.J., *Analectes pour servir à l'histoire ecclésiastique de la Belgique* (1872).

34 These 16 Jesuits together with Intorcetta were among the 22 who were exiled to Canton during the minority of the Kang Xi emperor. They were under house arrest in their church from 1665 to 1671, together with three Dominicans, among them Domingo Navarrete, and the Franciscan Antonio de S. Maria Caballero. What happened there is vividly depicted in J.S. Cumming's book, see Note 31. – Bayer, who had not seen the book, must have taken all these names – introducing some strange errors – from Lambeck's Catalogue, see Note 5 to *De Eclipsi Sinica*.

35 Athanasius Kircher, see Note 76.

36 *Confucius Sinarum Philosophus sive Scientia Sinensis, latine exposita studio et opere Prosperi Intorcetta, Christiani Herdtrich, Francisci Rougemont, Philippi Couplet, Patrum Societatis Jesu* (1687). It contains a 105-page Proëmialis Declaratio, signed by Couplet, a *Life of Confucius*, and a complete translation, or rather paraphrase of the *Great Learning*, the *Doctrine of the Mean* and the *Analects*. As appendices were printed the two-part 'Tabula chronologica Monarchiae Sinicae', both dated 1668, and the 'Tabula genealogica trium familiarum imperialium Monarchiae Sinicae' – For Prosper Intorcetta, see Note 33. – Christian Herdtrich (1625-84), Austrian Jesuit missionary, in China 1660-84. – François de Rougemont, see Note 29. – Philippe Couplet (1622-93), Flemish Jesuit missionary, in China 1659-81). Procurator of the Society in Europe 1682-93, died *en route* to China in 1693. While in Paris he arranged the edition of the *Confucius Sinarum Philosophus*. He was and still sometimes is called the author of this work, perhaps because he signed the important 'Proëmialis Declaratio' of which he may have written the last part. Cf. Knud Lundbæk, the article mentioned in Note 39.

while something had been added about the Siamese legation.[37] *Also, the Chinese characters were omitted. The words in the first book of this work have raised numerals, referring to Chinese characters, that should have been printed separately. However, I have never been able to find out what happened to these characters.*[38]

Couplet also brought with him to Europe a lengthy text containing commentaries by Confucian scholars, copied by the most learned among the Jesuits, and afterwards polished up by some Chinese scholars. (I think that these were the same commentaries that Intorcetta already had with him to Rome, and which Kircher edited, cf. Intorcetta's book about the miracles during the most recent persecutions in China, p. 393.)[39]

Less than a third of this text was printed in the above-mentioned edition. It was felt that all this should not be made public, and Couplet, or some other Jesuit in Paris or Rome, decided to keep it secret for further study. By ways unknown, this manuscript came into the hands of Aymon, the man who had edited the texts about the disturbances in Constantinople caused by the activity

---

37 A small embassy from the king of Siam was in Paris between November 1684 and March 1685 (see Lucien Lanier: *Étude historique sur les relations de la France et du royaume de Siam de 1662 à 1703* (1883).

38 The raised numerals after certain words in the text, obviously referring to Chinese characters, occur not only in the first work, the *Great Learning*, but also in the first part of the third work, the *Analects*. In the manuscript (see Note 40), these words are given in transliteration and open space is left for the addition of the Chinese characters. In supervising the edition in Paris Couplet had hoped to be able to print the Chinese text on separate sheets (Letter from Couplet to Christian Mentzel dated 6 march 1687. Hunter MS No 299). – The Yong Le emperor (reigned 1403-1425) issued a decree containing the words: ' I do homage to Confucius, the teacher of Emperors and Kings'. It was under the auspices of the same emperor that the great collection of Neo-Confucian philosophy, the *Xingli Daquan,* was printed. This work is prominent in the description of Chinese philosophy in the 'Proëmialis Declaratio' of the *Confucius Sinarum Philosophus,* Bayer mentioned it in his last-printed work 'On the Spring and Autumn Annals', see p. 180.

39 This parenthesis, which is printed as a footnote in Bayer's text, refers to a small treatise by Intorcetta about the miracles observed in China. It was printed in a work entitled *Historica Relation de Ortu et Progressu Fidei orthodoxae in Regno Chinensi per missionarios Societatis Jesu . . .* (1672). At the very end of this piece, dated Rome, 25 January, 1672, having mentioned some general works about China written by China Jesuits, Intorcetta writes: 'Those who desire a more profound insight into the political and moral sciences of the Chinese should wait patiently for the commentaries to the works of Confucius and Mencius, two Chinese philosophers, translated into Latin by Prosper Intorcetta. Father Athanasius Kircher is busily engaged in having them printed'. Apparently Bayer thought that such a work existed, but it never appeared.

Bayer cannot have seen the fourth volume of Melchisédech Thévenot's *Relations de divers voyages curieux* (1677), containing both the texts of Intorcetta's work, the *Life of Confucius* and the *Doctrine of the Mean,* which Intorcetta must have given to Thévenot in the early 1670s when he was in Europe. The *Life of Confucius* is in Latin and French, and there are some extracts of the *Doctrine of the Mean* in French translation. If he had, he would have

of Cirillo Lucaris.[40] *These spoils from the Far East would also have been published by him were it not – I think – for the fact that the editors shunned the expenses, or that something else stood in the way.*

Eighteen years ago, François Noël published his Sinensis Imperii Libri Sex *at Prague (1711). I have been looking for it, especially when I was in Leipzig, but without success, and to this day I have not been able to find a copy of it. The scholarly review in the* Acta Eruditorum *should requite me, but it does not satisfy me. For this Jesuit was extremely well versed in all Chinese matters, as I perceive from another small book of his which I shall discuss in a more suitable place.*[41]

In introducing Confucius, here, I was led away from a chronological presentation of the men who attained fame in this field in Europe.

Among the older generation, Claude Saumaise is said to have been one of the

---

commented on the editor's little note on p. 23, attached to these extracts: 'It is not enough to translate these thoughts of Confucius, they have to be commented upon to be understood. While we are waiting for the commentaries which Father Intorcetta has promised us, I put here (in French) a few that can be understood without help'. This seems to confirm Bayer's vague speculation. – Actually the first part of the 'Proëmialis Declaratio' of the *Confucius Sinarum Philosophus* seems to have been written about 1667 and it does contain commentaries, especially by Chang Chü-cheng (Zhang Ju-Zheng) – this part may well have been written by Intorcetta! (See Knud Lundbæk: 'Chief Grand Secretary Chang Chü-cheng and the early China Jesuits', *China Mission Studies (1550-1800) Bulletin,* III, pp. 2-11, 1981.)

40 Bayer had the story about parts of the manuscript not being printed from a short note in *Acta Eruditorum,* January, 1713, by Jean Aymon (1661- after 1734), the notorious French writer and manuscript thief. In 1706, while living in the Séminaire des Missions Etrangeres in Paris he bacame assistant librarian in the Bibliothèque royale where he stole several manuscripts. Fleeing with them to Holland, he had some of them printed there, among others the *Lettres anecdotes de Cyrille Lucar,* the much-talked about Patriarch of Constantinople, airing Calvinist views. In 1709 Aymon was forced to deliver up some of the manuscripts. In the article in the *Acta Eruditorum,* a vicious and ignominous attack on the Jesuits, he says – but does not say how – that he has obtained the 950-page manuscript of the *Confucius Sinarum Philosophus* and threatens to publish a complete edition of it, since 'the Jesuits have supressed more than two-thirds of it'. The manuscript is now in the Bibliothèque nationale in Paris (Fonds Latin 6277, I-II). It has 682 pages, but a part of the 'Proëmialis Declaratio' is missing. It is true that large parts of it were not included when the book was printed in 1687. (See Knud Lundbæk: 'The image of Neo-Confucianism in *Confucius Sinarum Philosophus*', Journal of the History of Ideas, 44 (1983): 19-30.)

41 François Noël (1651-1729), Belgian Jesuit missionary, arrived in China in 1687. In Europe in 1703-06 and again from 1708 to his death. His *Sinensis Imperii Libri Classici Sex . . .* (1711) contains not only the first three of the *Four Books,* but also the fourth, the *Mencius,* not included in the *Confucius Sinarum Philosophus,* as well as two other Confucian Classics, the *Filial Piety* and the *Little Learning.* Apparently the impression was not a large one, for several other contemporary writers, e.g. Bülffinger and Fourmont, complain about not being able to obtain a copy of it. The review in *Acta Eruditorum* is in 1711, pp. 184-6 and 1712, pp. 123-8 and 224-9. For the 'small book' see Note 177. – See David E. Mungello: 'The first complete translation of the Confucian Four Books in the West'.

first to deal with such studies.[42] *But the time was not ripe and the facilities for Chinese studies were very small; probably he did not imagine how big a task it was. I do not know from where he got the idea that the Chinese language is similar to Scythian – it is as odd as when we find Teixera comparing Chinese and Usbequian matters.*[43]

Saumaise says that nearly all Chinese words are monosyllabic, only a few having more than one syllable. I have noticed, however, that in his astrological comments Saumaise includes several remarks from which one can see that he had somewhat more exact ideas about the Chinese language than Scaliger. These remarks seem to indicate that he worked with the Chinese as well as with the Coptic language, which he was the first to study in Europe, but he did not publish anything about his Chinese studies. On the other hand there are vestiges of his Coptic studies in his works – not much, but enough to convince the competent reader that his knowledge of this language was greater than that of many others who bragged about theirs. About Chinese, however, one finds only commonplaces, for the works that existed at that time were of no help to him. Europeans had to wait for somebody to meet a competent person returning from China, who could give better information.

One year after Saumaise's death Martino Martini came to Europe, bringing with him a young Chinese of considerable education (1654).[44] *Jacob Golius had acquired a nice collection of Chinese books, but he did not understand a single character in them, for he had never met anybody who knew Chinese, either in Europe or in Asia.*[45] *When he heard that Martini was in Amsterdam he*

---

42 Claude Saumaise (Salmacius), (1588-1653), French Protestant classical scholar, professor in Leiden from 1631. His main work is the huge *Plinianae Exercitationes in Solini Polyhistora* (1629).

43 Pedro Texeira, born c. 1540 Portuguese historian and world traveller, author of *Relaciones de Pedro Texeira . . .* s.l. 1610, with a history of the Persian kings and descriptions of his voyages. – Bayer took these two bits of information from Andreas Müller's *Monumenti Sinici . . . lectio . . .*, Commentarium grammaticum, p. 14 (see Note 78).

44 Martino Martini, (1614-61), Tirolean Jesuit missionary, in China 1643-50 and 1659-61. While in Europe as procurator for the Society he arranged the publication of his three great works: the *Novus Atlas Sinensis* (1655), which is not only an Atlas but a Geography of China, taken from various local sources, the short *De Bello tartarica Historia* (1654), based largely on his own experiences during the fall of the Ming dynasty, and the *Sinicae Historiae Decas prima* (1658), the first history of ancient China to become available in Europe. These works were of immense importance for the knowledge of China in seventeenth century Europe. The Atlas was published in four languages, the ancient history in Latin and French, and the Tartar War became a bestseller, appearing in 27 editions in many languages, including Swedish and Danish. See Ma Yong: 'Martino Martini, Pioneer of modern European Sinology', in *Lishi Yanjiu*, 1980, No. 6, pp. 153-68 (in Chinese).

45 Jacobus Golius (Gohl), (1596-1667), Dutch orientalist, Professor of Mathematics and Arabic in Leiden. Travelled for several years in Syria and Arabia. His *Additions about the Kingdom of China* was printed in Martini's Atlas, including tables of the decimal and duodecimal

could hardly wait to join him there. However, as he knew that he was very busy at the time with preparing the edition of his Atlas Sinensis, *he preferred to wait for him in Leiden. Martini came there on his way to Brabant, greeted Golius very warmly and took him with him so that he could entertain him each day for a whole week. While in Antwerp Martini provided Golius with all kinds of information, and Jacques Edelheer, the mayor of the town, invited both of them to the Chinese studio he had arranged in his house, where they engaged in learned discussions among the many things he had collected. At their first meeting they discussed certain astronomical problems that Golius had from a text by Nasir al-din.*

Many years before – in 1581 – Joseph Scaliger had obtained from Ignatius, the Patriarch of Antioch, a copy of the twelve characters of the Cathaian cycle, deriving, I suppose, from Nasir al-din, but horribly distorted.[46] *This had led Saumaise, who knew from Ignatius's information to Scaliger that the Persians and the Turks arranged the names of animals in a cycle of twelve, to believe that the Chinese did the same. But as he knew – I do not know from where – that the Chinese names of these animals were quite different from these Cathaian ones, he concluded that the Cathaian characters were Tartaric, not Chinese. But here he was wrong. For although the Chinese peasants and some of the neighbouring peoples do use the names of animals for their twelve character cycle, the ones that Scaliger arranged in his cycle are not the names of these animals; they are clearly Chinese characters, but in themselves they have no meaning. They only serve the astronomers to designate the six (double) hours of the day and those of the night. As rightly suspected by Saumaise, they also denote the twelve signs of the zodiac. These signs are made into animals' names by the Chinese peasants and by Tartars and Turks.*

Étienne Le Moyne inserted the same cycle into his Varia Sacra *edition of the Sarravianus Codex.*[47]

John Greaves[48] *published these and other kinds of cycles when he translated*

---

cycles, the 60-year cycle, etc., in Chinese and in Arabic. Bayer took most of this story about Martini and Golius from Golius' own description of his raptures during the conversations with Martini. See also J.J.L. Duyvendak: *Holland's Contributions to Chinese Studies* (1950) – Jacques Edelheer (1597-1657) was a Belgian statesman and jurist. His rich collections of books, manuscripts and paintings were visited by many guests. – For Nasir al-din see Note 5.

46 Scaliger, see Note 22.

47 Le Moyne, Étienne, (1624-89), French Protestant, Professor of Theology in Leiden. His *Varia sacra, ceu sylloge variorum opusculorum graecorum* . . . came in two editions in 1685 and 1694.

48 John Greaves (1602-52), English mathematician and student of Persian astronomy. Among his many publications are *Epochae celebriores astronomicis, historicis, chronologicis Chataiorum* . . . *ex traditione Ulug Begi* (1650) and the *Binae Tabulae geographicae, una Nessir Eddini Persae, altera Ulug Beigi Tatari* . . . (1652) – Bayer probably had all this information about the history of astronomy from his friend Joseph Nicolas Delisle.

the Epochae . . . Cathaiorum *of Ulugh Beg, the King of Turkestan, from Persian into Latin. This remarkable work was falsely attributed to Ulugh Beg; actually it is Nasir al-din's work, word for word, as Golius discovered. In the same way Nasir al-din's* Geography *was published as having been written by Ulugh Beg. I am sure that nobody will deny this statement, if he has compared Greaves' edition of Nasir al-din's and Ulugh Beg's* Geography. *Similarly, I am sure that the* Tables of the Fixed Stars, *edited by Thomas Hyde as a work of Ulugh Beg, was composed by Nasir al-din. Ulugh Beg being a prince and a very bright and learned person, it may well have happened that works written more than a hundred years earlier were ascribed to him, either by adulation or by ignorance, for I just cannot believe that he himself would have stolen the glory of these works from Nasir al-din.*[49]

Now, returning to the different forms of the names as they occur in the various editions we are discussing here, and comparing them as Andreas Müller did in his Disquisitio de Cathaia,[50] *it is not possible to agree with Golius that they were badly written by Nasir al-din. It is quite clear from the great differences in the aberrations that Nasir al-din's text is the right one. However, it has become obsolete because it was distorted by the negligence of the copyists.*

In the Atlas Sinensis, *besides the characters of the cycles which Martini had written for him in Chinese, as mentioned before, Golius also added his own remarks, but not without grateful acknowledgement of the teacher from whom he had obtained them. Another result of the discussions between these two learned persons was that Golius obtained some grammatical rules and a list of words from Martini. I greatly admire the honesty of that man, who openly admits his debts to another.*

I myself have obtained useful information from Martini's manuscripts, and it is especially therefore that I want to mention here what I know about his death from a letter that Couplet wrote to Mentzel.[51] *In the sixth year after he had returned to China he died from what seems to have been a minor disorder (1661). Once, when he was troubled by indigestion, a Chinese physician prescribed a mild remedy. Martini, fearing that delay would lead to more severe disease, preferred to use the medicine he had himself – and took one drachm of rhubarb. When the physician heard that, he declared that there was no hope for him, and left him to die shortly afterwards.*

---

49 Ulug Beg (1394-1449), the 'astronomer king', grandson of Timur Lang and ruler of the Western part of his empire, including Persia. In 1420 he founded a new astronomical observatory at Samarkand to replace Nasir al-din's equally famous one which had ceased to function a century before. This observatory, beautifully restored, is now a tourist attraction in Samarkand.

50 Müller, see Note 73 and 77.

51 Mentzel, see Note 125. – The following long digression on the use of rhubarb is taken nearly *verbatim* from the letter dated Paris, 26 April 1684 from Couplet to Mentzel, the court physician, where it seems more appropriate than here in Bayer's text. (Hunter MS No. 299.)

(Chinese doctors never use rhubarb (Rheum officinale) *without mixing it with other ingredients to mitigate its coldness, which they think is extreme. All in all they hardly ever use emetics or (pure) laxatives, nor do they practise phlebotomy. They think it better to leave it to nature than to use violent methods that must hurt the body, sooner or later. They cut the rhubarb into tiny pieces, put a pot over the fire and place the pieces on a net that covers the mouth of the pot, so that they are imbued by the hot steam. Afterwards they expose them for six hours to fresh air in bright sunshine, and they repeat this attenuating procedure nine times. This is what they call "Kieu chim, kieu xai", nine times humidified, nine times exposed to the sun. The Portuguese in Macao, however, cut the rhubarb into pieces and boil it in water and drink this water the following day to alleviate constipation. Couplet infers from this that the blood of the Europeans is more spiritual and vigorous than that of the Chinese, since they can tolerate the crude rhubarb. The Chinese live a regular and sober life and are seldom affected by violent diseases. Their physicians do not use the same medicine in the northern and in the southern provinces. People in the south are thought to be of a milder and more natural disposition.)*

Now I will go on to the time and the state of life of those others who dealt with Chinese matters, starting with Spizelius, who lived at the time I am speaking about here.[52] *In 1661 he produced a small book called* De Re Litteraria Sinensium Commentarius, *a poor and insignificant piece of work, for it contains nothing that we did not know already from Mendoça, Semedo, Longobardi, Trigault and Martini.*[53] *There is a Chinese proverb for that: 'Twice nine is not more than eighteen'.*[54] *The book is stuffed with perfectly ridiculous quotations from works of all nations and all times, and the little there is about its subject matter is miserable. However, in this I think we should blame the bad habits of his time, more than the man himself.*

Spizelius also took material from Athanasius Kircher's work, not, however, from his China . . . illustrata *for it had not yet been published. This author had often mentioned Chinese matters in his books, but not produced anything of interest, except when he published the Nestorian Stele text.*[55] *This monument, a*

---

52 Theophilus Spizelius (1639-91), German theologian and polyhistor. In his *De Re literaria* . . . (1661) he quotes from Ruggieri's little translation from the *Great Learning,* printed in Possevino's *Bibliotheca Selecta,* but without mentioning either Ruggieri or Possevino. (See Note 25.)
53 Longobardi, see Note 13 to 'After the *Museum Sinicum*'.
54 By a slip of the pen Bayer came to the mysterious formulation 'twice eight is not more than eighteen'! He took this proverb from Andres Müller's *Monumenti Sinici . . . lectio . . .* Müller took it from Martino Martini.
55 The Nestorian Stele is the modern name for the 'Monumentum Sinicum', discussed and commented on again and again in the seventeenth and eighteenth centuries. The 2½ metre high tablet with its inscription in Chinese and a few lines in Syriac is still to be seen in the fine Forest of Steles Museum in Xian. The long Chinese text, written in high literary style, tells

testimony to the Christian religion once flourishing in China, had been discovered accidentally in 1625 under some ruins in Xian Fu, the capital of the Shenxi province. Its text, which had been published with marks of respect in a book written by Chinese magistrates, was translated into Portuguese and sent to Rome. There it was first published in Portuguese and Latin, and shortly afterwards Kircher included it in his Prodromus Coptus *(1631).*[56]

Later on, when the Polish missionary Michael Boym (his father had been court physician to King Sigismund) came to Rome as procurator for the Jesuit Society, accompanied by two Chinese by the names of Don Chin Andreas and Mattheus Sina, Kircher met them and enjoyed their company. Boym and these two young persons transcribed the text from the Chinese book mentioned above, compared it with the two copies of the Stele that were kept in the library of the Jesuit college and in the archives of the Professed House, and translated it into Latin.[57]

The Chinese text and the translation were included by Kircher in his China . . . illustrata. *However, some of the characters were copied wrongly, others were simply omitted, and all those along the edges of the Stele were left untranslated. As for the rest of this book, Kircher did not contribute significantly to the advancement of Chinese studies, except for some texts showing how the Christian religion was taught in Chinese, but only in transliteration, and something which Boym had taken from a Chinese book about how to write Chinese characters. The characters shown in this chapter are ancient Chinese ones, but they are figments of the mind.*[58]

about the Trinity, the Creator God and the Messiah (without mentioning the crucifixion and death of Christ), about the Nestorians coming from Da Quin (Syria or the Roman Empire) and their monasteries in China. It praises the Tang emperors, who protected the Christian religion. On many points this difficult text was above the capacity of seventeenth and eighteenth sinologists. In his correspondence with the Peking Jesuits we shall find Bayer asking again and again for a 'Chinese edition' of the Nestorian Stele text (see p. 162). – See A.C. Moule: *Christians in China before the year 1550* (1950). – There are several editions of the Chinese text in the Bibliothèque nationale in Paris (Courant 1185-92). One of them has a note by a certain Liang-an, dated 1625.

56 *Prodromus Coptus sive Aegyptiacus* (1636) was Atanasius Kircher's first linguistic work. The translation of the Stele text appears on pp. 53-69, Cap. III.

57 Michael Boym (1612-59), Polish Jesuit missionary, in the southern parts of China in 1646-50, shortly after the fall of the Ming Empire. In 1651 he was sent to Rome with letters to the Pope and to the Jesuit General by Helene, the Christian mother of the last Ming Emperor Yong Li. His appearance before the Doge of Venice displeased the General and he was not received by the Pope. He left Europe in 1656 but died on the frontier between Tonkin and China three years later. – There were no copies, i.e. replica of the Stele in Rome at the time (there is now), but probably several manuscript copies and perhaps rubbings.

58 Athanasius Kircher, see Note 76. – The fantastic 'ancient characters' are found in his *Oedipus Aegyptiacus* (1652-4), volume III, chapter II, pp. 10-21, and again (with one curious alteration) in his *China . . . illustrata* (1667), pp. 225-36. Kircher states that he took them from a book he had obtained from Michael Boym, the China Jesuit on visit to Europe in the 1650s.

However, Kircher had come to the point where he saw Egyptian hieroglyphs everywhere. Wherever he turned his eyes or his attention

> *There he saw worms, owls, pygmies, bones of fish,*
> *coiled snakes, mats, whirling flies,*
> *innumerable ridiculous things,*
> *meaningless in all their parts . . .*

as my Chrysorroas says.[59] *He therefore took it upon himself to place Ham and Trismegistus in Chinese history, imagining that the secret teachings of the hierophants had been transmitted to the Chinese and thus explained the whole migration of the Egyptians to that country. But having thought all this over carefully, he freely admitted that the Chinese characters are quite different from the Egyptian hieroglyphs. I am well aware of the fact that his* China . . . illustrata *was published in French, enriched by a Chinese vocabulary. However, I never had the opportunity of seeing this edition, let alone of studying it, so I cannot say anything about it.*[60]

I am not forgetting Boym's merits in Chinese medicine – he has no equal in this field in Europe. However, I shall not talk about the Flora Sinensis *which he prepared, for I believe this work is still unpublished.*[61] *But he has given an extensive description of the theory and practice of Chinese medicine, as he had received it from them.*

The book Boym had composed was sent by Couplet from Siam to Batavia to be forwarded to Europe. At that time the Dutch in Batavia were angry with the Jesuits because they believed that Adam Schall, the top Jesuit at the court, had

---

He gives the title of the book as *How to write Chinese Characters (Liber de formatione literarum chinicarum ratione)*. Actually it is chapter 11 of a small primitive encyclopedia entitled *Wenlin Shaqin Wanbao Quanshu*, printed in 1612. Kircher took his strange characters from leaves 17 to 23 of that chapter. The book is still kept in the Bibliotheca Apostolica Vaticana, Barb.Orient. 139. – Bayer's instincts were right, these characters obviously belong to Chinese folklore. – For more details about Kircher's *Vorlage* and a general discussion of these characters, including the notion about them in Europe, see Knud Lundbæk: 'Imaginary Ancient Chinese Characters', in *China Mission Studies (1550-1800) Bulletin*, V, pp. 5-23, 1983.

59 Chrysorroas, the flow of gold, was the Greek name Bayer had given his colleague and friend Christian Goldbach. He is mentioned many times in the Lacroze correspondence which also contains some of his poems. His eulogy of Leibniz, where he speaks of the great philosopher planting the Chinese philosophy in European earth, is printed in Kopelevič and Juškevič's Goldbach monography, See Note 11 to Introduction.

60 *La Chine . . . illustrée* (1670). For the problem of the authorship etc. of the vocabulary see Walter Simon's article in *Studia Serica Bernhard Karlgren dedicata* (Ed. S. Egerod and Else Glahn), (1959), pp. 265-70.

61 The *Flora Sinensis* had actually been published in Vienna in 1656. A French translation was printed in Vol. II of Melchisédech Thévenot's *Relations de divers voyages curieux* (1663-72).

in some way been responsible for the failure of the embassy they had sent to Peking. Therefore they threw away Boym's book, but Andreas Cleyer, the head physician of the Dutch East India Company in Batavia, rescued it and took over the care of this foundling, arranging for it to be printed in Germany, but without Boym's name.[62]

This fine volume contains Wang Shuhe's Treatise on the Pulses in four books, translated from the Chinese, and many other pieces and letters by various Jesuit missionaries. It includes some figures showing the blood vessels and the pulses of the human body, so crudely drawn that one would think they had been made for fun by a child, not by expert anatomists. This cannot be ascribed to Chinese ignorance, although it is true that the Chinese are below the Europeans as far as knowledge of the composition of the human body is concerned; there must be some other explanation why these vile pictures came into the hands of Cleyer, for I have seen much better and more elegant figures in Chinese books.

Moreover, mutilated sheets with Boym's own comments on the pulses as understood by the Chinese, which had been buried in oblivion for twenty years, were brought out by Couplet and Cleyer and sent to Europe. Here Couplet and Mentzel had them printed in the Annals of the Leopoldine Academy under the title of 'Boym's Clavis Medica'.[63]

Very little had been written by European authors about the Chinese language and Chinese literature till 1669 when John Webb appeared on the scene in England, having persuaded himself that this language was the oldest in the world and the mother of all other languages.[64] This idea was not rejected by the subtle and incredibly bright mind of Isaak Voss. However, this crazy and impious man had made himself ridiculous on many occasions by utterances that indicated that he would rather have been born in China than in our part of the world, perhaps because he was bored with our holy religion, perhaps just

---

62 *Specimen Medicinae Sinicae . . . edidit Andreas Cleyer . . .* (1682). – The crudely-drawn 'blood vessels and pulses' are the tracts connecting the acupuncture points! Except for the fact that they have been turned around when the xylographs were made, these plates are quite fine reproductions of pictures in traditional Chinese medical works.

63 'Clavis Medica ad Chinarum doctrinam de pulsibus', in *Miscellanea curiosa sive Ephemerides medico-physicae Germanicae Academiae Naturae Curiosorum* (1686) – For the complicated story about the authorship and the editors of this and the above-mentioned work see the article by Eva Kraft, mentioned in Note 125. – For a discussion of the contents of these works and their reception in Europe see Lu Gwei-Djen and Joseph Needham: *Celestial Lancets. A History and Rationale of Acupuncture and Moxa* (1980), pp. 269-94.

64 John Webb (1611-72), English architect and antiquarian. His book *A historical Essay endeavouring a Probability that the Language of the Empire of China is the primitive Language* (1669) is often regarded as a curiosity. Actually it is a well-informed and interesting work and a good example of the ideas about natural and artificial or 'philosophical' languages of the time. See Ch'en Shou-yi's article in *The Chinese Social and Political Review (Peking)*, 1935 and J. Bold's article in *Oxford Art Journal* (1981).

*out of frivolity.*⁶⁵

*On the contrary Louis Thomassin upheld, with more boldness than erudition, that all languages in the world were derived from Hebrew, and although he knew Chinese only from Semedo's book, he had convinced himself that something in that language came from the same source. However, he was an honest and modest man and dealt cautiously and sparingly with this question as with other problems about oriental matters.*⁶⁶

*Philippe Masson was a different man, vigorously, not to say passionately, explaining the Pentateuch with the help of Chinese.*⁶⁷ *It was he, I believe, who influenced Olaus Rudbeck, a very learned and very intelligent man, as was his father, who had insisted that Gothic, his mother tongue, was Hebrew. He indulged in strange and surprising speculations, expressed with nearly terrifying force and verbosity, confusing and carrying away even the most intelligent reader. He compared Gothic to Chinese, a fact which made him appear to be one of the strongest defenders of Masson.*⁶⁸

65 Isaac Vossius (Isaak Voss), (1618-89), eminent Dutch scholar, living most of his life in England, author of many learned works on theology, chronology, history and classical literature in which he 'gave free reign to his capricious imagination and his love of paradox'. His *Variarum Observationum Liber* (1685) contains an extravagant eulogy of the Chinese civilization in chapter 14: 'De artibus et scientiis Sinarum'. Bayer may have known about this work only from the long review of it in Tentzel's widely diffused *Monatliche Unterredungen . . .,* (1695), p. 298 ff. (See Note 83.)
66 Louis Thomassin (1619-95), French Oratorian, theologian and linguist. In his huge *Glossarium universale hebraicum . . .* (1697) he tried to show that nearly all languages are derived from Hebrew. He had difficulties with the eleven different ways of pronouncing a Chinese syllable and the corresponding eleven different meanings, which he had read about in Magaillan's work (see Note 29), but concludes that this anomaly is due to the 'rusticity' of the Chinese! (Praefatio, p. XCIX).
67 Philippe Masson (c. 1680-1750), French Protestant clergyman, living in Holland. He published three long articles on the relationship between Chinese and Hebrew in volumes II-IV of the *Histoire critique de la République des Lettres tant ancienne que moderne* (1712-18). The Chinese language, he says, is an old Hebrew dialect, a knowledge of Chinese helps one to understand certain words in the Old Testament. The nutritient that God sent to the children of Israel in the desert is called Manna, i.e. 'I do not understand it'. It is easily explained from the Chinese word *Man (Man tou)*, steam cooked bread, etc. etc. In volume V of the same journal Masson is called to order by Abbé Bignon (1662-1743), the powerful president of the Académie des Sciences, and the protector of Étienne Fourmont and Arcadius Hoang. – In volume III, pp. 272-6 (1713) there is a letter from *'un sçavant de Berlin'* to 'his friend in Utrecht'. It must be from Lacroze, the librarian of the Royal Library in Berlin, to Philippe Masson. Masson seems to have been writing to Lacroze about his 'etymological studies', for Lacroze writes: 'I agree with some of the things you tell me in your last letter, but there are other things which I hardly understand or not at all. To be able to judge it I would need a systematic exposition of your Chinese discoveries'. Bayer may have known of Masson and his ideas only from discussions with Lacroze in Berlin. (See also Note 35 to 'The Chinese Language'.)
68 Olaus Rudbeck jun. (1660-1740), son of Olaus Rudbeck sen. (1630-1702), Uppsala physician

Personally I do not like such things, not because I cannot accept the busy activity of enormously learned persons in this kind of study of the nature and, as it were, the philosophy of language – on the contrary, I admire them for their sharpness of wit and assiduity. However, what they produce is vague and superficial. It does not elucidate the problems, but rather steeps them in mist. Such studies, comparing all the languages of the world in search of the primordial one, are beyond the powers and the ingenuity of one man. Collaboration between several scholars would be necessary, but who would like to work in that way and how could they reach an agreement?

First of all, it is simply not possible today to discuss the relationship and connections between Asian languages. Those between the European languages are being elucidated now by many industrious and ingenious scholars, but those obtaining between the oriental languages are still hardly known at all. Therefore I admit that I prefer to follow the splendid and magnificent discourse of Rudbeck than to listen to William Nicholson, the Bishop of Gloucester, postulating that the Malebaric, the Chinese and the Japanese languages are related to each other.[69] *All the time it seems to me as if I heard the poem of Epicharmus:*

> *Reason has as two Laws:*
> *Be sober! Be critical!*[70]

On the other hand, I do not want to deny explicitly, as Abraham Hinckelman does, that ultimately the Chinese language may derive from Hebrew. I usually abstain from expressing opinions on unknown and abstruse matters.[71]

Now I shall revert to the path where I started. We have heard now about many authors who had wanted to contribute to the study of Chinese but lacked constancy and failed to obtain results. And yet we have just arrived at the time of Andreas Müller and Christian Mentzel! In these two persons we witness for

---

and polyhistor, author of the famous *Atland eller Manheim*, published in Uppsala in 1675 with Swedish and Latin text. Bayer polemized against it in several of his non-sinological works. Olaus Rudbeck jun. was a physician and a botanist and, like his father, dedicated to historical speculations. Of his immense *Thesaurus linguarum Asiae et Europae harmonicus* only a few pages were published in Uppsala in 1716. His comparison of Gothic and Chinese appeared in the *Specimen usus linguae gothicae . . . addita analogia linguae Gothicae cum Sinaca . . .*, Uppsala, 1717.

69 William Nicholson (1591-1672), Bishop of Gloucester, author of theological works and known as an enthusiastic grammarian.
70 Epicharmus, c. 540-450 B.C., Greek comic poet. Bayer probably took his quotation from Cicero's Greek quote in *Letters to Atticus*, I, 19,8.
71 Abraham Hinckelman (1652-95), German theologian and orientalist. He published the first Arabic Koran in Europe (1694). He died of 'apoplexy' at the age of 45 having read a particularly virulent attack on his works by theologian confrères.

the first time the combination of a passionate desire for understanding and an admirable productivity.

(I have never been able to find out what it was that a certain Nunnus of Canna at some time, I do not know when, is said to have written in Italian about the Chinese language.) [72]

Andreas Müller was born into a family of poor but honest citizens in Greiffenhagen in Pomerania, but in the course of his life he attained high positions in the church. I shall not relate what Gottfried Starck wrote about him in his biography but stick to what is pertinent in the present connection, most of which Starck omitted. [73]

When Müller was provost in Treptow he was called to London by Edmund Castell who was working on his great book – a rival of the Paris Polyglot *– together with Brian Walton, Thomas Hyde, Samuel Clarke, Thomas Greaves and other scholars: the Holy Scriptures with all the old commentaries of oriental authors, whether published or in manuscript form in libraries. Here Müller worked for some years with Castell on the glorious project, but he did not acquire any knowledge of Chinese. For there was nobody in England who knew Chinese, not even John Wilkins, the Bishop of Chester, the excellent constructor of a philosophical language. He obviously knew as little Chinese as Walton did. And yet Walton, discussing Asian languages in his Prolegomena in the* Biblia Polyglotta, *mentioned Chinese characters, pointing out how entirely different they are from Egyptian hieroglyphs, being made up of only nine different, very simple lines put together to form innumerable characters, the simple ones combining to form composite characters – this had not been said by anyone before. This tiny remark was enough for Müller to develop something*

---

72 This is from Andreas Müller's *Monumenti Sinici . . . lectio . . .* (Müller calls it *Della Scriptura delli Chini* and says he does not remember what it is. The present writer has also failed to identify this Nunnus.

73 Andreas Müller (c. 1630-94), German orientalist, born in Greiffenhagen close to Stettin in Pomerania. He was an infant prodigy, composing poems in Latin, Greek and Hebrew at the age of 16. Studied in Rostock, Greifswald and Wittenberg. In England 1660-1, perhaps working for a time with Edmund Castell. In 1667 he was nominated Provost of the Lutheran Nicolaikirche in Berlin, but gave up this post and moved to Stettin in 1685, where he lived for the rest of his life. He published many orientalist works, most of them on Chinese matters. For his biography and bibliography see August Müller: Eröffnungsrede, Zeitschrift d. Deutschen Morgenländischen Gesellschaft, Vol. 35, p. III-XVI, 1881. – S.G. Starck's Life of Andreas Müller was printed in the preface to his edition of Müller's *Alpha kai Omega, Alphabeta ac notae diversarum linguarum* (1703). Starck says, erroneously, that Müller collaborated for ten years in England with the scholars publishing the English Polyglot Bible. This was repeated many times till 1881 when August Müller corrected and explained the misunderstanding. – Bayer took large parts of his information about Müller's life and works from letters and various notes which Müller had sent to Tentzel, asking him to publish them in his *Monatliche Unterredungen* (see Note 83).

greater by careful reflection.[74]

Ten years later he returned to Germany and became provost of the churches in Bernow. But his interest in literature regularly attracted him to Berlin, where he studied the books in the Electoral Library. He concentrated on a book by the Tartar author Asisus Nesephaeus entitled About Divine Things, *which he translated from Turkish into Latin and dedicated to Friedrich Wilhelm, the Great Elector and Duke of Prussia.*[75] *At that period, however, he kept away from Chinese books because – as he says himself – he shuddered at the mere notion of the many difficulties. But then, in 1667, somebody sent him Athanasius Kircher's* China . . . illustrata *and immediately he started to arrange the characters of the Nestorian Stele under various headings.*[76] *The following year, when he happened to be reading a certain Arab author discussing another kind of script, Divine Providence – so he liked to tell himself and others – made him conceive of the idea of constructing a* Clavis Sinica, *a key to the Chinese language (18 November, 1668). I do not know what kind of script it was, nor who the Arab author might have been, but I am afraid that Müller*

74 The English Polyglot Bible – *Biblia Sacra Polyglotta* – published by Brian Walton (1600-61) and a number of learned co-workers in London 1653-7. It showed the whole or parts of the Bible in Hebrew, Greek, Latin, Vulgate and Septuagint, Chaldeic, Syriac, Samaritian, Arabic, Persian and Coptic. Its frontispiece was drawn by John Webb (see Note 64). – Castell (1606-85). After working with Walton on the Polyglot Bible he produced his great *Lexicon Polyglotton* . . . (1669). – Thomas Hyde, see Note 140. – Thomas Greaves (1612-76), English orientalist, a brother of John Greaves, the mathematician and student of Persian astronomy (see Note 48). – Samuel Clarke (1625-69), English orientalist. – The remarks Bayer quotes from the Prolegomena in the *Biblia Sacra Polyglotta*, Vo. VI, p. 10 are taken *vertabim* from Semedo's *Relatione delle grande Monarchia della Cina* (see Note 27) and Walton says so. Did Bayer only know Semedo from Walton? Together with some lines on p. 4 of the Prolegomena they contain all that he had said about Semedo. Anyhow, it is hard to understand what Bayer means with 'This had not been said before by anybody'. – John Wilkins, see Note 10 to 'Chinese Language'.
75 The Churfürstliche Bibliothek zu Cölln a.d. Spree (Berlin) was founded in 1660. From 1701 Königliche Bibliothek. – Müller's first book was entitled *Excerpta Manuscripti cujusdam Turci, quod ad cognitione Dei et Hominis ipsius a quodam Azizo Nesephaeo, Tartaro scriptum est* . . . (1665).
76 Athanasius Kircher S.J., (1602-80), the great German polyhistor who lived most of his life in the Collegio Romano in Rome. He published a great many huge tomes about mathematics, optics, magnetism, music, as well as books about the Tower of Babel and of Noah's Ark. His first presentation of the Nestorian Stele text in translation was in his *Prodromus Coptus sive Aegyptiacus* (1636). He included the Chinese text in his *China Monumentis qua sacris qua profanis* . . . *illustrata* (1667) translated into French in 1670 with a Chinese vocabulary. This work was of the greatest importance, arousing interest in China in Europe. Most of his works, being filled with hermetic and cabalistic speculations, influenced largely the European 'Figurists' as well as the Chinese ones. (See p. 138.) – There is an indifferent monograph about Kircher by Conor Really: *Athanasius Kircher, Master of a Hundred Arts* (1974) and a popular, profusely illustrated book entitled *Athanasius Kircher – a Renaissance Man in Quest for lost Knowledge* by Joscelyn Godwin (1979).

wanted to conceal his art and therefore purposely drew a veil over everything which this Arab had wonderfully invented. I rather think that it was while reading the few, but not insignificant, lines about Chinese characters in Al-Baidawi the Persian's book that he got this idea. And to be frank, in my opinion Walton had already suggested quite clearly what was the pivot of the system of Chinese characters. Anyhow, for Müller much tedious and exhaustive work remained to be done.

About that time – in 1669 – a certain person wrote to him that thirteen years before the appearance of Kircher's China . . . illustrata – *this was just at the time when Martino Martini had arrived in Europe* – he had received something about the Chinese language from somebody by the name of Johannes S. Maurus in Amsterdam, had learned it by heart, and had used it for translating certain Chinese texts. Using Kircher's book, he had then perfected his knowledge so that by now he understood how to analyse Chinese characters according to their principle and on the basis of their structural elements. Müller pressed him and urged him to disclose his secret, but he was unable to persuade him to do so. I am afraid, however, that here again Müller invents a story. I have come to the conclusion that such a thing would be quite in accordance with his ways and the turn of his mind.

It is clear from the books he published at that time that the work with the Clavis Sinica *was proceeding at a slow pace. As to his edition of Marco Polo, he might have emended and enriched it using the Berlin Codex, but actually he did very little in this direction. The companion volume, the* Disquisitio de Chataia, *is stuffed with statements about the country, drawn from all kinds of authors from all periods of time –*

> *So many men, so many minds,*
> *everyone has his point of view . . .*

Parading the opinion of one author, the assent of another, and the denial of a third, insisting that the problem should be considered more carefully, he ends up in utter uncertainties, even worse than those of Hegio in Terence's Phormio. *Sometimes he follows one author, at other times another, affirming, retracting, insisting without ever arriving at a personal opinion, not even a clear statement about the difference of other people's opinion; nor does he do as Golius used to do: indicate a personal preference, however small. He also put into his book the well-known notes on Chinese chronology from Golius, correcting the errors. His Chinese characters are very poor as usual and in this work they are so badly written that you have to know them beforehand to be able to recognize them. And even here, where an obvious occasion presented itself for him to unfold his ideas, his comments on the nature of the Chinese language are slender indeed.*[77]

At this time he was called to Berlin as provost of the Church, and could make free use of the Electoral Library for constructing his Clavis Sinica. However, his next book, the Monumenti Sinici ... lectio ..., dealing with the Nestorian Stele, does not give evidence that he was able to do so.[78] Here he expressed the tones of the Chinese syllables by the notes of a musical scale, as if we were to imagine a whole nation singing at a party – quarts, octaves and double octaves! It was stupid of him to let himself be taken in by the wild ideas of Kircher, who was so clever that he could teach even fish to sing, not to mention human beings.

Müller claimed that he had corrected Kircher's errors and supplied the parts of the text of the Nestorian Stele that Kircher had omitted, but actually he repeated his errors and even added some of his own. For at the end of the text, where it is badly corrupted, he did not even recognize the blemishes. In his comments he binds knots in the rush that a child could have undone – there was no need for a 'sharptongued advocate'.[79]

He mentions and exaggerates other scholars' difficulties with the Chinese language, and then he adds:

'As for me, I have no particular difficulty, for I have found out how to read it. However, I am not going to explain this prematurely and without being asked to do so. If only I could be as sure of obtaining financial rewards, ecclesiastic posts and peace, as I am sure of how to read Chinese characters, I trust that in the course of a year, or rather a month, or less than that, I could teach even women to read Chinese and Japanese books, and when they had understood the grammatical rules, to translate them'. But then he quotes from the Talmud about the man who possesses immense riches but cannot find a banker who is willing to accept them as security for a loan.[80]

Müller was also disturbed on hearing about a certain person – benevolently he does not mention his name – who had promised to publish an Introduction to Twelve Oriental Languages, including Chinese. This was all right if only he would not envy him his Monument book.

This man was August Pfeiffer, who lived in Silesia at the time and wrote something about sixteen languages of the Orient. However, his discussions of Chinese and Japanese can by no means be called introductions to these parts of

77 *Marci Pauli Veneti ... Libri III ... itemque de Chataja Disquisitio ...* (1671). – The quote is from Terence's *Phormio*, 454.
78 *Monumenti Sinici, quod Anno Domini MDCXXV terris in ipsa China erutum ... lectio seu phrasis, versio seu metaphrasis, translatio seu paraphrasis ...* (1672).
79 'To bind knots in the rush' is a Latin proverb. For the sharp-tongued advocate the text has 'Tenedios synegoros' in Greek, the Tenedos advocate, perhaps a quote from Stephan of Byzantium, fifth century grammarian whose works were edited many times in the seventeenth and eighteenth centuries. The words may refer to the first song of the Iliad.
80 The Talmud quote is in Hebrew in Müller's text – apparently no Hebrew fount was available in St Petersburg in Bayer's time.

the East – they hardly even tell us in which direction to go for it. It is as if he were pointing to some Samnite stronghold in the Caudine Forks, beyond the immense grove, hidden away among marshes and thick wood, not only unattainable, but simply invisible.[81]

Here, in the Monumenti Sinici . . . lectio, *Müller also collected material for building up the study of the Chinese language, but it is neither quarry stone, nor chalk nor sand, neither timber nor bricks, it is just something from everywhere, odds and ends, either insipid or self-contradictory – there is really nothing of value to build with. And as for the* Clavis Sinica, *the key to the Chinese language, he is like a locksmith who has iron and fine bronze but prefers to use metal dross for making a key – he produces something but he does not promote anything. He still does not dare to utter a word about the Chinese characters, as if they were secret Eleusian mysteries into which he had been initiated. His self-confidence made him split up and recombine the characters of the text of the Nestorian Stele, using his hermeneutical art to demonstrate some obscure and perverse meaning of them. However, I do not think he was able to do anything like that, nor that he could decide to do anything with the parts of the text on the sides and the edges of the Stele, left untranslated by Boym. There is one particular point that reveals to me his utter helplessness. That is the way he treats the term* rigo, *appearing in two places of the translation as the appellation of the divine persons. Looking at this term he trembles all over as if he had seen a ghost. He knew perfectly well that in Chinese there is no 'r' and no disyllables. What to do then? 'Perhaps', he says, now calming down and regaining his peace of mind, 'perhaps it is the Portuguese word* rigo, *a river'. From there on, believe it or not, he goes on to rave about the emanations of the Cabalists and the rivers of the Apocalypsis!*[82] *As a matter of fact, however, this* rigo *is just a slip of the pen or a misprint for the Chinese word* ngo, *the 'n' appearing as 'ri', and that character is so common that one learns it at the very beginning of the study of the language. Tentzel remarked on it, and Müller himself admitted his mistake later on in his notes on the Lord's Prayer in Chinese and Latin, printed together with his* Oeconomia Bibliothecae Sinicae.[83]

---

81 August Pfeiffer (1640-98), German Protestant theologian and orientalist, Professor of Oriental Languages in Wittenberg, known for his many polemic works, especially against the Jesuits. His little *Introductio ad Orientem* (1671) discusses 16 oriental languages, Chinese, Japanese, Annamite and Malay being despatched together on 1½ pages. In the Preface he writes: 'I could say more about Chinese, especially about how to resolve the characters, but I prefer to wait till Müller has published what he has promised'. – The lines about the Caudine Forks are allusions to Livy's account of the second Samnite war in the ninth book of his History.
82 *Monumenti Sinici . . . lectio,* see Note 78. – The passage Bayer discusses is in the Commentarius theologicus, p. 42, Dogmata II, b. – Ngo (Wo) is the first person singular ponoun: I.
83 Wilhelm Ernst Tentzel (1659-1707), eminent German philologist and numismatist. His journal *Monatliche Unterredungen einiger guten Freunden* (1689-98), followed by the *Curieuse*

At that time he also published his Hebdomas Observationum Sinicarum *with new, frustrating omissions. For example, in the discussion of the Ginseng root he writes: 'I would have printed the text with a translation as an example, had the circumstances permitted it.' He felt that at some time he would have to prove the – very doubtful – knowledge of which he boasted.*[84] *What adversity was it that prevented him from carrying out the noble project of a* Clavis Sinica *that had caused so many rumours and had aroused so much admiration, supported as he was at that time by the incredible favour, authority and encouragement of his Prince, Friedrich Wilhelm, the immortal hero? Later on, in the battlefield and even at critical moments, this learned Prince untiringly occupied his great mind with matters of public utility: again and again, with the greatest kindness and nearly flattering insistence, he urged Müller to finish his work. I have seen the letters he wrote to Müller while camping outside Stettin, bombarding this stronghold day and night. In these he thanks him for certain books, the titles of which Müller had explained to him, and talks about more books that are arriving from India. What more could he expect from that great Prince, a general first of all, and engaged in great undertakings? His wife, the Princess Dorothea of Holstein, felt the same for Müller as the Prince did.*

Besides the books the Prince purchased to help him in his studies, Müller himself had obtained other works of interest to him through people he had made friends with in Belgium and in India. Among these the most important was Nicolaas Witsen, who procured a considerable number of books for him, inter alia Giulio Aleni's Historia Evangelica.[85, 86] *This very learned burgomas-*

Bibliothec (1704-6) were very popular at the time. They contain a wealth of information about Chinese studies, including those of Müller, Mentzel and Leibniz. His remark here about Müller's error is printed in the *Monatliche Unterredungen* 1691, p. 294. Müller's admission of the mistake was printed in his *Oratio Dominica cumque versione et notis itemque Oeconomiae Bibliotheca Sinicae* (1676). He told Tentzel about it in an important letter printed in the *Monatliche Unterredungen* 1692, pp. 830-1, saying that he had noted the error in 'Kircher's edition', i.e. the *China . . . illustrata*, but too late to correct it in his *Monumenti Sinici . . . lectio*.

84 *Hebdomas Observationum de Rebus Sinicis* (1674).
85 Nicolaas Witsen (1641-1717), Dutch statesman, burgomaster of Amsterdam. His *Noord en Oost Tartaryen . . .* (1692 and 1705) was dedicated to Peter the Great, whom he knew from his stay in Holland.
86 The *Historia evangelica (Tianzhu Jiangsheng Chuxiang Jingjie* (1637)) is No. 1 in Müller's *Catalogus Librorum Sinicorum Bibliothecae Electoralis Brandenburgicae*. In the *De Eclipsi Sinica* Bayer had mentioned – as an example of impeccable Chinese books published by the Jesuits – an illustrated *Life of Jesus* by Giulio Aleni. In the grammar chapter Bayer wrote about a third book by Aleni (see p. 128). There are three important articles about Chinese books in the Electorial Library: Eva Kraft's 'Die chinesische Büchersammlung des Grossen Kurfürsten und seines Nachfolgers' and 'Ein Koffler Autograph', also Lieselotte Wiesinger and Eva Kraft's 'Die chinesische Bibliothek des Grossen Kurfürsten und ihre Bibliothekare', printed in the beautiful catalogue of the 'China und Europa' exhibition in Berlin in 1973 (pp. 18-25, 26-9 and 166-73).

ter was interested in Northern Asia and had plans of writing a major work about this area. He sent Chinese geographical maps to Müller, asking him to explain the information they contained about the regions beyond the Great Wall. If he could, Witsen would be pleased to let him have them. Nothing came out of it because the regions that interested Witsen were outside Müller's field of interest. However, after this failure Müller decided to write something about the geography of China, as we know from his letter to Johannes Hevelius.[87]

(I myself have found some well-preserved maps here, in which the names of the vast provinces outside the Great Wall are given in Mongolian. They are being used by my friend François Joseph Delisle, who is preparing a geographical work about the whole Russian Empire and the provinces adjacent to it in the East.)[87b]

Witsen had his work on Northern and Eastern Asia printed twice. The first edition of 1692 was withdrawn by himself because he felt that Peter the Great, to whom he sent it, was displeased in some way with it. The second edition of 1705, with some omissions and some additions, seems to have been mislaid somewhere. I sought for it eagerly and painstakingly, but never found it till I came to St Petersburg and could study it in the Imperial Library. Müller, who loved Chinese maps, wrote a Nomenclator geographicus, including longitudes and latitudes.[88] Generally the degress of his latitudes are in accordance with those reported for the sites of a great number of cities in the work published in Prague by François Noël (1710), but there are differences as to the minutes. The longitudes are all different by one or more degrees.[89] Müller also suggested to Witsen that he should have all the 'Chinese Annals' sent from India, then he, or some other person using his Clavis Sinica, could work on them in order to complete Martini's History of China, for that book contains only a part of the history of this country; there was another part which Melchisédec Thévenot printed in his Collection of Voyages. It is quite short and it may not even be by Martini.[90]

Also in 1680 Müller published versions of the Lord's Prayer and the alphabets of the languages of all people, in Berlin, under the pseudonyms

---

87a Johannes Hevelius (Höwelke) (1611-87), German astronomer in Stettin, the author of the last important star-catalogue based solely upon naked-eye observations. Müller's letter to him is printed on pp. 188-90 of Volume I of the *Museum Sinicum*. Hevelius's reply appears in a footnote to the Preface, pp. 92-3.
87b A number of letters from Delisle to Bignon (1720-30) deal with this project. (Bibliotèque nationale, Papiers de l'Abbé Bignon. Mémoires et correspondance, III. MS français 22.227).
88 *Imperii Sinensis Nomenclator geographicus* (1680) with a long dedication to Witsen.
89 For Noël's astronomical work, see Note 177.
90 The 'Historiae Sinicae Decas secunda', printed in Thévenot's *Voyages* (see Note 61). Bayer got his information about this work and his doubts about its author from one of Lacroze's letters to him in 1716 (Lacroze Correspondence, III, p. 8).

Thomas Ludeken and Hagius Barnimus.[91a] *Some copies of this work came out, others were neglected for many years until they were brought forth and published (omitting the Preface) by Sebastian Gottfried Starck, together with his Life of Andreas Müller. Müller had taken some copies of it with him to Stettin, in which an Irish, an Ethiopian and a Coptic alphabet – absent in the Berlin edition – had been added. These copies came into the hands of Gottfried Bartsch. I have one of them, on which Bartsch, during his stay in Königsberg, had written the title and his own name:*

> The Alphabets of the World
> together with related remarks
> listed in the following page
> Edited by Gotfried Bartsch, engraver
> Königsberg, Prussia, 1694

Then follows the Preface, written by Müller but signed by Bartsch. This book also contains various other things, including Chinese matters, such as Kircher's figures of birds and dragons forming characters, and the European alphabet in Chinese characters. However, one of the characters of the Lord's Prayer that had been missing in the earlier edition was still not supplied here, and one very poor character was still not improved.

From that period, with its heated discussions about the Clavis Sinica, we have printed letters from Müller and from some Jesuits about the invention.[91b] I cannot tell precisely what it was, but I am inclined to think that essentially all he did was to reduce the characters to their elements, studying the principle according to which they are combined, and their meaning. How this can be done I have explained in the present book. But while I have had help from others, Müller was working all by himself. If he really surmounted all the difficulties through his intellectual power and strength of mind, this must be regarded as the result of an incredible amount of hard work and profound meditation. We must forgive him, therefore, for enjoying particularly that which had cost him the greatest trouble to find out. When he had found it out he was not satisfied with it and hesitated, I believe, waiting for an occasion to perfect it.

(Leibniz, who knew Müller very well, wrote as follows in the Preface to his Novissima Sinica:

'It came to the point when this solitary man did what he had threatened to do many times – shortly before his death he burned his notes to withhold from us his knowledge – or his ignorance? I believe that he had reached important

---

91a *Oratio oratiorum . . . versiones praeter authenticam fere centum* . . . (1680). – For Kircher's figures of birds and dragons see Note 58.
91b Ed. Andreas Müller: *De invento sinico epistolae nonnullae* . . . s. 1. s.a.

results and was looking forward to more, which he might well have obtained, had he been properly supported. If only he had told his story quite frankly, no doubt he would have been able to complete his project with the help of mighty princes, in particular his own master.') [92]

Most of the things Müller promised to do were related to his invention, the Clavis Sinica, *but unfortunately his promises were vague statements and smart phrases that might delude even the informed reader, and made it look as if he had made major discoveries.*

I do dislike his greed – it was impossible to satisfy his demands, or perhaps he upheld them to conceal the meagerness of what he had to offer. Hence his favourite remark:

> *Everybody wants to know;*
> *nobody wants to pay.*

– it smacks too much of the mercenary for a scholar.[93]

Athanasius Kircher prompted the Pope to have the mysterious work printed under his auspices and at his expense, and Thévenot urged the councillors of Louis XIV to assume the responsibility, but the strongest recommendation of Müller's work came from the Jesuit Adam Adamandus Kochanski and from François Mesgnien Meniski, councillor and Knight of Malta, to Emperor Leopold in Vienna.[94] *The Emperor also sent Chinese and Mongol letters to Müller and is said to have been satisfied with his translations. When the rumour got around that the Emperor was negotiating about the publication of the* Clavis Sinica, *the Great Elector, Friedrich Wilhelm, intervened, offering to print, at his expense, whatever seemed of public utility in the project. When it was agreed that Müller should receive 1,000 thaler for the* Clavis Sinica, *or the 'Brandenburg Invention' as he called it in honour of his Prince, he asked to be relieved of his ecclesiastical duties. He got leave for three months, but then he also asked permission to go to Stettin and settle down with his project there, outside the domain of Brandenburg. When this wish was also granted he moved to Stettin.*[95]

While in Berlin Müller had prepared a set of wooden types with characters so

---

92 Ed. G.G.L. (Leibniz): *Novissima Sinica Historiam nostri Temporis illustratura* . . . (1697 and 1699). The citation printed in a parenthesis here occurs in the *Museum Sinicum* as a footnote.
93 He is said to have asked 2,000 Thaler, a very high sum, for his Clavis. See August Müller's Eröffnungsrede, Note 73.
94 Adam Adamandus Kochanski, S.J. (1631-1700), court mathematician to the Polish King. – François Mesgnien Meniski, (c. 1622-98), French orientalist. Lived many years in Constantinople, from 1671 in Vienna, where he published his great *Linguarum orientalium turcicae, arabicae, persicae institutiones* . . . (1680).
95 Hither Pomerania (Vorpommern), with the city of Stettin, was Swedish from the end of the Thirty Years War in 1648 to 1720.

that a Chinese text could be composed in the European way. This set he donated to the Electoral Library. Many of these types – I have seen them myself – are small enough to be used for printing. He promised to produce finer and more accurate ones in copper, if only somebody would pay for it, but the time was not ripe for such a project. Here, in his usual way, he found a thole pin and built a ship, as the saying goes.[96]

In Stettin Gottfried Bartsch, the engraver I mentioned above, stayed with Müller. He was a good man and not without education. He was born in Silesia into a very honest and honourable family; this was especially true of his father, who was a friend of Martin Opitz. He devoted himself to painting and worked for some time with Montcornet in Paris but later on he changed to engraving. From Paris he was called to Berlin to teach Crown Prince Friedrich to paint. After the death of his father, when Friedrich succeeded to the throne (1688), Bartsch, who was disgusted with the manners of the court, tendered his resignation, very much against the wish of the learned Elector.[97]

Working for some time in Stettin, he used all his money on Müller's works and was brought to the brink of poverty. As security for a loan he received some books and manuscripts from Müller, i.a. his Geographia mosaica, *which he published in Berlin at his own expense.*[98]

Finally Bartsch came to Königsberg, became a very good friend of my father and acted as sponsor when I was baptized. He used to tell my father a great deal about the Clavis Sinica *and other works of Müller, which he owned. From Königsberg he moved to Dantzig, where he died of gout in 1701 or 1702. He had no heirs, so all his books were taken into custody, but to this day I have not been able to find out what happened to them, either by personal enquiry, or through friends.*

While Müller was still in Berlin, Cleyer sent the 'Chinese Annals' from the Indies to the Elector.[99] *From these Müller copied the text about the solar eclipse that was thought to have occurred in China at the time when Christ was*

---

96 Müller's 'Typographia Sinica', 3284 coinshaped wooden types, including a few with Manchu script, is still in the Deutsche Staatsbibliothek in East Berlin, contained in its original cabinet. – Bayer got the remark about Müller's copper type project from the 'Catalogus librorum sinicorum . . . Andreas Mülleri Greiffenhagii . . .' published in Tentzel's *Monatliche Unterredungen*, March, 1697, pp. 182-92. (See Note 83.)

97 Johann Gotfried Bartsch, born in Schweidnitz in Silesia. Royal engraver in Berlin 1674-84. The list of his works includes a portrait of Friedrich Wilhelm, the Great Elector. The reference works I have consulted contain no information about his life, but Bayer says in his *De Eclipsi Sinica* that he had lived for a long time in Spain, Italy, France, England and Belgium. – Montcornet: probably Baltazar Montcornet (c. 1600-68), French Painter. – Martin Opitz (1597-1639), famous German poet, 'the father of German poetry'.

98 *Geographia mosaica generalis ex Genesios capite decimo . . . Sumptibus Godofredi Bartschii, Calchographi* (1689).

99 The Chinese Annals, see Note 2 to *'De Eclipsi Sinica'*. For Cleyer, see Note 127.

crucified. Shortly afterwards – in 1683 – he published it together with a list of Chinese kings, which he says he prepared from 276 books. But the reader must be careful not to let himself be deluded by ambiguous words and not to be overwhelmed by the thought of the great number of volumes Müller had worked his way through. In fact it is just one book, albeit a very big one, in several volumes and subdivided into a number of sections. Apparently the first thing he did was to note the number of volumes, then the sections of each of them, and finally the pages on which the history of each king begins – from 425 B.C. to A.D. 1329 – the books that had been sent from the Indies included only that period of time.[100]

(The Basilicon Sinense, *published already in 1679, contained nothing like this. For this he used Al-Baidawi, Mendoça, Martini and a Chinese manuscript that also began in 425 B.C.)*[101]

After this list of kings he again printed the catalogue of the Chinese books which were at the time in the Electoral Library and his own ones. In this, however, some books occur without titles, only with the names of those who bought them – just a nice way, I suppose, to conceal his ignorance. There are also some books that are not on the market, presumably obscene ones like those that were sent from the Chinese court to our Imperial Library.

In Stettin Müller did not accomplish much in the way of a Clavis Sinica, *but that was not his fault, he thought, attributing the blame to wicked and envious persons who wanted to prevent it.*

First Johannes Christopher Beckmann attacked him in a publication – just a few words, but virulent ones.[102] *Then he was assailed quite immoderately by a theologian from Frankfurt-on-the-Oder, by the name of Elias Grebnitz.*[103] *He*

---

100 This 1683 edition must be the German one which Bayer returns to below with the words 'as I said above', the *Deutsche Übersetzung und Erklärung . . . aus den Sinesischen Jahr-Büchern von der Sonnen-Finsterniss . . . Anno MDCLXXXIII . . . bey den Churfürstl. Durchläuchtigkeiten zu allererst unterthänigst offeriret*. The list of kings must be the last twelve sheets of Müller's *Andere Theil des Catalogi der Sinesischen Bücher bey der Churfürstl. Brandenburgischen Bibliothec . . .*, also printed in Berlin in 1683. For a detailed discussion of Müller's catalogues, see Eva Kraft: 'Die chinesische Büchersammlung des Grossen Kurfürsten und seines Nachfolgers' (see Note 86).
101 *Basilicon Sinense* (1679). – The catalogue of Müller's own books and manuscripts, noted in the following: Müller had sent it to Tentzel who printed it after his death in his *Monatliche Unterredungen . . .*, 1697, pp. 182-92.
102 Johannes Christopher Beckmann (1641-1717), German Reformed theologian, Professor of Theology in Frankfurt-on-the-Oder.
103 Elias Grebnitz (1627-89), another Reformed theology professor in Frankfurt-on-the-Oder. In a book printed in 1678 he had warned against the Chinese script. Being composed of pictograms, it showed the name of God as a picture which was an infringement upon the Second Commandment. Müller answered in his *Besser Unterricht von der Sineser Schrift und Druck*, printed privately in 1680. Grebnitz obtained a copy of it and published his rejoinder in 1681, a pamphlet which he posted on the doors of the Berlin churches. Only then did

had advanced some vague reproaches against Müller in relation to Chinese characters, and instead of neglecting them, Müller chose to lecture the grave old man and subtle controversialist about the Chinese script – quite modestly and mildly, but also weakly and unskilfully. Grebnitz took offence, or perhaps that was just what he had been waiting for. At any rate he seized the opportunity with delight, chastening Müller in the most insulting way and treating him as if he had been a schoolboy, completely ignorant of logic, the discipline Grebnitz had been teaching earlier in his life. He exhausted the scent-box of Aristotle and the rouge-pots of his pupils in his accusations of the honest man.[104]

Although I hate that kind of thing, and although Müller might very well have dismissed it altogether, I must admit that he had called the insults down upon his own head by his cunning ostentation and secretiveness. But what upset him more than anything else was that Grebnitz threatened him that, if he heard one more word from him, he was prepared to demonstrate that the work he was contemplating must necessarily be both injurious and criminal, and therefore, he said, the Clavis Sinica *was a worthless thing. But even under assault Müller could not be aroused from his sleep by the fact that Grebnitz, shrewdly recognizing his ways and his mind, seemed to be looking forward to the moment when Müller should decide to revenge himself properly by openly stating the content of his mystery . . . but enough of such disgusting matters!*

Some years later Müller published his De Eclipsi Passionali Disquisitio. *Here, as usual, he discusses the pros and cons without even reaching a conclusion.*[105] *First Adamus Adamandus Kochanski had urged him to find out what it was that Gabiani had found in the 'Chinese Annals' about the eclipse,*[106] *and shortly afterwards the great Friedrich Wilhelm himself had entreated him to explain the origin of the Chinese printing technique or to translate the text of the famous eclipse.*[107] *Therefore he first gave a small part of it in German translation to the Elector's wife, who was eager to learn about it. Now he published it in Latin without Chinese characters. I have two copies of this work in my library, one which the author, while in Stettin, had given to Michael Schreiber, Professor of Eloquence in Königsberg, later theologian, to whom I owe so much. The other is one that Bartsch had given to the Königsberg mathemati-*

Müller make public his *Besser Unterricht* . . . Two years later he published a new pamphlet, entitled *Andreae Mülleri Greiffenhagii Unschuld* . . ., Stettin, 1683. For more bibliographical details see August Müller, Note 73.

104 The last lines are modified from some lines in Cicero's *Letters to Atticus*, I, 1,1.
105 Müller's 'De Eclipsi Passionali Disquisitio' is printed in his *Specimen Lexici Mandarinici* (1684) as well as in the *Specimen Sinicorum . . . Decimae de Decimis . . .* (1685). See A. Müller, Note 73.
106 Kochanski, see Note 94. – Gabiani, see Note 29.
107 Müller sent a summary of a treatise about the Chinese printing technique entitled 'Typographiae Origo' to Tentzel, who printed it in his *Monatliche Unterredungen*, 1697, pp. 977-8.

cian David Blaesing.[108] *Neither of them is complete, some pages being missing in the one as well as in the other, but in both Müller had written some Chinese characters. He says that he is not quoting a complete passage from the 'Annals', but I have to correct that statement, for when I studied the 'Annals' in Berlin in 1716 I found just what Müller had translated. However, there were also a few small characters printed underneath – four or five, as I remember – I did not pay attention to them at the time, but now I would like to know what they were – supposedly just some scolium to that phrase.*[109]

Now a few words to explain which solar eclipse it is I am talking about. The Holy Scripture relates that when Christ was crucified, day changed to night, and several of the old interpreters explained it as a solar eclipse.[110] *Origen did not think it was, but rather felt that it must have been a profound darkness caused by a whirlwind of thick clouds covering only Jerusalem, or at most the whole of Judea.*[111] *However, the other interpretation has been accepted by a great number of authors. In defence of their opinion they quote the testimony of Phlegon of Tralles.*[112] *(I will not discuss the two letters by Dionysios Areopageta, known by all scholars to be falsifications.)*[113]

But in this connection I want to say that in another place I shall demonstrate that an abridged version of the work of Phlegon, the loss of which many authors have deplored, has actually survived – it is the Synagoge ton Olympiadon adespotos – *the Anonymous Summary of the 'Olympiads', edited by Scaliger.*[114] *Here are Phlegon's eclipses, most of them borrowed from Eratosthenes and included in the text, but some from other sources; and here we find the one the interpreters are talking about, but in a way completely different from theirs.*[115]

When the Jesuits, studying the 'Chinese Annals', thought they had found the description of a solar eclipse occurring about the time of Christ's death, Adrian

---

108 Michael Schreiber (1662-1717), Königsberg theologian, Professor of Rhetoric and librarian in the Wallenrodt Library of that city. – David Blæsing (1660-1719), Professor of Mathematics in Königsberg.
109 Müller writes correctly that he skips a passage in his translation. Bayer must have seen that when he looked up the history work in Berlin but forgotten about it afterwards. – The handwritten characters: In the copy in the Royal Library in Copenhagen the characters are found in xylography. – Scolium: The Greek 'kolion' in the text must be a misprint for 'skolion'. – The four or five small characters underneath are *fan-qie* indications of the correct pronunciation of the character *shang*, to send up.
110 Matth. XXVII, 45. Mark XV, 33. Luke XXIII, 44-5.
111 Origen (approx. 185-254), one of the greatest of all the theologians of the ancient Church.
112 Phlegon of Thralles, Greek historian of the second century A.D. His *Olympiads* was a historical compendium covering the years 776 B.C. to A.D. 137.
113 Dionysius the Areopagite, mentioned in Acts XVII, 34. A fifth century neoplatonist called the Pseudo-Areopagite attributed some of his writings to Dionysius.
114 Scaliger, see Note 22
115 Eratosthenes of Alexandria, Greek mathematician and astronomer, approx. 276-194 B.C.

Grelon, and shortly afterwards Giandominico Gabiani, began to inform the learned world about it.[116] *Gabiani asked the learned Vienna Jesuit Kochanski to examine the matter more closely, and he consulted with Müller about the problem.*[117] *Grelon obtained some help from Dominico Cassini, but this great astronomer immediately rejected all the statements about solar eclipses in the 'Chinese Annals'.*[118]

However, as stated above, Müller had produced the evidence by publishing the Chinese text in his De Eclipsi Passionali Disquisitio *and had settled the matter – albeit waveringly – in fact he did not conceal that he agreed with Gabiani and Grelon.*

(I myself have solved the problem in another book, translating the Chinese text quite differently from the way Müller did.[119] *The publication of that work led my friend, the great astronomer Christfried Kirch, to examine this eclipse very carefully, publishing his results both in the* Miscellanea Berolinensia *and in the* Bibliothèque Germanique, *supporting my conclusions with firm and undeniable arguments. If I had left some doubt in my book, Kirch dispatched it all so completely that I do not think anybody from now on will dare to adduce the Chinese eclipse in support of the eclipse hypothesis about the darkness over Golgatha.)*[120]

In Müller's book about the solar eclipse he printed, for the fifth time, his project about the Clavis Sinica. *He says he will not delay the publication of the* Clavis, *being afraid that after his death it might fall in bad hands. If only it could be arranged financially in such a way that part of it were paid for, and security were given for the rest of it, then he would finish the* Clavis Sinica *in six months or less, so that it would become available to those who might want it. Then – if they followed his instructions – even women and children would be able, in the course of a few days, to read Chinese texts in Latin, German, English, French, Dutch or whatever other language.*

The next year Philippe Couplet came to Berlin, bringing with him some Chinese books. He wanted very much to see Müller and is said to have enjoyed

---

116 Grelon and Gabiani, see Note 29.
117 Kochanski, see Note 94.
118 Giandominico Cassini (1625-1712), famous Italian astronomer. From 1669 director of the Paris Observatory.
119 The other book, of course, is his *De Eclipsi Sinica*, published in 1718. It may be significant that he does not give the title of this work with its attacks on the Jesuits.
120 Christfried Kirch (1694-1740), German astronomer. His father, whom he succeeded as Royal Astronomer in Berlin, had corresponded with Andreas Müller about the 'Chinese Eclipse'. Kirch was a great friend of Bayer and Delisle. Bayer may have met him in his young days in Königsberg, where he worked for some time. He is said to have declined a call from the St Petersburg Academy. His article about the solar eclipse appeared in the *Miscellanea Berolinensia*, Vol. II, pp. 133-9, 1723; the one in the *Bibliothèque Germanique* is found in its Vol. V, pp. 41-51.

his company when a meeting between them became possible.[121]

Shortly afterwards Filippo Grimaldi, a top Jesuit who had brought a message to Rome from the China Jesuits, was about to return to China via Poland and Russia. When he heard from Gottfried Wilhelm Leibniz about Müller's project, he looked for an opportunity to meet him. He did not succeed in this, but he spurred him on to pursue his work, personally as well as through Hiob Ludolf and Leibniz.[122]

It was at that time that Müller wrote a longer commentary on the Nestorian Stele – this manuscript was burned, as far as I know, together with his other papers. In a letter to Tentzel about Couplet's Confucius Sinarum Philosophus *and his* Chinese Chronology *he wrote that every time he compared this work with the Chinese text of the 'Annals' he noticed several departures from the original. Furthermore, he said that this translation was not the work of one man, nor of one century: Ricci had already begun it and had nearly finished it. And as to the Chronology, it did not have the authority of the 'Annals'; it was just a mutilated abridgement of that beautiful text.*[123]

Müller died in Stettin in 1694 – I remember to have heard that he left two daughters. Once when he thought he was seriously ill he did what he had threatened to do and burned his works.

There were rumours, however, that a commentary on the Clavis Sinica *had been stolen and that it still exists somewhere in Pomerania. And personally I know for certain that some of his books were stolen by his servant. I possess two volumes of excerpts, in one of which a certain Johannes Kranz has written that he bought it from the servant, who had destined it, together with other papers, to be used to wrap candlesticks, butter and cheese. One of these volumes is about the Cross, most of it printed already in his* Symbolae Syriacae,[124] *the other is about Caribbean words and words derived from this language. This*

---

121 Couplet, see Note 36. – The story about his visit to Berlin, meeting Müller and also Mentzel is shown to be legendary by Eva Kraft in her 'Frühe chinesische Studien in Berlin', *Medizinhistorische Journal*, Vol. 11, pp. 92-128, 1976.

122 Filippo Grimaldi (1638-1712), Italian Jesuit, in China 1669-86 and again from 1694 to his death. In Europe as procurator for the Society 1686-91. His plan of returning to China via Poland and Russia did not succeed. Bayer took this from Leibniz' *Novissima Sinica* (see Note 92) and from Tentzel's *Monatliche Unterredungen*, 1692, p. 829. – Hiob Ludolff (1624-1703), famous German statesman and linguist, is said to have known 25 languages. Many works on the Ethiopian language.

123 The letter is to be found in Tentzel's *Monatliche Unterredungen*, 1691, pp. 289-90. Müller had given him the title of his new Monument book, a very long one: *Monumentum Sinicum Kircherianum. I. Instauratum, h.e. ad infinitis erroribus Kircherianae editionis & Mentzelianae Sylloges repurgatus . . . Illustratum itemque examine facto . . . III. Vindicatum . . .* Then follows his criticism of Couplet's translation, slightly modified here by Bayer.

124 *Symbolae Syracae sive Epistolae duae Syriacae amobaeae* (1673). – Müller wrote to Tentzel about his 'pandectae' in 1692 and 1693 (*Monatliche Unterredungen*, 1697, pp. 172-3 and 176-

volume has a printed title page, saying 'Pandectae litterariae rerum et verborum'. Furthermore, it appears from this text that in the year 1691 Müller had conceived the praiseworthy idea of throwing his library open to the public, also suggesting a keeper, who should augment these Pandectae, and inviting people to make use of his manuscripts and orientalia and everything else he had. But his character, or the influence which the disease had upon him, made him suddenly change his mind, for it is said that after he realized that he was recovering, he regretted what he had done. Some of his books went to the Stettin Library – I went there to examine them, but although I found some good things, there was less of interest than I had expected.

Among his own published works there are only a few that are not mutilated in one way or other. In several cases, in order to obtain a complete copy, I had to buy two or three deficient ones, and I have still not got a complete collection of his works.

The next to study the Chinese language in Berlin was Christian Mentzel, the court physician.[125] He did not obtain the same fame as Müller, but he deserves it much more. He arranged to have several Chinese books sent through Georg Everhard Rumpf, a high official of the Dutch East India Company in Amboina on the Moluccas, as well as from Andreas Cleyer in Batavia.[126, 127] Indefatigably studying what he had learned from Cleyer and Couplet, he succeeded in

---

8). – In his *Monumenti Sinici . . . lectio . . .*, Commentarium grammaticum, p. 8 Müller mentions Caribbean languages, i.e. languages spoken by the aborigines of South America north of the Amazon and of the West Indies. They were said to have a tonal system.

125 Christian Mentzel (1622-1701), German physician and botanist, physician-in-orderly to Friedrich Wilhelm, the Great Elector in Berlin from 1660 to 1688. He became interested in the Chinese language in his old days and was warden of the Chinese collections of the Electorial Library from 1685. He retired in 1692 but continued with his Chinese studies. – Mentzel's life and works are described in great detail in three recent papers by Eva Kraft: 'Frühe chinesische Studien in Berlin' (see Note 121). – 'Christian Mentzels chinesische Geschenke für Kaiser Leopold I', in *Schloss Charlottenburg-Berlin-Preussen, Festschrift für Margarete Kühn* (1975), pp. 191-9. – 'Christian Mentzel, Philippe Couplet, Andreas Cleyer und die chinesische Medizin', in *Fernöstliche Kultur. Wolf Haenisch zugeeignet von seinem Margburger Studienkreis* (1975), pp. 158-96. – Nearly everything on the following pages about Mentzel, Couplet and Piques is taken, often *verbatim*, from the Mentzel papers which Bayer copied in Berlin in 1716 – the six letters from Couplet, 1687-9 and the one from Picques, written in 1687. (Hunter MS No. 299.)

126 Rumpf, Georg Everhard (1628-1702), Dutch naturalist and high official in the Dutch East India Company on the Moluccas, author of several works on the flora and fauna of these islands.

127 Andreas Cleyer (1634 to 1697 or 1698), German physician and botanist in the service of the Dutch East India Company in Batavia (Java). He corresponded with many other European scientist besides Mentzel. There are two early letters from him to the Danish anatomist and botanist Simon Paulli (1603-80), one of them with a fine picture of the tea plant (*Acta medica et philosophica Hafniensis*, Vol. IV, pp. 1-5, 1677). – When he met Couplet Cleyer was about to leave for his first visit to Japan.

contributing to the advancement of our knowledge about the Chinese civilization. He published only three works, and they are far below what this excellent man might have produced – I can say so, for I have read, with the greatest admiration, the drafts of his unpublished writings.

In 1685, when Müller had moved to Stettin, Mentzel published his Sylloge Minutiarum Lexici Sinici, *which he said he had composed from Chinese dictionaries, and gave as an example of the kind of work he was engaged in.*[128] *But something – I do not know what – must have happened to this excellent man, for I have seen the same dictionary in the Royal Library of Berlin, beautifully printed on red paper by the Jesuits of Peking, and sent to Berlin by Cleyer! I could find no difference between this Peking edition and Mentzel's book, except that the Peking Jesuits say that the Chinese word for ten is pronounced 'sipn', not 'xe' – Mentzel corrected that. I realized, therefore, that Mentzel was only human and, at that time not as good at Chinese as we know he later became. On the other hand, I often ask myself if it were the Peking Jesuits who reprinted Mentzel's book, but I cannot see what reason they could have had for putting such a book on the market, whether it was their own or a reproduction of Mentzel's book. Could they not have done better? As a matter of fact, this dictionary contains nothing more than Latin words followed by Chinese characters – namely those to be found on the Nestorian Stele! All the errors in Boym's translation are carried over to this lexicon and words referring obscurely and unsatisfactorily to their characters and characters left untranslated, are omitted here. How can we explain this? Were the Peking Jesuits not capable of correcting the errors of Boym, or rather of Kircher who edited the text?*[129]

---

128 *Sylloge Minutiarum Lexici Latino-Sinico-Characteristici* . . . (1685). Also as an appendix to the *Miscellanea curiosa sive Ephemerides med.-phys. Germ.Acad.Caes.-Leopold.nat.cur.*, Decur. II, annus III. – It consists of ten pages of grammatical notes and a dictionary of about 500 Latin words, arranged alphabetically, followed by the Chinese words, first in transliteration then the characters. At the end he says that he hopes later on to publish two more short word lists, one with characters followed by transliterations and then by the Latin words, 'in the Chinese way and according to the principles of Hiob Ludolff, very learned in Chinese characters and oriental matters', and another one arranged in the opposite way, first the transliterated words, then the characters and then the Latin words. 'These works will make it possible to understand the meaning of Chinese books . . .' – Hiob Ludolff, (see Note 122), a friend of Andreas Müller, seems to have tried to prevent the publication of the *Sylloge*. See Eva Kraft: 'Frühe chinesische Studien . . .', Note 121, and R. Wienau: 'Sylloge Minutiarum Lexici Latino-Sinico-Characteristici', in *Acta historica Leopoldina* (1975).

129 What Bayer says here about the possibility of the Jesuits having published Mentzel's little *Sylloge* in China seems preposterous, but he may have based his speculations on a paragraph in one of the Couplet's letters to Mentzel, dated 26 April 1687, which he omitted here. Mentzel had sent a number of copies of his book – it can only be the *Sylloge* – to Couplet. Couplet writes: 'I have distributed this monument of erudition and learned labour to colleagues who are able to appreciate it. And now, this year, some copies of it will be sailing to India and even to China, so that the name of the excellent Mentzel will be celebrated from

In this dictionary Mentzel included a short but excellent and correct preface dealing with Chinese characters. His own characters, however, are poorly written.

After this little work he printed some notes from Chinese pharmacopoeias about the Ginseng root in the Annals of the Academia Leopoldina,[130] *and finally his Chinese Chronologia which I shall return to later.*

(Mentzel writes as follows about his Ginseng project: 'I had decided a long time ago to publish something about the Ginseng root, which the Chinese esteem so highly, in gratitude to my colleagues Cleyer and Rumpf.[131] *However, I was detained from this design for several years by a certain very learned person, who had published the name of the plant in Chinese, with an engraving showing it, but since that had left the matter untouched and unfinished. Respecting his honour, I did not want to outstrip him'. Of course he was thinking of Müller, who said something about the Ginseng root and promised more, as I mentioned above.)*

When Couplet came to Europe, Mentzel moved the wise Elector to call this learned man to the court. For he had heard about the erudition of this man from Cleyer, who had met him when his ship called at the port of Batavia, and had taken very good care of him. For his part Couplet undertook to explain the Chinese pharmacopoeia in Latin to Cleyer, but he did not get beyond a few pages. It was too difficult, not only because of the names of the plants, but also because of the many descriptions of the nature and the virtues of each of them and their use in medicine. About some of them he read that they should be macerated in brine, some in vinegar, others again in other liquids. Then some of them should be roasted, others dried in the sun, in the shade, in a windy place, others again should be imbued in the steam of boiling water – all the kind of nonsense the Chinese physicians spend a lot of effort explaining.[132]

West to East (*a solis occasu usque ad ortum*)'. Even allowing for the gross flattery of the epistolary style of the time this seems outrageous, but is there a possible explanation? Can the Peking Jesuits have had a few copies of this little book – the dictionary is only 24 pages – printed in China with the purpose of sending one to the old court physician in Berlin? The fact that the Chinese book, 'beautifully printed on red paper', was actually in Berlin when Bayer visited there can hardly be doubted. He tells the same story on p. 8 of his *De Eclipsi Sinica* with its dedicatory letter to his friend Lacroze, the librarian. He would not have dared to invent the story. Moreover, Lacroze, in his letter to him, dated 30 April 1719, offers several specific comments and criticisms of the Eclipse book, but says nothing against the 'red book' in the Royal Library. (Lacroze Correspondence, III, pp. 47-9.)

130 'De radice Chinensium Gîn-Sên', in *Miscellanea curiosa sive Ephemerides med.-phys. Germ. Acad. Caes.-Leopold. Nat.cur.*, Decur. II, annus V, 1686, pp. 73-79.

131 By *Collegae* Mentzel means that the three of them are members of the Academia Naturae Curiosorum, see Wienau's article mentioned in Note 128.

132 Probably it was the classical pharmacopoeia called *Bencao (Gangmu)*. In the grammar chapter of the *Museum Sinicum* (p. 84) Bayer describes a copy of it, calling it *Caomu*, presumably one of Mentzel's books which he had seen in the Royal Library. The last page of

Moreover, Couplet was disabled by an inflammation of the eyes, and finally he had to stop translating because his ship was departing.

When Couplet came to Berlin the Elector paid him very handsomely for instructing his Mentzel.[133] *Later on Mentzel courted Couplet's favour in letters and with presents, and in turn received many learned and highly informative letters from him – I myself have profited very much from reading them. However, Couplet's Chinese characters were even worse than those of Mentzel – trying to unravel them has often delayed my work.*

In 1687 Couplet went to Paris, where he devoted himself to Melchisédec Thévenot, the Royal Librarian, a man proficient in many and various disciplines and an astute investigator of antiquities, as his associates rightly remark in their Collection of Ancient Mathematicians.[134] *He was keen to get information about the Chinese language, and Couplet gave him the explanation of the radicals which Mentzel had never received and which he could not wrench out of Thévenot's envious hands. He got it later, however, from elsewhere.*

Louis Picques of the Sorbonne was quite another man. Strongly interested in promoting the study of oriental languages, he undertook, with the greatest kindness, to help Mentzel in all possible ways. Realizing that his own duties would prevent him from working full time on Chinese – he had just been elected, on 16 September, by 53 votes, head librarian of Mazarin's Collège des Quatre-Nations – he generously helped Mentzel with various suggestions.[135]

I cannot refrain from quoting some lines from one of his letters to Mentzel, showing his sincerity and generosity:

'Being compelled by the burdens of my office', he writes, 'I am unable to give myself completely up to Chinese studies, but I shall help you as much as I can. Maybe my services will not be of disadvantage to you. Couplet is more and more obsessed by the idea of promoting your studies in that way; although I am really not qualified for it, he thinks that it is especially incumbent upon me to encourage you. As to myself, I have always feared loneliness: who would embark on such an undertaking without fellow students, without people to

---

Mentzel's *Clavis Sinica* (see Note 16 to 'The Chinese Language') contains a 36-character text with transliterations and translations about the gingseng root from a *Bencao Gangmu* edition. – Later on Bayer must have owned a copy of this work himself. We are going to hear about it in the chapter on his big Chinese dictionary.

133 For the legend about Couplet's visit to Berlin see Note 121.

134 Melchisédech Thévenot (ed): *Veterum Mathematicorum Athenaei* . . . (1693).

135 Louis Picques, French scholar, died 1699. He was chief librarian of the Bibliothèque Mazarine from its foundation in 1688. Retired in 1695' because he wanted to devote himself entirely to his studies'. He owned a rich collection of works in oriental languages. (See Alfred Franklin: *Histoire de la Bibliothèque Mazarine* (1901.) – By an amusing slip of the pen Bayer wrote 'Collegium Mandarinicum Quatuor Nationum' instead of 'Collegium Mazarinicum', as clearly written by himself when he copied Couplet's letter in 1716.

congratulate him? That was why Müller had to converse with a dormouse.[136] *You must find some bright young person and commit to him the results of your studies, that they shall not perish with you'.*

In that year Couplet published the Confucius Sinarum Philosophus *in Paris. He would have liked to include the Chinese characters and mentions that in a letter to Mentzel: 'It would have been desirable', he says, 'to add the Chinese characters to the translation, and I also planned to do so, but practical difficulties arose that made me change my mind.'*

At that time Mentzel received a copy of the Four Books *in Chinese.*[137] *Couplet congratulated him on it, admitting – to my surprise – that in China he had only studied one of them. In other words, it was not Couplet who made the translations contained in the* Confucius Sinarum Philosophus, *as most people believe; there were several others, among them Intorcetta, although in his* Catalogus *Couplet says that he only translated the Sayings of Confucius.*[138]

In Paris Couplet also left behind him a Chinese dictionary, beautifully written, which he had little hope of seeing published there. Had he been in Germany, he could have expected to have it printed in the course of a month, because at that time there was much more interest in that kind of study in Germany than in France.[139]

At the beginning of the year 1687, when Couplet wrote this, he sent his fellow-Jesuit Francesco Spinola and a young man of about 30 years from Nanking, by the name of Michael Chen Fuzong, ahead to Portugal, via Belgium and England. At that time the famous Thomas Hyde, versed in all oriental languages but particularly in Persian, lived in Oxford. Until then he had not devoted himself to the Chinese language apart from reading something about it, written by European authors. Now he gave all his attention to this young Michael – he saw that he was a very talented and extremely diligent student of literature and regarded him as a colleague and friend. He alone among the Chinese converts had learned to speak Latin. Hyde shared the fruits of their

---

136 The meaning is clear enough, but I do not know if it is a proverb or if Picques is referring to a story that belonged to the Müller legend. It may refer to something which Mentzel had written to him. There are no copies of Mentzel's letters among the Glasgow Bayeriana.
137 The *Four Books,* see Note 40 to 'The Chinese Language'.
138 *Catalogus S.J. qui post obitum Sti. Francisci Xaverii . . . in Imperio Sinarum Jesu Christi Fidem propagarunt* (1686). However, there is nothing in this Catalogue about Intorcetta's translations in the *Confucius Sinarum Philosophus.* Later on Bayer wanted to publish a new edition of it and asked the Peking Jesuits to help him to bring the record up to the present.
139 In two of his letters to Mentzel Couplet speaks in a very definite way about leaving this dictionary in Paris. It is not known who the author was or what became of it – oddly enough Fourmont never mentions it. Couplet also says that once he is in Portugal he will try to make a vocabulary himself and send it to Mentzel, if time permits, adding that when he gets back to China he will look into what happened to Christian Herdtrich's Chinese-Latin dictionary. 'It was being printed when I left, but the work may have been interrupted when Father Herdtrich died'. (See Abel Remusat's *Mélanges Asiatiques* (1826), Vol. II, p. 67.)

conversations with all of us. For in 1688 he published his 'Letter to Edward Bernard about Chinese Measures and Weights', and some years later – in 1694 – when he composed the many sections of his De Ludis Orientalibus, *he explained several Chinese games. In his* Historia Religionis Veterum Persarum . . . , *published in 1700, he deals with problems of Chinese chronology, somewhat more exactly than Golius had done. However, the information he had obtained about Chinese idolatry, their ideas about God, Heaven and Hell, and what he had learned during their conversations about Chinese criminal law, the geomantic and the nautical compass, as well as about literature, books, paper, the principles and antiquity of bookprinting, epistolary style and colloquialisms, also the Apostolic Creed and the Ten Commandments – all these things he had hoped to publish, but they never appeared.*[140]

Couplet went from England to Lisbon and left the young Chinese in the seminary there, while he hurried to Madrid and then back to China.

However, to return to Mentzel: he also got much help from Claudio Filippo Grimaldi when this Jesuit was in Berlin.

Some time later, in 1696, he published his Chronology of the Chinese Kings in German, adducing the Chinese characters he found in a small book called Xiao Er Lun *to the names of the kings.*[141] *The rest is simply a translation – sometimes incorrect – of Couplet's Chronology. To give some examples: Under*

---

140 Thomas Hyde (1636-1703), famous Oxford orientalist, master of Turkish, Arabic, Syriac, Persian, Hebrew and Malay. He was responsible for most of the Persian texts in Walton's Polyglot Bible. – 'Epistolae de Mensuris et Ponderibus Serum sive Sinensium', in Edward Bernard's *De Mensuris et Ponderibus antiquis Libri tres* (1688). – *'De Ludis orientalibus Libri II'. in Mandragorias seu Historia Shahiludi* (1694). In Part II of the *Mandragorias (Historia Nerdiludii),* p. 87-8, Hyde writes about this young Chinese calling him 'my Chinese . . . my brilliant friend Mr. Michael Chin Fo Çum'. – Six letters from him to Thomas Hyde are found in the Appendix on the Chinese language in Gregory Sharpe's edition of the *Syntagma Dissertationum quos olim Thomas Hyde separatim edidit . . .* (1767). This interesting and important Appendix, composed by the editor, a classical and oriental scholar, also contains a Bayer bibliography (see p. 219) and a description of a *Za Zi,* a kind of primitive Chinese primer – we are going to hear more of *Za Zi's* in the chapter on the *Xiao Er Lun.* – Chin Fo Çum (Chen Fuzong) (? to 1692), Chinese Jesuit. After having been with Couplet in Europe from 1681 to 1692 he died on his way back to China.

141 *Kurtze Chinesische Chronologia oder Zeit-Register Aller Chinesischen Kayser . . . auch mit zween Chinesischen erklärten Tafeln . . . bezogen aus der Chineser Kinderlehre Sia Ul Hio oder Lun genande . . .* (1696) – The chronology from Huang Di onwards is an abbreviation of Couplet's chronology. Mentzel does not say so, although he does mention Couplet, namely as the author of the 'Proëmialis Declaratio' of the *Confucius Sinarum Philosophus.* He writes that he has made this short historical catalogue from the 'Chinese Annals' in the Electoral Library, for the use of future librarians. This is true in so far as he found the individual emperor's names in the 'Annals' and added them to his summaries from Couplet's chronology. I have inserted the page numbers from Couplet in the text. – The first part of the chronology is taken from a Chinese children's book, a primitive primer (*Za Zi*). See p. 135.

Kang Wan (p. 10) Mentzel notes that the country enjoyed peace and everything was done to cultivate the soil, to the extent that criminals released from prison went to work in the fields. What Couplet had said, however, was that at that time the sense of justice was so highly developed that prisoners released to cultivate the soil returned to their chains of their own free will as soon as the work in the fields was over. Mentzel relates that King Er Shi Huangdi was ordered to commit suicide by his brother. But in Couplet's Chronology we read that the father had designated his eldest son to succeed him, but that Er Shi Huangdi, who was the second son, ordered his elder brother to kill himself (p. 17). Mentzel writes that Zhao Di gave solemn amnesty to and concluded a peace treaty with the Tartars. But Couplet had said that when peace was concluded with the Tartars, the king proclaimed a general amnesty in the whole country, following the benevolent example of his ancestors (p. 19). Mentzel says that King An Di married one of his concubines, but as she did not bear him any children, he adopted the son of another concubine, whom he poisoned. However, Couplet had said that without telling the king the wife had taken a newborn child from another concubine, whom she then killed (p. 40). Mentzel speaks about Muhammadans coming to China during the reign of Tai Zu. He ought to have said, as Couplet does, that it occurred during the dynasty to which the king belonged or – as others have it – in the one before (p. 66). A careful comparison of these two texts reveals several things like this.

Mentzel's Chronology starts with the first pages of the Xiao Er Lun ('Siao Ul Lun'), translated from the Chinese. I have decided to include it in the present work with my own commentary.

However, Mentzel also contemplated a major work. When he received two copies of the Zi Hui dictionary from the Indies he took one of them apart and interleaved it with sheets of European paper, forming eight big volumes, so that he could add his translations. When he thought his work was progressing, he published a prospectus about it:

> A Chinese Dictionary, entitled
> Zi Hui, i.e. the genera and
> species of the Chinese characters,
> arranged according to the
> radicals and their composite
> forms evolving from primary
> ones, with pronunciation and
> Latin translations, corrected
> and augmented with new characters
> from the Zheng Zi Tong dictionary
> and many important ones from
> other sources.

Vol. I
by Christian Mentzel, MD.[142]

In 1698 he bestowed upon the Elector, Friedrich the Wise, vast amounts of important observations from Martini's Grammar, Couplet's letters, Francisco Diaz's Vocabulary and other sources, the results of his indefatigable labours. These things now adorn the Royal Library in Berlin.

Gottfried Wilhelm Leibniz was among the most passionate promoters of Mentzel's studies. His profound insights into the constitution of the Universe, created according to God's providence, was only rivalled by his genius as a humanist: it was as if he lived inside the monuments of the humanities, and he laid the proper foundation of the philosophy of language, a discipline not yet cultivated for the benefit of the understanding of history. His powerful mind had made him acquainted with nearly all the languages and their mutual interrelations. He realized that not even a Hercules could master all of them, and therefore he was pleased to support anybody who applied his mind and his energy to any part of such problems, helping them, without jealousy, as much as he could with his comments, advice and praise. So he tried to awaken Müller's dull mind, and when that man proved as unbreakable as the marble of Paros he turned his attention to Mentzel. After Mentzel's death he tried in all possible ways to find some bright person whom he could get started on this honourable career.[143]

---

142 Mentzel's dictionary disappeared from the Deutsche Staatsbibliothek during the Second World War. It is described by Tautz as 'containing the characters cut out from the pages of the Zi Hui dictionary . . . with the addition of some from the *Zheng Zi Tong*, many of them with Portuguese transliterations, some of them (*gelegentlich*) with Latin translations' (Kurt Tautz: *Die Bibliothekare der Churfürstlichen Bibliothek zu Cölln an der Spree* (1925). Bayer must have seen it, but he could also find information about it in Tentzel's *Monatliche Unterredungen* 1690, pp. 900-1. It would have been natural to mention here Mentzel's *Clavis Sinica* but for some reason Bayer preferred to wait till he came to the discussion of Polycarp Leyser.

143 Gottfried Wilhelm Leibniz (1646-1716), the great German philisopher and universal genius. His general interest in all the languages must have been known to Bayer from his *Collectanea Etymologica*, edited by I.G. Eccard in 1717 and from his 'Brevis designatio meditationum de originibus gentium, ductis potissimum ex indicio linguarum', printed in the *Miscellanea Berolinensia*, Vol. I, 1-16, 1710. In this first volume of the acts of the Societas Regia Scientiarum his universality was demonstrated by the inclusion of no less than eleven articles dealing with many different subjects in mathematics, physics and humanities. He had shown his interest in China by his publication of the *Novissima Sinica* in 1697 and in 1699 (see Note 92). His correspondence in 1700-2 with the China Jesuit Joachim Bouvet, (1656-1730) led to their recognition of a certain similarity between Leibniz's dyadic number system and the *Yi Jing* hexagrams in the so-called 'Prior to Heaven' arrangement, believed to have been invented by Fu Xi, the 'first Chinese emperor'. In 1703, the astounding discovery that Fu Xi, the father of the Chinese civilization, had understood the science of combinations and the dyadic principle was published in *Histoire de l'Académie royale des sciences*, pp. 85-9. –

Leibniz was on friendly terms with Couplet and Grimaldi. When Bouvet was looking after the affairs of the Society of Jesus in France, he corresponded with him, asking him to comment on the natural history of the Chinese. Bouvet answered him kindly when he was about to sail from La Rochelle, promising to send him ample information about that matter. Grimaldi treated him just as kindly, writing to him from Goa about his wishes and interests. They wrote to each other several times and I believe that the world would have reaped the fruits of this interchange if only Leibniz had lived a few more years.

He gave us his Novissima Sinica *with Joseph Suarez's little text about the recent imperial decree legalizing the Christian religion in China, and also the 'Portrait of Emperor Kang Xi', painted in lively and brilliant colours by Bouvet and translated by Leibniz from French into Latin. He does not state that it is his translation, but I know his elegant style and immediately recognized his hand.*[144]

In the Miscellanea Berolinensia *he also inserted something about a Chinese game from a volume of Chinese pictures in Berlin, but his explanations are not very useful. He had them only from Trigault's book, and he himself felt that something had gone wrong with the text. He had never seen Thomas Hyde's book about Chinese games, in which the rules of this game called Weiqi – a kind of encircling game – are explained.*[145]

When Friedrich the Wise made Prussia into a kingdom he made plans for the foundation of the Societas Regia Scientiarum, *the Academy which flourishes to this day in Berlin. By his decree discussions were initiated about the introduction and propagation of Christianity in China, about the promotion of knowledge of the nature of the peoples and the languages of the vast regions*

> Bayer commented on this matter in the chapter containing his speculations about the origin of Chinese characters (see p. 114), and his *De Horis Sinicis* (1735) shows that he was familiar at that time with the 'Prior to Heaven' arrangement of the hexagrams (see p. 172). See David E. Mungello: *Leibniz and Confucianism – the Search for Accord* (1977). Also an article by A.J. Aiton and W. Shimao: 'Gorai Kinzo's Study of Leibniz and the I Ching Hexagrams', *Annals of Science* (1981). – Curiously, in this section of the Preface Bayer does not mention Leibniz's many attempts to get Lacroze to concentrate on the study of the Chinese language – he knew about it as is seen from his dedicatory letter to Lacroze in his *De Eclipsi Sinica* (1718). These attempts can be followed in the more and more insistant letters Leibniz sent to Lacroze between 1705 and 1710 (Chr. Kortholt (Ed) *Leibniz: Epistolae ad diversos* . . . Vol. I, 1734).

144 See Note 92. – The second edition, published in 1699, included the 'Icon Regia Monarchae Sinarum nunc regnantis delineata a R.P. Joach. Bouveto Jesuita Gallo, e Gallico versa', a translation of the *Portrait historique de l'Empereur de la Chine* (1697). – In his *Bibliotheca Sinica*, Col. 835, Henri Cordier mentions a copy of this edition in the library of the great sinologist Alexander Wylie (1815-87). It had belonged to T.S. Bayer and had a great number of marginal notes from his hand.

145 G.W. Leibniz: 'Annotatio de quibusdam ludis: imprimis de ludo quodam sinico . . .' *Miscellanea Berolinensia*, I, pp. 22-26, 1710. – Thomas Hyde: see Note 140.

stretching between China and Prussia, and about studying all the oriental languages accurately.

This Society boasts two illustrious members, the eminent and brilliant old scholar Mathurin Veyssière de Lacroze and Alphonse des Vignoles. Lacroze has perfected the study of Coptic and Armenian for the understanding of history – more than anybody else today, in former times and maybe in times to come. As to Chinese he used to tell me that he had given only so much time and attention to that language as to satisfy his curiosity.[146] *Alphonse des Vignoles works only on ancient chronology and for that purpose includes the study of Chinese to be able to obtain information about eclipses and other astronomical observations from their Annals. I have also heard that he has taken up the study of Chinese geography.*[147]

It should also be mentioned here that the diligent Engelbert Kaempfer, while staying in Japan, had endeavoured to become acquainted with the language of that country. The Japanese use the same characters as the Chinese, but pronounce them in their own way. So when Kaempfer published his Amoenitates *in Europe he included the names of plants and other natural things, in beautifully written Chinese, but with the Japanese pronunciation.*[148]

Polycarp Leyser, known for his many and various studies, had a rather ambitious plan in the field of Chinese studies.[149] *If I remember rightly it was Lacroze who gave him Mentzel's* Clavis Sinica *together with some short grammatical notes in 1717. He included this information in his* Apparatus literarius, *but the most important thing for him was to demonstrate that he had done what*

146 Lacroze, see p. 92.
147 Alphonse Des Vignoles (1649-1744), French chronologist, parson in Reformed churches in the neighbourhood of Berlin. He was a member of the Berlin Academy from the start (1701) and became its president in 1727. Co-editor of the *Bibliotheque Germanique*. Author of the *Chronologie de l'histoire sainte et des histoires étrangères* . . . (1738), and a great number of articles in various journals.
148 Engelbert Kaempfer (1651-1716), German physician and traveller, in Dutch service in the Far East for years. – *Amoenitatum exoticarum* . . . (1712).
149 Polycarp Leyser (IV) (1690-1728), German polyhistor, Professor of Poetry in Helmstadt. The *Apparatus literarius* . . . (1717-18), published by a club of erudites, contains miscellaneous short papers dealing with literary and theological subjects. Most of them were written by Polycarp Leyser. In his 'Clavis Linguae Sinicae Mullerianae orbi literato restituenda' (Vol. I, pp. 31-8) Leyser discusses a *Clavis Sinica* he has obtained from a famous scholar versed in the Chinese language, the name of whom he does not want to divulge. It is clear from the short presentation of it that it was in fact Mentzel's *Clavis*, i.a. from the two characters given as examples – they are to be found in Tabula 7 of this work, exactly in the way Leyser describes them. Comparing his copy with the vague notes Andreas Müller had given about his *Clavis,* Leyser concludes that they are identical! This *Clavis,* however, is 'grammatical, not philosophical'; it is not possible to understand the meaning of a character at a glance, but he has now found out that there is a system behind it. He has corrected the *Clavis,* using Chinese works, and supplied an infinite number of additions to it. It is ready to print and he hopes to have it published in some way, perhaps in Belgium or England . . .

Müller had only promised to do. He said that he had obtained a certain Clavis Sinica, *so badly written that it was clear to him that the author had known as little Chinese as Kircher or the person whose copy of the text of the Nestorian Stele he had used.* To me there is no doubt that it was Mentzel's Clavis – I will never conceal this man's merits or suffer him to be denigrated by others. It is true that his Chinese characters were very poor – but this was due to his trembling old hand, not to ignorance or negligence. Actually it is not difficult to discern the correct strokes in his characters, if only one has learned not only the characters the Chinese cut in the wooden boards they use in book production, but also the type of script they use when writing rapidly. Mentzel used to write in that way.

(On the other hand I do not see what problems there should be with the Nestorian Stele text in Kircher's China . . . illustrata – no great learning is required to make out the correct strokes in its characters at a glance.)

But to return to the Clavis which Leyser had, he writes that he has perfected it, comparing its characters with those of Chinese books and supplying his own corrections and additions. He imagined that there would be many persons who would financially support the printing of this work, and therefore I do not know why he gave it up – either because his hopes had been exaggerated or because he became distracted by more important matters. Anyhow, unfortunately, this work did not appear.

I also know, from an announcement in the catalogue of the Vienna Library, that Nessel, the successor of Lambeck, had thought of publishing a collection of articles about Chinese matters, especially about the life and the miracles of Christ as drawn by a Chinese artist, with a short commentary in Chinese. It was also to include geographical and astronomical notes, but he never published it. I do not know how competent he was.[150]

In 1716 Johann Jakob Mascov was departing for Italy.[151] I knew about his erudition and the fame of his works in the learned world, and also that he was an extremely kind and mild person. Therefore, and because I knew his great flair and diligence, it seemed to me that nobody could be more useful to me than that excellent man. So I took the opportunity to ask him, while staying in Italy, to be on the look-out for persons who were interested in Chinese studies. He wrote to me that he had become familiar with Maigrot, the Bishop of Conon

---

150 Daniel de Nessel (1644-1711), German scholar, the successor of Peter Lambeck as librarian of the Imperial Library in Vienna. He published the *Catalogus sive recensio specialis omnium manuscriptorum graecorum nec non orientalium* . . . (1610), an abbreviated edition of Lambeck's *Commentarii.* (See Note 5 to *De Eclipsi Sinica.*)

151 Johann Jacob Mascov (1689-1761), German historian and jurist. In 1712-14 and again in 1717-18 he was in Italy, visiting libraries and meeting many famous scholars. He was admired by his contemporaries for his works as well as for his amiable manners. He was a great friend of Lacroze.

and Pontifical Vicar to the Chinese Empire, who had acquired a profound knowledge of Chinese culture during his twenty-year stay in the country. Mascov had also heard about the proficiency, both in Chinese and Manchu, of Visdelou, Bishop of Claudiopolis and Pontifical Vicar in the province of China, who lived at the time in Pondicherry, the French town on the Coromandel coast.[152]

At that time I also asked Apostolo Zeno, through the distinguished Paul Joseph Pasqualin, if he knew anybody in Italy who was well versed in the Chinese language. He answered me that he knew several people, the most eminent among them being the Pope – this Zeno had told Pásqualin that he had heard once when he was in Rome.[153]

I would have liked to deal with the studies of the eminent French authors in the same way as with the other ones I have discussed here, if only I had known them better.

The works and fame of Abbé Jean Paul Bignon in the promotion of all disciplines are far beyond my praise.[154] *It was he who seized upon the opportunity to promote the study of Chinese when the young and learned Arcadius Huang came to Paris in the company of the Bishop of Rosalia.*[155] *First he was attached to the Collège des Missions Étrangères, where he just subsisted meagrely. However, becoming infatuated with the splendour of that city and the ways of the French, he married a French girl. The daughter she bore him looked quite Chinese, her traits and colours were just those that distinguish a*

---

152 At the turn of the century the Rites Controversy reached a high point in China and in Europe. Charles Maigrot (1652-1730) from the Societé des Missions étrangères issued a proclamation against the Chinese rites that caused much unrest (1693). Exiled from China in 1706, he lived the rest of his life in Rome. For the virulent anti-Jesuit book he published in 1714 under the name of Minorelli, see p. 158. – Claude de Visdelou (1656-1737), learned China Jesuit, historian specializing in the history of Central Asian peoples. He became entangled in the problems raised by de Tournon, the papal envoy who quarrelled with the Kang Xi emperor. He fled from China in 1708, came to Pondicherry and had to stay there for the rest of his life, being forbidden by the Duke of Orleans, the French Regent, to return to Europe. (See Note 162.) – Clement IX, Pope from 1700 to 1721, was against the accommodation practice in China.

153 Apostolo Zeno (1668-1750), Venetian dramatist and historian. – Paolo Guiseppe Pasqualino, Italian man of letters (?), born in Tirol. Bayer must have got his address from his friend Christian Goldbach who had met him on his travels and corresponded with him. (Ju.Ch. Kopelevič and A.P. Juškevič: *Christian Goldbach – 1690-1764*) (in Russian) Moscow, 1983, p. 50)

154 Bignon, see Note 67.

155 Arcadius Huang (Arcade Hoang) (1679-1716), the young Chinese who worked with Fourmont and Fréret in the Royal Library in Paris. Born into a Christian mandarin family in the Fukien Province he came to France with Artus de Lionne (1655-1713), Bishop of Rosalia, in 1702. His importance for the birth of French sinology, depreciated in the writings of Fourmont, is discussed in Danielle Elisséeff-Poisle's book, *Nicolas Fréret (1688-1749). Reflexions d'un humaniste du XVIIIe siecle sur la Chine*, Paris 1978.

Chinese from a European. Later on Bignon hired him for a small salary to translate from the Chinese books in the Royal Library. Here he founded the catalogue of Chinese books and began the composition of a grammar and dictionaries of the Chinese language. Fréret, the eminent scholar, versed in the languages and the geography of the East, ancient as well as modern, attached himself to Arcadius and benefited from his directions and advice.[156]

Besides Fréret there are two other excellent orientalists in the Académie des inscriptions et belles-lettres, the brothers Fourmont, both of them interpreters in the Royal Library. Étienne Fourmont, the older one, is Professor of Arabic at the Collège de France. His younger brother Michel is Professor of Syriac in the same institution. (Rumour has it that he is at present on his way to Constantinople.) Both of them, but in particular Etienne, continued with Chinese studies by themselves. Therefore they gained access to all the Chinese books that had been deposited in the Royal Library before, as well as those that Arcadius had brought with him and those that were kept in the Collège des Missions Étrangères and elsewhere.[157]

I have heard that Arcadius had had 50,000 Chinese characters cut in wood for a dictionary, and that more were in preparation, making up 70,000. I often heard about these matters from my friend François Joseph Delisle, who was a friend of Arcadius, living close to him in Paris, and who held Fréret and the

---

[156] Nicolas Fréret (1688-1749), French historian, member of the Académie des inscriptions et belles-lettres. His long dissertation entitled 'Reflexions sur les principes généraux de l'art d'écrire et en particulier sur les fondements de l'écriture chinoise' was printed in the *Histoire de l'Académie royale des inscriptions et belles-lettres . . . avec les Memoires de litterature . . .*, Vol. VI (*Memoires*), pp. 609-35 (1729). In Volume V (*Histoire*), pp. 303-12 (1729) there is a summary of a paper he had read in the Academy, 'Sur la langue chinoise'. Bayer probably did not know these two articles when he wrote his *Museum Sinicum*, but he knew Fréret's translation of a Chinese poem, printed in Vol. III (*Histoire*), pp. 289-91 (1717). – In a long letter to the French China Jesuit Gaubil, written in 1735, Fréret gives vent to his contempt for the *Museum Sinicum*. However, from his emotional and vague remarks it seems that he does not remember it very well – he is mostly irritated by the fact that Bayer had included his translation from the little Chinese poem in it. (Vigile Pinot: *Documents inédits relatifs à la connaissance de la Chine en France de 1685 a 1740* (1932).) On Fréret, see the biography by Danielle Elisséeff-Poisle, Note 155. – One of two letters Bayer wrote a few days before he died, dealing with Fourmont's attack on him, was to Nicolas Fréret, the other was to Souciet (See p. 208.)

[157] Étienne Fourmont (1683-1745), French sinologist, member of the Académie des inscriptions et belles-lettres. His *Meditationes Sinicae . . .* appeared in Paris in 1737. It contained nearly three pages of harsh and insulting remarks about Bayer and his *Museum Sinicum*. Bayer only got time to read a review of it before he died. (See p. 204.) Fourmont's next work, the *Linguae Sinarum Mandarinicae Hieroglyphicae Grammatica Duplex . . .* was published in 1742. – Bayer knew of his fame as a sinologist from his friend Delisle and from reading a review of a paper he gave at the Academy in 1722. (See Notes 8 and 9 to the *Museum Sinicum* – 'The Chinese Language'.) – The great importance of that man for Bayer's thoughts will be apparent in many places in the following.

Fourmont brothers in the highest respect. In his home here in St Petersburg he showed me a list of Chinese astronomical works that are kept in the Royal Library of Paris. This colleague of mine, with whom I share so many interests, undertook a study of Chinese astronomy, arriving at conclusions very different from those of Cassini.[158] *When we were together he often praised the* Shu Jing, *one of the oldest of the Chinese classics, and showed me the passages dealing with the first five emperors after Çao. He had gone through that book with the help of Arcadius. Thus nothing detained Delisle from publishing his results except that he knew that the Jesuit Étienne Souciet, who worked in the same field, had perfected the Chinese chronology with the help of the excellent works he had received from Peking in the course of the years.*[159]

This work of Souciet is now famous and acclaimed by the most erudite persons, but it did not reach me. I have not even been able to obtain the volume of the Mémoires de l'Académie des inscriptions et belles-lettres *in which Fourmont presents his results. I have read, however, the notes on Chinese literature extracted from the* Mémoires de Trevoux *by the excellent Georg Bernhard Bülffinger (1724). They are really to the point, for here – in my opinion – my learned colleague has cleared up both dubious and obscure problems.*[160]

I had nearly forgotten Abbé Eusèbe Renaudot, who was extremely well versed in the literature and history of all oriental nations and possessed a very useful library.[161] *His many excellent studies had been admired by the learned society, but the admiration did not last because of his habit of offending venerable scholars with his insults. Finally, the many enemies he thus made for himself came to hate him and made him an object of derision, rightly or*

---

158 Cassini, see Note 118.
159 The first five emperors after Çao: It is not clear what Bayer means here. Çao may be an error or a misprint for Yao, the emperor dealt with in the first chapter of the *Book of History*, the *Shu Jing*. According to tradition Yao lived from 2357 to 2258 B.C. In this chapter they would be reading about two 'astronomers' by name Xi and He and about the orders they receive from the emperor about observing the movements of the sun, the moon and the stars, and regulating the calender. – Étienne Souciet, S.J. (1671-1744), librarian in the College Louis-le-Grand in Paris. Co-editor of the *Mémoires de Trevoux*. Just before Bayer finished his *Museum Sinicum* the first volume of his work had appeared, the *Observations mathématiques . . . par les Pères de la Compagnie de Jesus* (1729).
160 Bülffinger, see Note 12 to 'The Chinese Language'.
161 Renaudot, Eusèbe (1646-1720), influential French theologian and orientalist, member of the Académie française and the Académie des inscriptions et belles-lettres. One of his targets was Hiob Ludolff (see Notes 122 and 128) – he had misunderstood the nature of the Coptic church. Another one was Bayer's old friend Lacroze in Berlin, who got extremely upset about it. (Lacroze Correspondence, Vol. I, p. 9 and 39, Vol. III, p. 4.) The works of Renaudot discussed here are his *Historia Patriarchorum Alexandrinorum Jacobitorum . . .* (1713), and the *Anciennes relations des Indes et de la Chine . . . de deux voyageurs mahométans . . .* with four appendices, one of them entitled 'Les sciences des chinois' (1718).

wrongly, either because he had abused themselves, their friends or acquaintances, or because they felt that he was aiming at them while slandering other persons. I do not like to detract from that man's great merits and I am not surprised that working in so many fields he sometimes made mistakes, but one thing is clear: he knew practically nothing about Chinese. Yet, however, he contributed greatly to the understanding of Chinese history by his studies of Arabic texts.

He disputed the veracity and the authority of the Nestorian Stele, and this called scholars from other fields to its defence, adducing testimony from Persian, Arabic and Syrian sources. Among the first of them was the abovementioned Melchisédec Thévenot, who had found evidence in Muhammadan authors that the Christian faith had actually been carried to China by the Nestorians. Later on Barthélemy Herbelot translated a description of a voyage through Usbekistan to Cathay or China for the Grand-Duke of Tuscany, which contains indications of a flourishing Christianity in that region.[162] Leibniz asked Antonio Magliabechi to edit this text, which was kept in the Bibliotheca Medicaea. I do not know what came of it, but Renaudot and Guiseppe Assemani supplied the necessary information.[163]

First, however, about the French translation of an Arabic voyage through India and China, which Renaudot published in 1718. He estimated that the author had travelled in these regions about the year 1173. His commentaries on this voyage are numerous and full of brilliant erudition. Going through all the various disciplines he demonstrated the superiority of the Europeans in fields such as metaphysics, physics, astronomy and all other branches of science. Here his opinion differed strikingly from that of Voss, but he came closer to the

---

162 Barthélemy d'Herbelot de Molainville (1625-95), French orientalist. Interpreter of Eastern languages to the French king, professor of Syriac in the Collège de France from 1692. Ferdinand II, the learned Grand-Duke of Tuscany, had presented him with many oriental manuscripts. His huge *Bibliothèque orientale* . . . was published posthumously by Antoine Galland (1646-1715), professor of Arabic at the Collège de France (1697). A *Supplement à la Bibliothèque orientale de M. D'Herbelot* by Visdelou, S.J. (see Note 152) and C. Galland appeared in 1780. It contains comments on d'Herbelot's book and two important works by Claude de Visdelou, his long 'Histoire de la Tartarie' (pp. 18-133) and a new translation of the Nestorian Stele text, The 'Monument de la religion chrétienne' (pp. 165-190). The last text was written by Visdelou in Pondichery in 1719. Unfortunately Bayer, who in his later years was asking the Peking Jesuits for a Chinese book with the Stele text, was unaware of the fact, and so, apparently, were his friends in Peking.

163 Antonio Magliabechi (1633-1714), erudite Italian, organized the Medici Library for GrandDuke Cosimo III in Florence. Bayer took his information about this man and the one about Thévenot from Leibniz's *Novissima Sinica*. – Guiseppe Simonio Assemani (1687-1718), Lebanese Marionite, librarian at the Vatican Library from 1730. His *Bibliotheca orientalis Clementino-Vaticana*, 1719-28, contained editions of many manuscripts which he himself had collected on his travels in the Near East. Bayer had seen Volume I of this work in the Municipal Library in Königsberg (Wolff Correspondence, Sup.Ep. 114, approx. 1721).

truth. As to their moral and political doctrines, he esteemed them to consist partially of utterly vulgar and commonplace opinions, partly of unsystematically arranged and confused rules of life. He criticized several points in their chronology, and in their literature it seemed to him that there was absolutely no sign of intelligence or wisdom.

These postulates called forth several persons who attacked him for having falsely accused the Chinese. Fourmont castigated him for his complete lack of knowledge of Chinese literature. I would not say that there is no reason or wisdom in the many books and collections of works of the Chinese, but I do think that there is much more ingenuity and sense of proportion in the European ones, and I believe the Chinese would agree with me.

But why was it that Renaudot found such great satisfaction in tearing to pieces our praise of China as if it were complete nonsense? Obviously he knew nothing about Chinese literature.

As to Christianity, he himself had proved that the Nestorians went as far as China. That was in his Historia Patriacharum Alexandrinarum, *published in 1713, and his evidence at that time was not only the Nestorian Stele but also other sources he had discovered. Moreover, the fact that there were many Christian churches in India appears already from the works of Cosmas Indicopleustes, and he was a Nestorian. This has been proved beyond doubt by Lacroze, refuting the opinion of Bernard de Montfaucon.*[164] *There is also clear evidence of Christian churches in China. Not to mention Marco Polo, Guiseppe Assemani, the excellent doctor of the Maronite church, has brought others to light from the Vatican Library, and I myself possess some pieces of evidence, so that this matter should be settled by now.*

I realize that now I also have to say something about myself and about my own studies. I shall do it frankly and modestly as it suits an honest man.

Since my earliest youth I have been drawn towards the humanities, my greatest pleasure being to read ancient history. I was still a child when I started to read Tertullian, admiring his acumen, richness and dignity. This made a great impression upon me, especially as at that time I read it with the commentaries of d'Aubespine.[165] *Thus, little by little, I became strongly attracted by the problems of the Eastern churches. I soon realized, however, that the study of these problems required some knowledge of the relevant oriental languages, as well as a more intimate acquaintance with the history of Asia, the part of the*

---

164 Bernard de Montfaucon (1655-1741), French Benedictine, edited the *Collectio nova Patrum et Scriptorum graecorum* (1706). Lacroze criticized him in his *Histoire du christianisme des Indes*, for not understanding that Cosmas was a Nestorian (1724).

165 Tertullian (approx. 155-222), the great and fiery church writer. – Gabriel de l'Aubespine (1559?-1630), French patrist. He wrote *Observations de veteribus Ecclesiae Ritibus* (1623) and a treatise on Tertullian.

world I was particularly interested in; and, as if with the help of my good fortune, it so happened that I got the opportunity to learn the elements of the Hebrew language properly.

I shall never forget the benevolent and efficient instructions I received from Abraham Wolff, the eminent Hebraist, now Professor of Theology and Oriental Languages in Königsberg. I remember gratefully his kind admonitions and I do not regret my own hard work. All in all my studies were not too difficult, for I worked with the related languages according to the principles that Wolff had used in teaching me Hebrew. All the extra help I have had was a few days of Arabic with Salomon Assedeus of Damascus, exceedingly well versed in European sciences too – he died recently in England – and of Coptic with the gentle Lacroze.[166]

In the year 1713, while I was staying in the country, something happened to me – all of a sudden I was overwhelmed by a desire to learn Chinese. In the period that followed I worked and thought – or rather dreamed – about how to penetrate that mysterious discipline. If only I could produce some small thing in that field I would count myself grandson of the gods and king of kings. Like a pregnant rabbit, I collected everything in my burrow, whatever I could find to make up some kind of dictionary and some introduction to the rules of the Chinese language and to Chinese literature. The Nestorian Stele text as well as Thomas Hyde's and Christian Mentzel's works, which I possessed, were very useful to me. Most of all I looked for Andreas Müller's publications, but even today they annoy me – I get angry with him for his tricks and deceits.[167]

But then, in 1716, I came to Berlin and met Mathurin Veyssière de Lacroze – what a difference! How learned, how gentle he was! As all my readers will know, it was he who admonished me not to let the Chinese things I had learned deteriorate but to take upon me to cultivate this hitherto neglected field. Whatever I wanted to see in the Royal Library, wherever it was hidden or stored away, he brought it out for me and let me use it. And more than that, some time later when he heard that Leibniz was looking for a young man engaged in Chinese studies who could assist him with his knowledge and advice, Lacroze recommended me to the great man. Unfortunately, however, just as he was endeavouring to arrange that matter, Leibniz passed away.[168]

---

166 Abraham Wolff (1680-1731), Pietist theologian, Professor of Theology in Königsberg.

167 The oldest of the Bayeriana in the Glasgow University Library is a manuscript entitled 'Glossarium Sinicum' (Hunter MSS No. 139). Under the title Bayer wrote: 'Begun 22 May 1713'. As he says, the characters are from Mentzel (the Xiao Er Lun of the *Kleine Chinesische Chronologia*), from Hyde's books, and finally 'Monumenti Sinici omnes', numbered from 796 to 2577, i.e. the approx. 1800 characters on the large folding table in Kircher's *China . . . illustrata,* including the ones not translated.

168 These events are dramatically told in four letters exchanged between Bayer and Lacroze in the winter 1716-17. (Lacroze Correspondence I, pp. 7-9 and III, pp. 14-18). – Leibniz died on 14 November 1716.

After I had enriched myself with Chinese matters in Berlin I now and then got an opportunity to return to these studies in my spare time. As a result of such labours and in order to prevent myself from languishing in passivity and sloth, I had a small treatise printed at Königsberg, dealing with a solar eclipse in China and including some preliminary rules of the Chinese language and literature.[169] *It was part of a larger project about the Christian churches once flourishing in China and the Northern parts of Asia. However, I do not regret having kept it to myself, for later on, after I had learned much more and had had access to more of the sources, a more elaborate work came out of it.*[170]

After I had been called to the St Petersburg Academy I began to think of what to do with my Chinese. I felt that other subjects drew me away from these studies but I also thought that the things I had acquired by hard work ought not simply to remain in my desk drawer. Moreover, I was urged to publish it and was supported by the wise Theophanes Prokopowitsch, Archbishop of Novgorod and President of the Holy Synod. And thus it has come to pass that what nobody has succeeded in doing is here offered to the public through the munificence of the St Petersburg Academy.[171]

I have called my book Museum Sinicum, *because that was the name that first occurred to me and because I could not find any better.*[172] *It is not a large book, but I wanted to have it printed in two volumes so that a number of engraved plates could be included, making it easy for the reader to form his own opinion. I thought that there might be some readers who would want the tables mounted so that they could be unfolded outside the pages of the book – this would be difficult with one bulky volume.*

It is not for me to set forth in detail what it is that I have accomplished in these two volumes, nor how or to what extent I have failed – it is up to the reader to judge it for himself.

Volume I contains two books, one on the Chinese language, the other on Chinese literature. The first one I composed mainly on the basis of the gram-

169 Here again Bayer does not give the title of his *De Eclipsi Sinica.*
170 Bayer did not get time to write that work. He mentions it often in his correspondence with Lacroze and Benzelius in the first years, and in one of his last letters to the Peking Jesuits (1735) he enumerates what seems to be the titles of the many chapters of such a book (see p. 164). Drafts for some of these chapters are preserved in the Glasgow University Library.
171 Theophanes Prokopowitsch (1681-1736), Ukrainian theologian, the head of the Russian church, a favourite of Peter the Great as well as of the empresses Catherine I and Anne. A lively and independent spirit, he helped Czar Peter to reduce the power of the old Russian clergy. He had studied in Rome in his youth and was tolerant towards Catholics and Protestants. The *Museum Sinicum* has a long dedication to Theophanes. – In a letter to J.Chr. Wolff (1 August 1735) Bayer writes that he has visited Theophanes twice in his country house close to Peterhof (Wolff Correspondence, Sup.Ep. 122, Bl. 95-8).
172 At the time *Museum* usually meant library or collection of books. *Museum Sinicum* is a humble title, as different as one can imagine from that of the next 'Textbook of Chinese', Étienne Fourmont's *Meditationes Sinicae* . . . published in Paris in 1737.

mar of Martino Martini, which he gave to Golius, and that of Philippe Couplet who gave it to Picques, but also on the basis of the information from a third one.

In the description of any language the most important thing is to present a detailed and precise formulation of the rules of composition, i.e. the syntax of the language. However, the reader will find that I do not deal with that at all, for although I have obtained some insights into these matters, they seem to me to be still so crude and even uncertain that I prefer to look forward to another man presenting them, rather than to offer my ideas to others.

In the other book I describe the nature of Chinese literature, mainly from Couplet's very precise letters to Mentzel, from Mentzel's own notes, and from the Diaz Vocabulary, but also from my own observations and experience. I admit that what I say about Chinese style is very little – I hope that another person will study and describe it more fully, for although my studies are on a primitive level, they may still help others to achieve more important results. While being fully aware of my weaknesses I still believe that this book will be acknowledged by honest and impartial critics, especially when they contemplate how extremely difficult it must have been for me to penetrate this new field.

After these sections there follow a grammar of the Chin ceu (Zhangzhou) dialect, which I found in the Royal Library in Berlin. It is written in Spanish on thin Chinese paper, supposedly by some Franciscan friar, for the name of St Francis occurs in the liturgy. This book contains not only grammatical rules, but also a dictionary and many religious texts translated into Chinese. However, the Spanish is so poor that although I copied it out, I understood very little of it. Still, I thought it worthwhile to present it here to show the rules of one of the Chinese dialects. In translating the text I was assisted by Bernardo Ribera, one time Professor of the Sacred Languages in the Spanish Academy, now priest for the members of the Spanish embassy under the worthy Duke of Liria. For that I am grateful to this learned and kind man and want to thank him here for his friendliness and his help. While we were translating the text it turned out to be completely confused, to the astonishment and amusement of the venerable Spaniard. I have rebuilt the whole structure in another way, using his text as my quarry stones.

I believe that Chin ceu or Chin cheo is a place in the province of Heguang close to the border of the Guangdong province. In this region – besides Chin ceu, according to Martini's Atlas *a big and crowded and noble city, there are many small towns, as listed in the* Atlas.[173] *It is hoped that somebody will*

---

[173] The Heguang province was the big province in central China that was divided up in Hebei and Henan during the reign of the Kang Xi emperor. Bayer did not know that Chin ceu was the city called Zhangzhou on the coast of the Fukien province. He must have spent much time to find a city with the name of Chin ceu on the many maps of Martini's *Atlas Sinensis!*

publish specimens from all the Chinese provincial dialects or at least of the most important ones. In the proper place below I shall discuss the benefits to be derived from such endeavours.

Finally, this volume contains three pieces which I believe the reader will be interested in. The letter the missionaries in Tranquebar sent me is so learned and contains such a variety of information that I want to share it with other scholars. I decided also to print Müller's Proposition for a Key to the Chinese Language, *because all his small works are rare. Moreover, it reveals so clearly his hopes or his treasures . . . I think the reader should have the opportunity to consider it so as to be able to compare it with the contents of the present work. Finally, I print Müller's letter to Hevelius from the original. I obtained it through the kindness of my excellent friend Delisle who, while visiting in Dantzig, bought all Hevelius' manuscripts and correspondence. Hevelius answered that he had not observed the eclipse which Müller had questioned him about.*[174]

And now about Volume II. It contains two Chinese dictionaries and some articles. In the first dictionary I show how the Chinese characters should be arranged in classes and how they should be referred to their primary elements. I would have liked to have treated these matters in a more accurate way but I could not have done so without producing an enormous book with 80,000 or more characters, a task beyond my intent and certainly beyond my means. Actually, till now I have collected only 10,000 characters or a little more, and even those I did not dare to spread over the pages of this book for fear of making it too expensive. It actually contains less than 2,200 characters with some variants and it is not my fault if they are not perfect.[175]

As to the characters of the dictionary, I wanted them to be disposed and arranged in such a way that all secondary characters were arranged below the primary ones, under the secondary only the tertiary, under the tertiary only the quartary and so on. That would have been the best system, but I am only pointing the way and so I have put not only the tertiary but also the quartary and the quintary under the secondary, the sixth, seventh and eighth orders under the tertiary and so forth. To be frank, I did so for economic reasons. I wanted to help the reader and this was all I could do.

Perhaps this system of mine will be more copiously filled in by the Fourmont brothers – I am sure that my work will incite them to proceed further. I am also sure that the Paris Academy will not suffer our Academy to surpass it in munificence but join us in a noble contest. Lack of funds also explains why I have left some of the classes empty. Afterwards I felt that much more could be

---

174 Hevelius, see Note 87.
175 This statement probably refers to the poor quality of the Chinese characters in the *Museum Sinicum*. Bayer was to return to that argument in his defence against Fourmont's attacks, printed after his death.

done about the arrangement of the characters, but I have not gone deeper into it.[176]

(The reader should not suppose that the kind of accuracy which I hope is present in my work and which I expect to find in a future work by the Fourmont brothers, is to be found in the dictionaries of the Chinese. On the contrary, they are quite chaotic by European standards.)

However, a dictionary constructed according to this principle will be useful only for translating a Chinese text into Latin, for in order to write in Chinese or to translate from Latin into Chinese very different kinds of dictionaries are clearly needed. Those who want only to write Chinese for special purposes – say merchants or ambassadors – should compose special dictionaries. I have included a specimen here of such a dictionary, listing the titles of the civil and military servants to the Chinese court. It may be useful to Europeans who want to get information about the state of the Chinese Empire.

The first of the articles that follow contains the Life of Confucius *from the Goa edition, including the parts that Couplet changed in the* Confucius Sinarum Philosophus *published in Paris. I also add the Chinese characters from the edition printed in Goa. There follows a work by Confucius,* The Great Learning, *in Chinese and in Latin with my notes, and the first part of a book called* Xiao Er Lun *with my comments about the origin of the Chinese as an example of how to proceed in interpreting a Chinese text. This fragment from the* Xiao Er Lun *has already been published by Mentzel but I bring it here with better Chinese characters and with a new translation.*

In my commentaries on the origin of the Chinese I have tried to show what they have retained as a memory about the creation of the world, so that we do not have to be afraid that their history and chronology might bring prejudice to our holy doctrines. It was the eminent Theophanes Prokopowitsch, the Archbishop of Novgorod, who urged me to write this about three years ago, and I have tried here to convince that exceedingly learned and polite man that this is so.

To this commentary I have added an article about the time system of the Chinese, taken from Golius, Hyde and François Noël and some of my own notes, and also another one about Chinese weights and measures from the same sources. These are all the facts I have been able to collect, but I shall be surprised if I can convince others more than I have convinced myself about them.

I am grateful to François Noël, S.J., whose work informed me about these matters more clearly than any other work published by members of the Society. What he may have omitted and what I have been unable to track down else-

---

176 Of course, Bayer expounded his lexicographic system in the chapters on the Chinese language, but he must have felt it was necessary to give a sketch of it here – however incomprehensible it were – after all this system was his main concern.

where, will be for future scholars to find out about. His mathematical observations are not as well known as they ought to be, in my opinion. I owe him a debt of gratitude because I have taken large amounts of information from him, whenever they suited my discussions and my work in general.[177]

Finally I have added something about tables of solar eclipses that I hope may be of interest even to astronomers.

Last Part of the Preface

Until now we have heard Bayer speaking directly, telling his 'History of Sinology' as it appeared to him, concluding with a self-portrait – Bayer the sinologist. The last part of the Preface, up to page 145 of the *Museum Sinicum*, will be presented here only by some remarks and comments. It consists of a series of loosely connected divagations on various matters more or less related to his subject, with stray remarks on Japanese, Korean, Annamite, Siamese, Malebaric – and Finnish. It is clear that he lets his pen run on and cannot get himself to stop. On p. 136 he says: 'Now I must be brief lest this Preface swells to a book', and he repeats it on p. 140. In one place, near the end, he addresses his reader directly, saying: 'I had intended to stop here, but while they are printing these pages I come to think of something that I have forgotten to tell you'.

The following are short presentations of some of the themes he discusses.

Taking up again the much discussed problem of the primordial language and the relationship between Chinese and other languages, he takes issue with Golius – and with Leibniz. Golius's idea that the Chinese language is an artificial language, invented by some genius in antiquity, is against reason, even though the great Leibniz seems to have accepted this as a possibility. In the article Bayer is thinking about, Leibniz had said that languages are not invented, they arise in a natural way. Their sounds are the expressions of the affections and the movements of the human mind – the origin of words is to be found in a kind of mental onomatopoetica. In the German word *Ruck*, a thrust, the 'r' indicates a violent movement, while the final 'k' denotes its cessation. 'I except the artificial languages, such as that invented by Bishop Wilkins . . . and also the Chinese language. Golius surmised it to be an artificial language, and he is worth listening to'. Leibniz adds: 'If God had taught a language to human beings, it would have been like Chinese'.[178]

Supposedly it is the spoken Chinese language Bayer is referring to in his

---

177 The title of Noël's book is *Observationes matematicae et physicae in India et China facta . . . ab anno 1684 usque ad annum 1708*. It was reviewed in the *Mémoires de Trevoux* in 1712, pp. 654-703.

178 The article on language in the *Miscellanea Berolinensia* is mentioned in Note 143.

criticism of Golius and Leibniz. As to the Chinese script, he always thought, as we shall see later, that it was an invention of 'some genius'; otherwise how could one explain the *system* according to which, in his opinion, it is constructed. But it is not clear, and there is even one place where he seems to forget himself and accept an idea which elsewhere he rejects. In connection with a discussion of Chinese 'dialects' he says that a language with an alphabetic script is less liable to change and variation than a language, such as the Chinese, that is written by arranging *pictures of things!* (p. 105).

In his St Petersburg years Bayer also tried to obtain information about Central Asian scripts – Mongol, Manchu and Tibetan – and published some articles about their alphabets in the *Commentarii* of the Academy.[179] Here, in the last part of his Preface, he demonstrates his interest in the Tibetan.

About 1720 a document written in Tibetan script had been found in Southern Siberia, close to a place called Semipalatinsk, in the present Kazakhstan SSR. It was brought to Peter the Great, who sent it to Paris in 1722, supposing that there would be somebody there who could read it. Étienne and Michel Fourmont, of the Académie des inscriptions et belles-lettres, undertook to interpret it with the help of a small list of Tibetan words in the Bibliothèque royale and sent the Czar a translation and a transliteration of it. It was rumours of this feat, spreading all over Europe, together with the publication of a summary of the lecture on the Chinese language, printed in the same year in the *Mémoires de Trevoux,* that made the fame of Étienne Fourmont.

Bayer found the document and the pseudo-translation in the archives of the St Petersburg Academy, took it at its face value and printed the translation with transliteration over fourteen pages in his Preface, thus showing his profound admiration for the two Paris scholars.[180]

In another place he goes back to an earlier sinological study, a paper by the Dutch orientalist Adriaan Reeland, printed in his *Dissertationes Miscellanea*.[181] Here Reeland speaks about a notebook that had belonged to Golius,

---

179 'Elementa litteraturae brahmanicae, tangutanae, mungalicae', in Vol. III, 1732, pp. 389-422.
– 'Elementa brahmanica, tangutana, mungalica', in Vol. IV, 1735, pp. 289-301. – 'De litteratura mangjurica', in Vol. VI, 1739, pp. 325-38.

180 Lacroze had heard about this translation and mentions it in a letter to Bayer in 1723, adding: 'I hope it will be published at some time' (Lacroze Correspondence III, p. 59). – G.F. Müller, in his article 'De scriptis Tanguticis . . .', printed in the *Commentarii,* Vol. X, pp. 420-68, 1742, mentions this translation:
'Bayer believed in it and inserted it in the Preface of his *Museum Sinicum* from a handwritten copy kept in the Academy, paying his respect to Étienne and Michele Fourmont'. Müller adds: 'I wish that the first of them had dealt less unfairly with Bayer's excellent works and great merits in Chinese studies. *Sat sapienti.*'

181 Adriaan Reeland (1676-1718), Professor of Oriental Languages and Ecclesiastic Antiquities in Utrecht. He became famous in his short life for his studies in Rabbinic literature and Islam, knew Arabic, Persian and Malay. His *Dissertationum Miscellarium Partes tres* was

in which Martini and his Chinese famulus Dominico had written some words and sentences in Chinese, Japanese and Annamite, among other things the Lord's Prayer.

Reeland had included a number of characters in his article, indicating the different way in which they are pronounced by the Chinese, the Japanese and the Annamites. He discussed the relationship between the Chinese and Japanese script, but Bayer reminds the reader of what he said before, speaking about Kaempfer's book: Japanese is written with Chinese characters, either the 'Correct Style' characters or the so called 'Grass Script'. He adds that the Lord's Prayer, which Reeland inserted later in John Chamberlayn's collection, is obviously written in 'Grass Script', in contrast to the 'Correct Style' characters used for that holy text by Andreas Müller at an earlier date.[182]

On the following page Bayer came to write about the *Qian Zi Wen*, the *Thousand Character Book*, in a way that seems to indicate, more sharply than anywhere else, a complete rejection of the idea about Chinese characters being, or having ever been, pictographs.[183] He tells his reader that Reeland took the bits of the *Qian Zi Wen* from Golius' notebook. This famous Chinese book had been composed by a learned person while in prison – the King admired it so much that he set the author free. It is printed in China with white characters on black paper, and, as the title says, it consists of one thousand characters. Reeland had explained them, not from their 'true roots', but from certain pictures of material things, like those that Kircher printed in his *China ... illustrata*. One of his illustrations shows a half moon followed by the character for 'moon' written in the 'Correct Style' to demonstrate that this character derives from a picture of the moon. He dealt similarly with the characters for 'sun' and for other things. However, says Bayer, all this is nonsense – 'let us not waste our time on that Master!'[184]

---

printed in Utrecht in 1706-07 and again in 1713, and is said to have been 'more pilled than quoted'.

182 John Chamberlayn (1666-1723), English miscellaneous writer. He was said to know sixteen languages. He edited the *Oratio Dominica* (1715) with the Lord's Prayer in 150 languages. The Chinese one is written with a brush in Running Hand (not Grass Script), presumably by Dominico, the famulus of Martino Martini. – Andreas Müller's Lord Prayer had been printed in his *Oratio Orationum* in 1680 and again in the posthumous *Alpha kai Omega* in 1703. – In Bayer's correspondence with the Peking Jesuits he writes that he is helping a London clergyman with a new edition of Chamberlayn's book (see p. 160).

183 The *Thousand Character Book*, a text written with 1,000 different characters, was used by Chinese children after perusing the *Three Character Book*, and before entering upon the *Four Books*. It was translated several times in Europe in the nineteenth century.

183 To express his contempt for Reeland's proposition Bayer inserted here a four-line quote from Plautus's *Miles Gloriosus*, 209-12, as usual without mentioning author or title. Here the soldier is depicted gesticulating ridiculously to indicate his deep thoughts. It is meaninglessly

After all that, there follows, rather abruptly, a long section about what Lorenz Lange, the Czar's agent in China just back from Peking, has told him about the disastrous situation of the missionaries in China after the death of the Kang Xi emperor in 1722. Bayer also prints the information which Lange had given him about the terms for weights and measures in China, and adds a section about Chinese calenders.[185]

Finally, on two strange pages, Bayer tells his reader about Chinese books newly arrived at or on their way to the Academy, at the moment when he has finished his manuscript and while the book is being printed.

> Quite recently we received in the Library a copy of the *Wu Jing*, the *Five Classics*, bound in one volume. The first work in this Pentabiblion is the *Yi Jing*, the Book of Changes. This book contains the characters or rather the lines, invented by Huang Di (*sic*) with two commentaries. It is not a large work in comparison with European books, making up only one fascicle of 30 leaves. The next work is the *Shu Jing*, the Classic of History. Couplet says that it consists of six books, but here there are only two, one of 45, the other of 71 leaves – four are missing. The third work is the *Shi Jing*, the Book of Odes, in four fascicles of 71, 52, 34 and 18 leaves respectively. The fourth work is the *Li Jing*, the Classic of Ceremony, in six fascicles, numbering 62, 58, 69, 66, 49 and 57 leaves. The fifth and last work is the *Chun Qiu*, the Spring and Autumn Classic, written by Confucius, four fascicles with 29, 29, 43 and 33 leaves respectively. I cannot say more about this Pentabiblion than what Couplet said (in the Preface to the *Confucius Sinarum Philosophus*) as these works are far beyond the powers of my rudimentary knowledge of Chinese, and because I have only had a few days to examine them. We also received the *San Guo*, i.e. the Three Kingdoms, in two volumes. It contains 120 comedies (*sic*), each one preceded by two pictures. And we are looking forward to the *Hai Pian* and *Zi Hui* dictionaries, as well as to a handwritten Chinese-Latin dictionary, due to arrive from Moscow.

These pitiful pages describe to us with admirable clarity the situation of the young scholar who had conceived of the idea of writing a book on Chinese language and literature in the wilderness of Peter the Great's Russia. The book is finished and being printed; there is no time to make corrections or additions. And now the material is arriving which he should have had all the time – the fundamental texts and dictionaries!

---

out of context and could have been understood only by those of his readers who knew their Plautus by heart.

185 Lorenz Lange, died 1743. Swedish officer in the service of the Russian court. He is said to have visited China eight times from 1718 and onwards. In 1739 he was made vice-governor of Irkutsk. – In China he was favoured with the friendship of the old Kang Xi emperor. – He was in China in 1726-8 with Count Sawa Raguzinskij Vladislavich. – His sympathetic personality and his experiences in Peking are vividly depicted in one of his own books, the *Journal de la résidence du Sieur Lange à la cour de la Chine* . . . (1726). – His name appears in many of the letters to Bayer from the Peking Jesuits, 1732-7.

Resigned, but still as if in defiance, he counts the pages of these treasures and notes them down for his readers. Is there a tone of bitterness or irony on these pages? Bayer did not have it in him – neither irony nor bitterness.

He concludes his long Preface with the following words:

Now you, whoever you are, who read me, be fair to me and to my writings, also to the present one about Chinese matters. Farewell, St Petersburg, 15 July 1730.

6
THE CHINESE LANGUAGE

The main content of the *Museum Sinicum* is its 'Grammatica Sinica' with appendices. Following the long Preface we find two books on Mandarin and one on a 'dialect', the 'Chin ceu language'. Volume II contains Bayer's 'Lexicon Sinicum', 42 engraved plates with Chinese characters and 119 pages with transliterations and translations. There are also three small texts that may be regarded as the chrestomathy of this 'Textbook of Chinese'.

In the following we shall first discuss the sources of inspiration for Bayer's ideas about the Chinese writing system – Leibniz, Fourmont and Bülffinger – and after that the material on which he based his insight into the nature of the Chinese script. Then, after a shorter section on his speculations about the beginning of the Chinese writing system, we shall present his reflections on the nature of the present-day Chinese characters and his attempts to disclose an underlying *system*, leading up to the production of his own *dictionary*. The next short chapter is on the *grammar* of the Chinese language, and finally, after a brief look at his Chin ceu grammar, we shall deal with the *chrestomathy*, the three texts he included as aids for learning Chinese.

SOURCES OF INSPIRATION

Among the few works that Leibniz himself published was the *Dissertatio de Arte Combinatoria*, written when he was twenty years old and printed in Leipzig in 1666. It deals with the rules of combination and permutation, applying these mathematical procedures to theology, music, poetry etc.

In the manuscripts published after his death we find him coming back again and again to these problems. There is a note, written about 1685, in which he says:

> If there were an exact language – some call it the Adamitic language – or just a truly philosophical script based upon a kind of alphabet of human concepts derived directly from facts, it could lead to some kind of *calculus* similar to the one we use to solve arithmetical and geometrical problems – this would be the mystical vocabulary of the Cabala or the Pythagorean numerology or the characteristics of the magi or sages. Already when I was a child I nourished ideas of such sublime things and I inserted something about it in my *De Arte Combinatoria*.[1]

There is another manuscript from about 1700 entitled 'The history of (my) universal language of characteristics, with a recommendation', an enthusiastic

---

1 J.E. Erdmann (Ed.): *Gottfried Wilhelm Leibniz: Opera philosophica* . . . (1840), p. 83.

piece where Leibniz refers to this work of his youth, saying that he does not regret having published it, for it has pleased many very intelligent persons. Now, he says, he realizes that nothing is more important than to take up these ideas again and to construct the necessary grammar and dictionary of such a universal language. A few well-chosen persons could accomplish it in the course of five years.[2]

Leibniz does not include the Chinese language in these reflections, but we know that he was keenly interested in it, and undoubtedly his speculations about the universal language were connected in his mind with this interest. He knew, of course, about Andreas Müller's proposed *Clavis Sinica,* and Christian Mentzel had told him that he was working on one himself.[3] In one of Leibniz's letters to Lacroze, the Berlin orientalist, written between 1705 and 1712, where he urges him to take up the study of Chinese, he wrote: 'This study seems to me to be of utmost importance, for if we could discover the key to the Chinese characters we would find something useful for the analysis of thought' (8 October, 1707).[4] And in his great language article in the *Miscellanea Berolinensia* in 1710 Leibniz said that if God had taught mankind a language it would have been something like Chinese.[5]

Lacroze did not rise to the bait, but, as we have heard, in 1716 he recommended his young friend T.S. Bayer to Leibniz, only too late, for the philosopher died before he could even answer Lacroze's letter of recommendation.

The most interesting texts in connection with Bayer's studies are two letters that Leibniz wrote to the mathematician Remond de Montmort in Paris in 1714. They were published in 1720, a few years after his death. In the letter dated 10 January he wrote:

If I had been less distracted or if I were younger or had the assistance of talented young persons, I would hope to produce a kind of universal symbolistic (Spécieuse Générale), in which all the truths of reason were reduced to a sort of calculation. It might be at the same time a kind of language or universal script . . . It would be very difficult to formulate or invent this language or characteristic (caractéristique), but once formed it would be very easy to learn it without a dictionary . . .[6]

He returned to the point in a letter to Remond de Montmort, dated 14 March:

2 ibid., pp. 162-4.
3 Letter from Leibniz to Hiob Ludolff, 12 December 1698, in Joachim Friedrich Feller (Ed.): *Otium Hannoveranum sive miscellanea ex ore et schedis Leibnitii* . . . (1717), pp. 118-21.
4 Christian Kortholt (Ed.): *Viri Illustris Godofridi Guilielmi Leibnitii Epistola ad diversos* . . ., Vol. I (1734), pp. 377-8.
5 *Miscellanea Berolinensia,* see Note 143 to Preface.
6 Erdmann (see Note 1 above), pp. 701-2.

I have spoken to Marquis de L'Hôpital and others about my universal symbolistic but they paid no more attention to it than if I had told them about a dream I had dreamed. I should have to support it too by some obvious applications, but to achieve this it would be necessary to work out at least a part of my characteristic – a task which is not easy, especially in my present condition and without the advantage of discussions with men who could stimulate me and help me in work of this nature . . .[7]

These letters were read by one of his great admirers, the young Tübingen philosopher Georg Bernhard Bülffinger, who commented upon them in the long appendix on the Chinese language to the book he published four years later, the *Specimen Doctrinae Veterum Sinarum* ..., printed in Frankfurt-on-Main in 1724. Bayer may have known about this book before meeting the author in 1726 at the St Petersburg Academy, where they were going to be colleagues for the next five years.

However, between the publication of Leibniz's letters and the appearance of Bülffinger's China book, something else had happened which impressed Bülffinger and became of the greatest importance for Bayer; this was a speech about the Chinese language, given in 1722 in Paris by the learned Étienne Fourmont.

We will look at that before returning to Bülffinger and his influence on T. S. Bayer.

Étienne Fourmont, of whom we have heard so much in the Preface, made his first contribution to sinology in 1722. On 14 April of that year he gave a paper on the Chinese language at a meeting of the Académie des inscriptions et belles-lettres in Paris. An extract of it was published in the July issue of the influential and widely circulated *Journal de Trevoux*.[8]

This 'Dissertation de M. Fourmont sur la littérature chinoise' – six pages in all – starts with the death of Arcadius Huang, the young Chinese who was charged, it says, by Louis XIV to work on a Chinese dictionary. After his demise, Fourmont was directed by the Duke of Orleans, the Regent, to examine the papers left by 'this interpreter', especially to look into the state of his dictionary, and to report to him about it. That done, he was ordered to

---

7 ibid., pp. 702-4. – Pierre Remond de Montmort, to whom this and the foregoing letter were addressed, was the brother of Nicolas de Remond with whom Leibniz also corresponded and to whom he wrote his important 'Lettre sur la philosophie chinoise' (see pp. 113,·180). The letters to Remond de Montmort were printed already in Pierre des Maizeaux's *Recuil de diverses pieces sur la philosophie* . . . *par Messieurs Leibniz, Clarke, Newton etc.* (1720). – Remond de Montmort was interested in games, as Leibniz was, and is the author of one of the first studies of probability, the *Essay d'analyse sur les jeux de hazard* (1713).

8 *Journal de Trevoux* or *Mémoires de Trevoux* was the name commonly used for the *Mémoires pour l'Histoire des Sciences et des beaux Arts*, published at Trevoux in France. It was regarded as the mouthpiece of the French Jesuits.

continue the work on it, and now he had produced not one but several Chinese dictionaries and a number of works to facilitate the study of that language, all in all twelve to fourteen volumes *in folio*.

After a short section on the studies of the China Jesuits and a few European scholars – Golius, Reland, Muller, Meultzen (*sic*), Masson, Fréret and Renaudot – there are a few lines about the small number of syllables in the spoken Chinese language.

Then follows the description of the Chinese script. It takes up only about half of one of the small pages, but it made a profound impression in the learned world and served to establish the fame of Fourmont as the world's leading Chinese scholar:

The Chinese script system is immense; there are 80,000 characters; each thing has its own character; in reality they are hieroglyphs. But according to M. Fourmont, the beautiful order the Chinese keep in composing their characters is a philosophical and a geometrical order, more analogical than that obtaining in any other language. Because of this order the difficulty felt at first in the face of the innumerable characters is considerably reduced. M. Fourmont asserts that *the composition of the Chinese characters is the noblest achievement (effort) of the human race; there is no system in physics (système physique) that approaches it in perfection*.[9]

It was not till fifteen years later, with the publication of the *Meditationes Sinicae* in 1737, that Fourmont revealed to the world the grounds for this extraordinary postulate. Bayer was not to be favoured with the exposition of the great discovery. He saw the review of the book in the *Journal des Sçavans* and learned about the insults of him, contained in it, but he died before he got the opportunity to examine the book itself.

In the meantime these few lines seem to have been taken at their face value by most scholars – except by the China Jesuits, who knew better, and by their brothers in Europe with whom they corresponded. As a matter of fact, during

---

9 The extract of Fourmont's paper appears on pp. 1575-80 (1722). – A secretary's summary of the speech was printed in 1729 in the *Histoire de l'Académie royale des inscriptions et belles-lettres*, Vol. V, pp. 312-19. Here we find some lines about the 214 radicals or *keys* (caractères simples ou radicaux, que l'on nomme clefs à la Chine). Fourmont had mentioned radicals or keys for man, woman . . . prince . . . heaven, earth, air, water . . . horse, insect . . . etc. He had also indicated that under each of these keys (in the Chinese dictionaries) one found characters for words related to them 'by their properties, accidents or just metaphorically', giving a few examples. Bayer probably never saw this text – he never refers to it. – Arcadius Huang, see Note 155 to Preface. In the extract in the *Journal de Trevoux* Fourmont does not mention the help he had obtained from Huang during the five years they worked together in the Royal Library. In the summary mentioned above he is reported to have mentioned the help he had obtained 'from Huang's papers'. In the summary of Fréret's speech on the Chinese language, printed immediately before that of Fourmont's (pp. 303-12) we hear about the 'many conversations he (Fréret) had with Huang'.

these years, from 1722 to 1737, Fourmont's words in the *Journal de Trevoux* functioned very much like Andreas Müller's *Propositions for a Clavis Sinica* in the preceding century, only that greater credence was given to the words of a member of one of the famous Paris Academies than to those of an obscure pastor in Berlin. Fourmont did not say that he could teach anyone to read Chinese in a week, but he stated emphatically that *there was a system*, and that he had found out about it.

As we have seen, and as we are going to see again, Bayer's admiration for Fourmont was boundless. He knew that earlier authors, such as the China Jesuit Semedo, and Bishop Wilkins, the famous creator of an artificial, philosophical language, had spoken more or less clearly of the Chinese script as a system.[10] To Bayer Fourmont's postulate was, if not the origin, then at least the strongest support for his own ideas about the Chinese script as a combinatory system. The Chinese themselves might have forgotten about it, but Fourmont had discovered it and he, Bayer, just wanted to emulate, in his own feeble way, the great man in Paris. Apart from the force of the postulate, there was no help for Bayer to find in Fourmont's words. It is important to note that in the extract in the *Journal de Trevoux* the 214 radical system is not mentioned, there is no reference at all to any classifying systems.[11]

It is possible that Bayer never saw the article in the *Journal de Trevoux*, but he knew it from Bülffinger's *Specimen Doctrinae Veterum Sinarum ...*, where the important section, quoted above, is printed *verbatim* in a footnote in French.

The language section which Bülffinger attached to his *Specimen Doctrinae Veterum Sinarum* is a 70-page treatise that deserves to be studied on its own merits. Here we shall have to limit ourselves to the parts that were of import-

---

10 John Wilkins (1614-72), bishop of Chester, famous for the great book he published under the title of *Essay towards a real character and a philosophical language* (1668), in which he developed a systematically worked out artificial language, written and spoken. He actually compares it with the Chinese language (pp. 450-2), but finds this language inferior to his own because of the difficulty of pronouncing the Chinese words and the many homonyms, and because of the complexity of the characters which he demonstrates by a page with the Lord's Prayer in characters and in transliteration. He quotes Semedo's examples of meaningful radicals, adding: 'The meeting with this passage was no small satisfaction to me, in reference to that way which I had *before* pitched upon for the most natural expression of things' (My italics). However, he says, according to Semedo this is not a constant rule among them. There is reason to doubt, he concludes, 'whether they had (sic) any such general Theory of Philosophy, as might serve for all other things and notions'. – Bayer mentions Wilkins, as we have seen, in the Preface, calling him the excellent constructor of a philosophical language, but he probably never saw the book. If he had, and if he had been able to read its English, he would have commented upon the author's remarks about the Chinese language. – Bülffinger mentions it in his *Specimen* . . . p. 333, but says that he has not seen it. See Note 12.

11 See Note 9.

ance for Bayer.[12]

Bülffinger starts with admitting that he knows very little about the Chinese language, having read only the books of Semedo, Spizelius, and Le Comte – and the extract from Fourmont's speech in the Académie des inscriptions et belles-lettres. However, he knows something about it, and that is enough, he thinks, for him to dare to present these notes to the public.

After several interesting chapters on semantics in general – he seems to have invented the word – he proceeds to the Chinese script.

> As for the Chinese characters, undoubtedly they contain some similarities and dissimilarities that can be understood in a general way. For if this was not the case no dictionary could be composed where one could look up the meaning of the characters. Who would work his way through thousands of characters in search of a single one? There can be no doubt, therefore, that there are some kind of genera and species, indicated by the strokes of the characters, by which they are referred, as it were, into their special classes. However, such a system only makes it easier to find a character in a dictionary; it could not help in memorizing it if it did not also have a semantic regularity, appearing from the arrangements of the individual simple strokes. I have not seen a Chinese dictionary with my own eyes, but I trust the testimony of other scholars.

He then refers to the *Clavis Sinica,* promised but never given, by Andreas Müller. It is not possible, he says, to determine today if it had any value, but now there is hope – he is happy to inform his readers of a recent study by the illustrious Fourmont.

> I have read with great pleasure the passage in the *Journal de Trevoux,* where he asserts that in the composition of their characters the Chinese observed a clear and exact philosophical order. This is a genial system and the characters reveal a high point of human endeavour, attaining to a perfection not present in any physical system.

---

12 Georg Bernhard Bülffinger (Bilfinger), (1693-1750), German philosopher and statesman. In 1719 to 1721 he studied at the University of Halle under the famous philosopher Christian Wolff (1679-1754), a follower (with modifications) of Leibniz's philosophy. (Wolff was a great sinophile, his *De Sapientia Sinensium Oratio* was published in Trevoux in 1725 without the author's permission – see Note 17 to 'After the *Museum Sinicum*'.) Bülffinger became Professor of Philosophy in Tübingen in 1721, where he published several works in defence of Leibniz's theories, as well as his *Specimen Doctrinae Veterum Sinarum Moralis et Politica* . . . (1724), a systematization of the *Confucius Sinarum Philosophus*. The long appendix on the Chinese language, 'De litteratura Sinensi dissertatio extemporalis' is to be found, together with a piece on the *Book of Changes* and the 'Expositio Mysterii Leibnitio-Bouvetiana' on pp. 289-360. – From 1726 to 1731 he was a colleague of Bayer's in the Academy of Sciences in St Petersburg. – After returning to Tübingen he became Minister of State in Würtemberg, and was occupied with the organization of institutes of higher learning as well as with studies of the art of fortification.

Bülffinger quotes the passage from the *Journal de Trevoux,* adding that to some it will appear as an exaggeration to compare the art of composing characters to that of the sciences, to equate them or even to put the composition of characters above science. 'What I am now going to write will seem scandalous to some readers'.

He then turns his attention to Leibniz, quoting from the letters to Remond de Montmort mentioned above. Here, he says, Leibniz spoke as if in enigmas.

His own explanations and speculations run as follows:

'As I understand it, this is what the great man postulates or promises:
If someone could isolate and collect all the simplest kinds and principles of all things, *if someone* would study all their relations and arrange them in classes, *if he* invented characters for things and relations in such a way that composite ones could be produced from simple ones, according to the connections of the things themselves, *if he* found the rules by which equivalent terms could be substituted for each other, then I think that this man would have come close to the idea of the great philosopher. And such a thing is *possible,* by continued effort – I do not despair of that. For there *are* certain universal genera and principles – essence, existence, substances, modes, order and similitude, etc. There are also mutual relations and cohesions of all things in general – original and originated, causes and effects, subjects and adjuncts, impulses, activities, resistance and acceptance, powers and oppositions, coexistence and succession and other similar concepts that ought to be arranged in classes. Now, if these [concepts] were represented by characters and signs in such a way that composite ones could be made out of the simple ones . . . , and, furthermore, if a method was worked out, based on the nature of the relations, for substituting equivalent concepts, a method corresponding in its own way to that which the Algebraists derive from the relation of magnitudes, then metaphysical truths could be handled by calculation just as is done now in mathematics.

Bülffinger goes on to express his hopes and doubts that the Chinese script is such a system *or that it could be made into one* – it is hoped that Fourmont will get time and obtain the necessary support to carry through what he has so splendidly begun.

This System Builder's Creed reads, almost to a point, like the way we shall find Bayer discussing his ideas about the Chinese script system. As we have seen in the Preface, Bayer's reference to that Appendix is short and noncommittal – 'Everything in it is very true indeed', and apart from this little passage Bülffinger's name occurs only in one small footnote about Leibniz and Bouvet in Book II of the Chinese Grammar.

We know, however, how carefully Bayer studied this Appendix on the Chinese language, for the handwritten 'Grammatica Sinica', a draft of the grammar to be printed in the *Museum Sinicum,* begins with four pages of small excerpts, notes and remarks about it.[13]

Here Bayer says that Bülffinger had collected everything about the Chinese language in the earlier European literature, but not as Spizelius had done (simply by accumulating quotes) – 'he deals with the problem in a philosophical way'. He remarks that Bülffinger looked for things that he, Bayer, had already found, and made mistakes because his principles were wrong and because he lacked information. However, on the last of these pages he notes: 'How excellently B. saw many things, pp. 326-7!' – This is where Bülffinger concludes that the mere existence of dictionaries proves that there *must* be a system.

THE MATERIALS

The materials Bayer had at his disposal for composing the grammar and the dictionary of his *Museum Sinicum* were manuscripts he had seen and copied from in Berlin in 1716: Diaz's Vocabulary and Mentzel's papers.

The *Vocabulario de Letra China con la Explication Castellana,* composed by the Dominican Francesco Diaz in the 1640s, had been described by Lacroze in an article published in *Miscellanea Berolinensia* in 1710, and Bayer may well have seen that article before he met Lacroze in Berlin. Lacroze says that the vocabulary comprises 598 pages, the text being arranged in three columns on the pages. The Chinese characters are very elegant, he says, even better than those of printed Chinese books; the Spanish translations, some short, some long, include references to synonyms in other places in the work. 'Undoubtedly this dictionary is better for the study of the Chinese language than any other one in Europe'.[14]

As mentioned above, Bayer may have had it on loan for some time in the 1720s, but if so he can only have copied small parts of it, for in a letter written from St Petersburg in 1732 he says that he would like to get it – or a copy of it – from Berlin (see p. 189). This dictionary disappeared during the Second World War, but there is a copy of it in the Vatican Library.[15]

---

13 'Grammatica Sinica', Hunter MSS, No 350. The title says 'written in St Petersburg' but gives no date.

14 *Miscellanea Berolinensia*, Vol. I, pp. 84-8, 1710. – It was described again by Julius Klaproth in his *Verzeichniss der chinesischen und mandchurischen Büchern und Handschriften der kgl. Bibliothek zu Berlin* (1822), pp. 129-36, with comments about a revised copy of it in the Bibliothèque nationale in Paris, the one that Fourmont had had at his disposal. – The Berlin dictionary comprised 7169 characters.

15 This copy is a fine, closely written manuscript of 91 pages with six columns per page (Vatican Library, Borgia Cinese, 412). It was made for Antonio Montucci (1762-1829) Italian sinologist. For his great but unsuccessful lexicographic endeavours, see his interesting book *Urh-Chih-Tsze-Tëen-Se-Yin-Pe-Keaou*, London, 1817.

The bound volume of *Mentzeliana,* various manuscripts dealing with the Chinese language and produced in the last part of the seventeenth century, which was in the Royal Library in Berlin, has also been lost. However, a copy of it is preserved among the Bayeriana in the Glasgow University Library. Bayer copied it in September 1716 and gave his copy the title 'Agathe tyche'.[16]

The first 40 pages of it comprise the 'Grammatica Sinica a M. Martinio consignata'. Mentzel had written on it that he had received it in 1689 from Andreas Cleyer in Batavia. Its last 15 pages contain a list of 331 radicals.[17] Then, after a few pages with about 50 characters extracted from the Diaz Vocabulary, there follows the 'Martinio Cupletiana Grammatica Sinica' – this is Bayer's transcript of Mentzel's *Clavis Sinica.* Here Bayer found a list of about 800 Chinese characters, arranged according to another radical system with 214 units, and an alphabetical vocabulary of about 500 transliterated words, with the addition of their location in the preceding list of characters.

Mentzel's *Clavis Sinica* also contained a long section on the Chinese grammar 'compiled by Jesuits', but Bayer only took extracts from it – six pages in all. Curiously enough Bayer did not copy the last four pages of Mentzel's book – at any rate they are not among the Glasgow Bayeriana. These pages with the *Lord's Prayer,* small parts of the *Great Learning* and the *Doctrine of*

16 'Agathe tyche' (By God's Help), Hunter MSS, No 299, 205 pages. – The original manuscript of Mentzel's *Clavis Sinica* is kept in the Deutsche Staatsbibliothek (Libri Sinici, Alte Sammlung, No. 14 (new No. 19): 'Varia Sinica et Mandschurica, dabei Mentzel's *Clavis Sinica*'). It consists of 124 folio pages. Pages 1-4 contains a list of Chinese numerals. Pages 5-54 comprise a small 214-radical dictionary, arranged as in the *Zi Hui* dictionary. Each character is followed by its pronunciation and the translation. Pages 55-89 contain the alphabetic list of words which Mentzel had constructed with the help of the Diaz Vocabulary, supposedly in preparation of his own dictionary. Bayer copied all but omitted the Chinese characters in the alphabetic list and in fact they are superfluous because the list refers to the characters in the dictionary. Then follow, on pages 90-120, a 'Grammaticalia quaedam a P.P. Societatis (*sic*) observata . . .', i.e. rules about tones, about substantives and their declinations, pronouns, etc. all of it explained with Chinese characters. At the end – pages 121-4 – there are four paradigms, the Lord's Prayer, the first 58 characters of the *Great Learning,* the first 62 characters of the *Doctrine of the Mean* and finally 36 characters about the Ginseng root taken from a *Bencao* edition. Bayer did not copy these last pages, but after he returned to Königsberg he wrote to Lacroze and asked him to copy out the piece from the *Great Learning* (see p. 35). There is no title in the Berlin manuscript or in Bayer's copy of it, but Henri Cordier has seen one and presents it in his *Bibliotheca Sinica,* Col. 1635: *Clavis Sinica . . . fabrefacta a Christiano Mentzelio . . .* – One may wonder why Mentzel chose this word, the same that Andreas Müller had used when speaking about his own mysterious key ot the Chinese language. There is nothing mysterious about Mentzel's *Clavis,* it is a straightforward introduction to the Chinese language: a small dictionary, a grammar and four paradigms, i.e. a chrestomathy. It is obviously the result of much hard work and may well be called admirable, taking into consideration the few means that Mentzel had at his disposal. It is on this manuscript that Bayer based his respect, so often expressed, for old Dr. Mentzel.

17 The 331 radicals in this list include all those of the 214 radical system, the rest being variants or characters appearing as derivates of other radicals in that system. It seems as if something

the Mean, and a small section from a pharmacopoeia – all in Chinese characters with transliterations and translations – should have interested Bayer. Apparently what interested him most – already at that time – was the Chinese writing system itself.

The last part of the 'Agathe tyche' contains a 'Grammatica Sinica' by Louis Picques – 11 pages – and finally we find copies of a number of letters about the Chinese language. There is a German translation of a letter from Thomas Hyde in Oxford to Christian Mentzel, written in 1683. There are seven letters from Philippe Couplet to Mentzel, written between April and September 1687, and one from Picques to Mentzel, also of 1687. There is an undated letter from Couplet to Andreas Cleyer in Batavia, 'written on Chinese paper'. And finally there are two letters of earlier date, Andreas Müller's letter to the astronomer Hevelius and Hevelius' reply, both of them written in 1679. As we have seen Bayer included them in the *Museum Sinicum.*

These letters, especially those from Couplet, were of great importance for Bayer in his first attempts to learn about the Chinese language.

Together with his old 'Glossarium Sinicum', containing the 1800 characters from the Nestorian Stele, this was all that Bayer had when he started to compose the grammar and the dictionary of his *Museum Sinicum.* He had seen the *Zi Hui* and the *Zheng Zi Tong* dictionaries in Berlin in 1716 but perhaps only briefly and in all probability he did not profit from seeing them. He may not even have realized at the time that their characters were arranged according to the same 214 radical system he had learned about when he copied Mentzel's *Clavis Sinica.* More importantly, he cannot have noticed the many picture-like seal characters in the *Zheng Zi Tong* dictionary.[18]

Working in St Petersburg in the late 1720s he had no Chinese books. At the end of the Preface, as we have seen, he says that now he is looking forward to two Chinese dictionaries arriving from Moscow.

THE ORIGIN OF THE CHINESE SCRIPT

Before entering upon a discussion of the nature of the Chinese characters, Bayer inserted a section – Chapter two of Book II – about the origin of the

has been lost at the beginning, for there are only two one-stroke characters, namely the last ones among the six one-stroke characters of the 214 radical system. However, there is no sign of a page having been torn out. – All in all it gives the impression of being a hastily written list of 'radicals', some of the entries appear to be included rather at haphazard. It looks as if it were written with a brush, coarsely but evidently by someone who was used to writing Chinese characters, on very poor paper. The transliterations and translations are added with a fine pen. – Bayer took some of these 'radicals' and added a number of his own. – This list and its origin needs further study.

18 See Note 39a to 'After the *Museum Sinicum*'.

Chinese script.

In the early literature about China the European reader had been told that originally the characters were pictures of things. In Martini's China history, the widely-read *Sinicae Historiae Decas Prima,* there was a woodcut showing the 'old forms' of the characters for mountain, sun, dragon, bird and hen beside their modern equivalents (very badly drawn). The first four look like some of those found in seal-character dictionaries, but the bird and the hen are simply European-style pictures. In the case of the characters for mountain and sun, the old ones may have appeared as acceptable forerunners of the new ones. As for the dragon and the king, the relationship was invisible, and the idea that the picture of the bird and the hen should be prototypes of the bird and hen characters must have seemed – and is – ridiculous. Martini just said that these old characters were invented by Fu Xi, the first emperor, and that they were pictures of things.

To Bayer, the idea of a pictographic origin of the Chinese characters was quite unacceptable; he derides it, as we have seen, several times in the Preface, and he desists from showing these 'fanciful things', i.e. the illustrations in Martini's book. The reason for his complete rejection of the pictographic theory was partly that he had never seen or noticed seal characters in a Chinese dictionary. Had he seen them, and had he accepted them as genuine ancient characters, he would have recognized that many of them are obviously pictures of things. But, of course, the strongest reason for his rejection of the theory was that it was incompatible with his own idea of the characters as a combinatory system of simple strokes.

In this connection Bayer also mention the 'ancient characters' in Kircher's *China . . . illustrata,* but only to declare, as in the Preface, that they are fanciful inventions of idle minds, adding now that they are similar to the decorative letters of the Armenians, forgetting, however, to mention Kircher's opinion that these ancient forms were actually made by the Chinese 'using the things as they presented themselves to their eyes'. We know, Bayer says, that some primitive peoples, e.g. the Mexicans, used pictures for writing, but this is quite different from the Chinese system, which he is going to explain in the following. As to the much discussed question of the resemblance and possible relationship between Egyptian hieroglyphs and Chinese characters, he quotes from Kircher, saying that the scarab in the obelisk script does not mean the dung beetle, but the sun. This again is quite different from the Chinese way; their characters are devoid of such symbolic mysteries. If one wants to compare the Chinese characters with anything they look more like the ciphers of the ancient Romans, but these were formed without any kind of system, contrary to the Chinese characters, which 'arise, as it were, from certain stems and therefore function with a kind of analogy, their meaning deriving from the way they are composed.[19]

THE CHINESE LANGUAGE

This is the first time Bayer tries to formulate his idea; he will be trying again and again to clarify it in the following and also in his later writings.

As we might expect of a system enthusiast, he is more in favour of the hexagrams as the cradle of the Chinese script: their combinations of whole and broken lines do suggest some kind of system. We should begin, he says, by looking at the tables of the 64 hexagrams from the *Yi Jing*, the venerable old *Book of Changes*, as they are printed in the *Confucius Sinarum Philosophus*.

At this place Bayer makes an obscure aside about Leibniz: this old Chinese book had recently been drawn into a philosophical discussion by the great philosopher! Bayer seems to take it for granted that his readers were acquainted with one or the other papers in which Leibniz had written about the similarity of his binary arithmetic and the table showing the special arrangement of the hexagrams, the 'Prior to Heaven' arrangement, which he had learnt about from the China Jesuit Joachim Bouvet. Bayer writes:

> Bouvet was much too subtle when he compared Leibniz' binary arithmetic with this table. It is, indeed, incredible how things may resemble each other, but what Leibniz had invented was far too sublime to have been observed by the first human races on earth.[20]

However, Bayer proceeds along the Leibnizian lines of *Ars Combinatoria:*

> I hold it a great merit for an ancient Chinese philosopher and an invention worthy a hecatomb if he has come to consider how many times two or three or more simple figures can be changed by altering their place and order.

Showing the system of whole and broken lines composing doubles, then the eight trigrams, and finally four of the 64 hexagrams, Bayer speaks of it as a combinatory system:

> Look at the first two simple figures, the whole and the broken line. From them they make four composite ones, from those again eight more complex ones and from these

---

19 Bayer had probably seen such Armenian 'decorative' letters in Andreas Müller's *Alpha kai Omega* (1703) (see Note 73 to Preface), but there are similar ones in Athanasius Kircher's *Oedipus Aegyptiacus*, Vol. III, p. 41. – Ciphers, *notae*, is a term used in the works of Latin authors for a secret script and for the abbreviated forms used in stenography, but sometimes said explicitly to be 'one *nota* for one word' (Cicero: *Oratio pro Murena*, 11, 25).

20 This table: Leibniz had published his and Bouvet's 'discovery' that this arrangement of the hexagrams could be read as a binary system in the *Histoire de l'Academie royale des Sciences*, 1703, pp. 58-63, and had sent more details to Tentzel who published a long article about it in his *Curieuse Bibliothec*, 1705, pp. 81-112. He had told the story again at the end of his 'Lettre sur la philosophie chinoise' (see pp. 104, 180), of which it is an integral part, not an accidental addition as sometimes believed.

complex ones they form the 64 hexagrams – that is how the *Book of Changes* is composed. This kind of thing did not belong to old popular ideas of the people, but it caught the eye and seemed to these primitive human beings to be something divine and of eternal significance. If this invention was employed by them, then I believe that the ancient people may well have used the symbols as words – even today they (the eight trigrams) are said to mean something, namely Heaven, Pools, collected in the Mountains, Fire, Thunder, Wind, Water, Mountain and Earth.[21]

This was Bayer's contribution to the everlasting discussion of the mysteries of the *Book of Changes*. It can be read as if he imagined a two-step process, the system itself being invented at the dawn of time, other people later, though still in the dark past, using it for a script. Such a sequence was in fact adumbrated in the Proëmialis Declaratio of the *Confucius Sinarum Philosophus* and Bayer may have sensed it. But he did not *know* at the time about the Fu Xi, or 'Prior to Heaven', and the King Wen, or 'Posterior to Heaven' arrangements of the hexagrams. The only person in Europe who did was Leibniz and he never showed his hand.[22] We shall return to this problem in Part III, chapter 2, dealing with Bayer's *De Horis Sinicis*.

Immediately after his explanation of the hexagrams, however, Bayer adds a note of caution:

I shall not regard it as being of great moment whether this idea is accepted or not. It is, however, extremely likely that the Chinese, playing around with such combinations, went on to form simple characters, out of which came more and more complicated ones – even today the magistrates may invent and add new characters!

This was Bayer's way – he disliked the interminably vague pros and cons of Andreas Müller, the father-idol he criticized all his life. Bayer preferred to state what he meant and leave it to others to correct him.

---

21 Bayer had that from the table facing p. XLIII in the Proëmialis Declaratio of the *Confucius Sinarum Philosophus*.
22 In the article mentioned above Leibniz does not say in so many words that he had obtained a certain Chinese *figure* from Bouvet, one in which the hexagrams can be read as a binary system (not a binary *number* system). Later on Bayer was going to become acquainted with this figure (see Part III, chapter 2). – It is reproduced from the original preserved in the Niedersächsische Landesbibliothek in Hannover, with the square and circular arrangement of the hexagrams from the numerological works of Shao Yong (1011-77), in David Mungello's *Leibniz and Confucianism* (see Note 143 to Preface). – Hans J. Zacher's important study, the *Die Hauptschriften zur Dyadik von G.W. Leibniz* (1973) brought much new about these problems, but more work has to be done to elucidate Leibniz's intention in publishing his discovery the way he did. One who wondered intelligently about it at the time was Johan Thomas Haupt in his *Neue und volständige Auslegung des . . . Ye-Kim,* printed in Rostock and Wismar in 1753.

THE NATURE OF THE CHINESE CHARACTERS

Bayer's ideas about the Chinese script, the result of his reflections on the system he assumed to underly the confusing variety of these signs, are presented in the third chapter of the second book of the 'Grammatica Sinica', called 'On the nature and the analogy of the Chinese characters'.

Now we shall follow him on his way through these speculations, and afterwards we are to see him bringing these ideas into practice in composing his dictionary.

First there are some very simple characters, single strokes, which, however, all mean something. From these the other characters are composed, gradually and step by step. The first simple characters, nine in all, are shown below.

The nine characters, shown here in Fig. 7, are presented in the *Museum Sinicum* with transliterations (two of them by mistake in inverted order) and with translations of those he understood.[23] Omitting his transliterations and adding in parentheses the number of the character in the 214 radical system, the list looks as follows:

1. (1) One
2. (2) A relationship between something above and something below
3. (6) A hook, a connection
4. (4) Primordial heat
5. (?) Humidity
6. (3) Sovereignty
7. (?) A lateral sign
8. (?) The same sign turned around. This and the one before have some meaning which I have not been informed about. I do not want to speculate about it.
9. (5) One. Although this seems to consist of more than one stroke the Chinese regard it as a one-stroke character; it is as if it were the first of these nine strokes, written cursorily.

It is not clear where Bayer got the idea that the Chinese characters are built up from nine elementary or basal strokes, and that they are the ones he shows here. In all his printed and unprinted works and letters he stresses the fact that they are nine in number – 'neither more nor less' – and also that they all mean something. He may have arrived at the conviction about nine elementary forms from remembering Semedo's words: *'Per formare tuta questa moltitudine de lettere adoperano solamente nove tratti'*. We have seen in the Pre-

---

[23] Bayer took this mistake from Mentzel's mistake on p. 11 of his *Kurtze Chinesische Chronologia*. He corrected it later on in his big Chinese-Latin dictionary (see Part III, chapter 5).

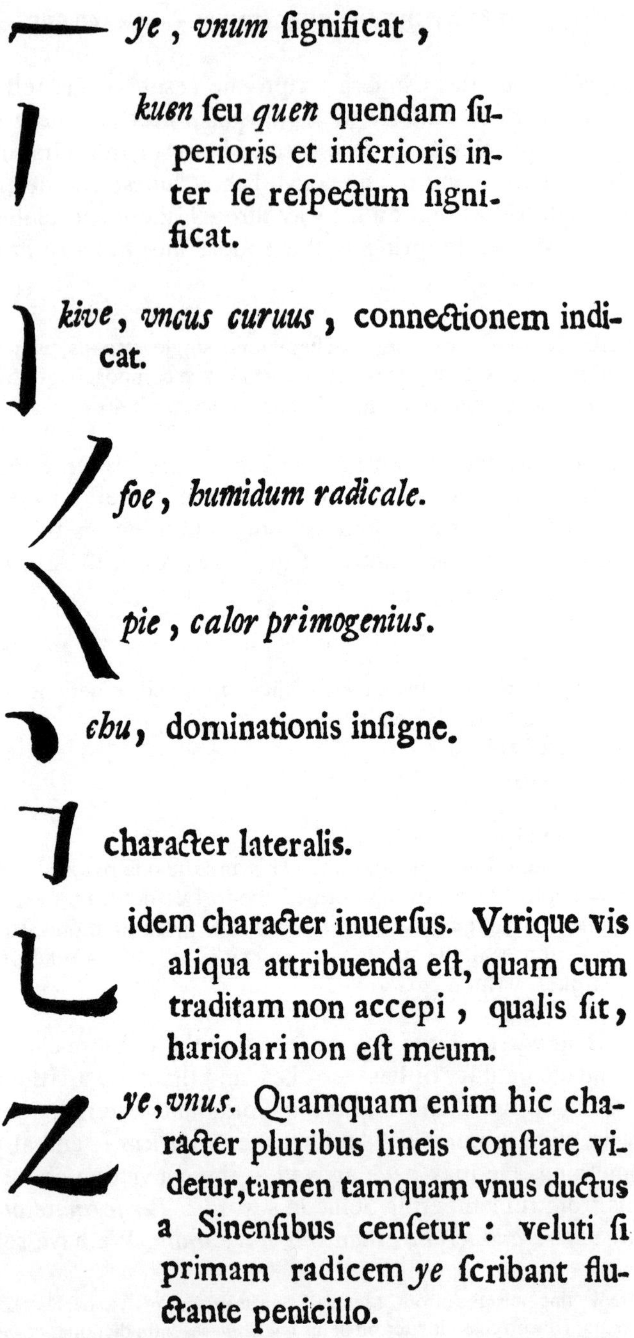

── *ye*, *vnum* significat,

│ *kuen* seu *quen* quendam superioris et inferioris inter se respectum significat.

) *kive*, *vncus curuus*, connectionem indicat.

⟨ *foe*, *humidum radicale*.

pie, *calor primogenius*.

chu, dominationis insigne.

⏋ character lateralis.

⌴ idem character inuersus. Vtrique vis aliqua attribuenda est, quam cum traditam non accepi, qualis sit, hariolari non est meum.

Z *ye*, *vnus*. Quamquam enim hic character pluribus lineis constare videtur, tamen tamquam vnus ductus a Sinensibus censetur: veluti si primam radicem *ye* scribant fluctante penicillo.

Fig. 7. The nine elementary characters, from Bayer's *Museum Sinicum*, 1730.

face that he regarded the little language section in the *Relatione della Grande Monarchia della Cina* (1643) as the finest description of the Chinese language in print.

However, it is interesting that in the draft of the 'Grammatica Sinica', preserved among the Glasgow Bayeriana, he says that the 'very simplest characters' are 'about seven' (*ad septem*), referring to a table which is not in the manuscript (Hunter MS 350). We do not know, therefore, what these 'about seven' characters were, but in Mentzel's *Sylloge Minutiarum Lexici* . . . (1685), which he knew and admired, there is a similarly vague expression – 'about six' (*fere sex*), followed by a woodcut showing seven simple characters! Mentzel was working on a 214 radical dictionary based on the *Zi Hui* dictionary, and the characters he gives are the six one-stroke characters of this work, but with an interpolated character of the form like No. 5 in Bayer's list. I do not know whence he took his simple characters Nos. 7 and 8, of which he claims not to know the meaning.

Bayer proceeds as follows:

This is the first set of characters. Two such characters, joined together, make up the secondary set, three the tertiary, four the quaternary and so forth, but they are still called simple characters. Then all these (simple) characters – binary, tertiary or quaternary, etc. – are combined to form other (complex) characters. Such characters, if made up of two simple characters, are the origins or as it were, the roots of characters in which a third simple character is joined to the first two, and this again is the root of those in which a fourth simple character is joined to the three, and so forth. Thus, in this system each character is a root as well as a branch. It is the branch of a simpler character and the root of a more complex one. But all this will become more clear in the dictionary.

Having proposed these general ideas, to which he is to return at the end of the following chapter, Bayer sets forth some more practical rules:

Now note the following points:
1. Some characters are simple, although they look as if they were complex. I said this about the ninth character in the above list of the simplest characters, and more examples will occur later.
2. The simple characters may vary a little in their form, especially in the grass script (five examples are given).
3. In the complex characters one often encounters great variation of the constituent simple characters, differences that hardly occur when they stand alone.
4. Some simple characters, when included in complex ones, lose their original form and take on another form, which has no meaning outside the complex character (13 pairs are shown).

In the following small section Bayer speaks more clearly about *analogy* than anywhere else in the book.

In the component parts of the complex characters a certain system of analogies obtains, a subtle indication of the meaning of the character, something about the use of something, or some quality. From this you may suspect what the character means, even before the teacher tells you. This phenomenon is most obvious when a character is composed of several simpler ones.

The example he gives, an analysis of the character for *huang,* sovereignty, is fanciful to a degree, even more so than the example shown on p. 137 of his dissection of the name of the mythological queen, Nü Gua. More acceptable (today!) are his short examples of characters containing the word, or the radical as we would say, Mountain. And the following list of 'partial characters' that point to something dealing with river, tree, plant, bird, fish, serpent or stone looks respectable to a modern reader.

There is no contradiction between the idea of analogical structures and that of a combinatory system. Of course, a certain combination of strokes may mean something or point to something, and do so wherever it occurs, thus opening the way for analogical interpretation. But Bayer was wary about stressing the concept of analogy and we know why: he did not have the meaning of the simpler characters at his disposal.

It was left to Étienne Fourmont to emphasize 'analogy' at the expense of 'geometry', as he said. However, that is beyond the scope of the present book, for Bayer did not survive to read the *Meditationes Sinicae.*

Chapter four is entitled 'On Chinese Dictionaries'. There are a few words about the *Zi Hui,* the *Zheng Zi Tong* and the *Hai Pian* dictionaries, as well as, once more, about the Diaz Vocabulary – 'I admit that it has been useful to me'.

Then follows an important section on the pronunciation of the characters as indicated in the dictionaries – 'either they show another character, it is hoped better known, which has the same pronunciation, or they proceed more subtly'. And then his readers found a clear exposition with many examples of the traditional *fan qie* technique. In this technique two well-known characters are shown and the pronunciation is found by joining the first part of the first of them to the second part of the second.

THE DICTIONARY

The last few pages of the chapter on Chinese dictionaries set out to deal with the way the characters are arranged in them, but actually they are mostly about his own dictionary. He starts by talking about his ambitious project, taking up the arguments – with some repetition – of his discussion of the nature of the Chinese characters. However, writing here he seems to realize more acutely than before that what he wrote a moment ago is not quite clear.

For the sake of brevity I shall only deal with my own dictionary and its relationship to the *Zheng Zi Tong* dictionary. From this it will become apparent not only how the Chinese construct their dictionaries, but also where I have followed them and what I think others, who might want to be more complete and accurate, should do.

In the following he tries to describe his dictionary system in a comprehensive way:

The first class in my dictionary contains the nine very simple characters, the tiny elements out of which all Chinese characters are formed . . .
The second class is made up of characters formed by the combination of two one-stroke characters in the first class. These characters, which I shall call secondary, are arranged like those of the first class. For example, the first character in the first class being a horizontal stroke, is followed by a vertical stroke. Similarly, the first character in the second class is made up of two horizontal strokes, followed by a vertical line crossing a horizontal one. In the second class each character that functions as a root is followed by other characters that are its branches. The characters thus formed as branches from their roots are also given in the third and fourth classes as roots.
The third class, containing the three-stroke roots, is arranged in the same manner. Remember the order in which each of the characters in the second class was examined for its origin and in which order it was placed. Here again you will see that each root is followed by the derived characters – the branches – that function as roots in the next class. But there are also complex characters for which a suitable root could not be found later in the system.
In the fourth and fifth classes – the roots made up of four or five strokes – characters gradually begin to appear that are made up not only of the simple ones in the first class, for now there are also some which are composed of two of the characters in the second class. Otherwise, however, everything is arranged as in the previous classes, and so it is in the following ones. The eighth class contains many roots made up of relatively simple ones among the complex ones and this tendency becomes more and more pronounced in the rest of the classes.

In the last part of the chapter Bayer sets forth a principle he was going to follow even more rigorously in the big dictionary he composed in his later years:

In constituting and forming the roots and arranging them properly, we ought to take into account only those parts of the characters that appear on top of or at the left border of the composite one, but sometimes when parts of composite characters at the bottom or on the right side are very conspicuous the Chinese also accept them as roots. I have followed them in that. But the result is that sometimes characters, especially the most complex ones, appear under more than one root.

Finally he adds some odd and some significant reflections to this difficult exposition:

> I know that I might have solved all this in a more exact way. More roots should have been used, and as they increase gradually in complexity, generating new ones, they should have been arranged in their proper classes. Using such a new procedure I would have lived up to European expectations of accuracy – as for the Chinese they do not bother about such matters. But this would have meant composing a giant dictionary – that was not my intention and anyhow I am afraid that poverty would have prevented me from doing otherwise than I did. Other persons after me may be more fortunate and able to produce a nobler work in this field. The complex characters should have been placed more subtly and arranged under their respective roots. But I hope what I have done will not be rejected; it has been very hard work and I think I have done enough in having demonstrated on a small scale the material and the method to be used in a major work.[24]

Actually Bayer did compose a 'giant dictionary' later in life, but at that time he had partially given up the system he invented for his *Museum Sinicum*. We shall return to that in the chapter on 'Bayer's Big Dictionary'.

The dictionary found in the *Museum Sinicum* contains 2,251 characters, but a large number of them are repetitions. They appear on 40 engraved plates and are numbered in such a way that their pronunciation and meaning can be found in the accompanying 107-page list. In about 20 cases the pronunciation, the translation or both are missing. Bayer added a few of them in his private copy.[25]

The characters are arranged under 407 roots in 18 sections, from the nine elementary ones in the first section to those written with 18 strokes in the last one. As he had explained, each root is followed by a number of derivates or branches.

Bayer knew the 214 radical system from the Martini-Couplet grammar – Mentzel's *Clavis Sinica* – he had copied in Berlin and he had read about these radicals (*radicales litterae*) in two of Couplet's letters to Mentzel, where he says that he has given a list of radicals – supposedly the 214 – to 'the librarian' in Paris, meaning Thévenot, as Bayer rightly guessed. However, in another place in one of these letters Couplet asserts that there are 'about 400 *radicales litterae,* from which the composite characters are formed', and Bayer had seen and copied a 331 radical list at the end of the Martini grammar, also among

---

24 Here, of course, Bayer was thinking of Étienne Fourmont.
25 Glasgow University Library, Hunter Books, Ee, 2.1,2.

the Mentzeliana in Berlin. Oddly enough he never mentions Martini's 331 radicals, nor the sentence about 'approximately 400 radicals' in Couplet's letter. He must have thought that both were Chinese systems and may have imagined that there were others – he did not *know* there were, and at the time he probably did not even know about the *Kang Xi* dictionary, published in 1716, in which the 214 radical system was made authoritative and obligatory. At any rate, he felt free to invent his own system, looking for what seemed to him to be the most conspicuous features of the characters and perhaps aiming at 'about 400'.[26]

However, it was not just a matter of feeling free to do this; the desire to make something better of his own invention may have been uppermost in his mind: all the time we must imagine him to be looking over his shoulder, so to speak, at Fourmont in Paris, the great man who had said that *there was a system,* and that he had discovered it. The Chinese 214 radical system which he knew from the specimens in the Martini-Couplet grammar could really not qualify as a system. He had to reject it and trust to his own intellectual powers.

Technically, how did he go about it when he arranged his dictionary? We can only guess.

Working with the 500 transliterated and translated words in his transcript of the Martini-Couplet grammar and a number from the Diaz Vocabulary, he may have copied out a certain number of them, those that seemed to him to be the most important ones. Then, having decided on his 407 roots and having arranged them according to the number of strokes, he had to accommodate the characters under each of them. Perhaps he had written out each of them, with its pronunciation and the Latin translation, on separate slips of paper – standing on edge these would have filled a box 15-20 cm long. All the way he had to make decisions about where to place them as secondary, tertiary, etc. characters in the system, making concessions and exceptions, breaking his own strict rules, as he says himself . . .

Figs. 8a and 8b show the first two pages of the 'Lexicon Sinicum' in the *Museum Sinicum.*

Section I presents the nine elementary strokes (characters). In Section II, which continues on the following four pages, we find all the roots consisting of two elementary strokes, and their derivates. First there is the character made up of two horizontal strokes, i.e. twice the first of the elementary strokes – let us call it a 1-1 combination. This is followed by only one derivate, namely

---

26 There is one small sentence in section IX of the chapter on Chinese characters in general (p. 102) that seems slightly out of place and may have been added at a late time during the writing of the manuscript: 'In these, then, (the books of the Chinese) the number of radicals (*litterae radicales*) is about 400; that of the composite characters is much larger (*sic*). Seven thousand are said to suffice for reading and interpreting the easier types of books . . .'

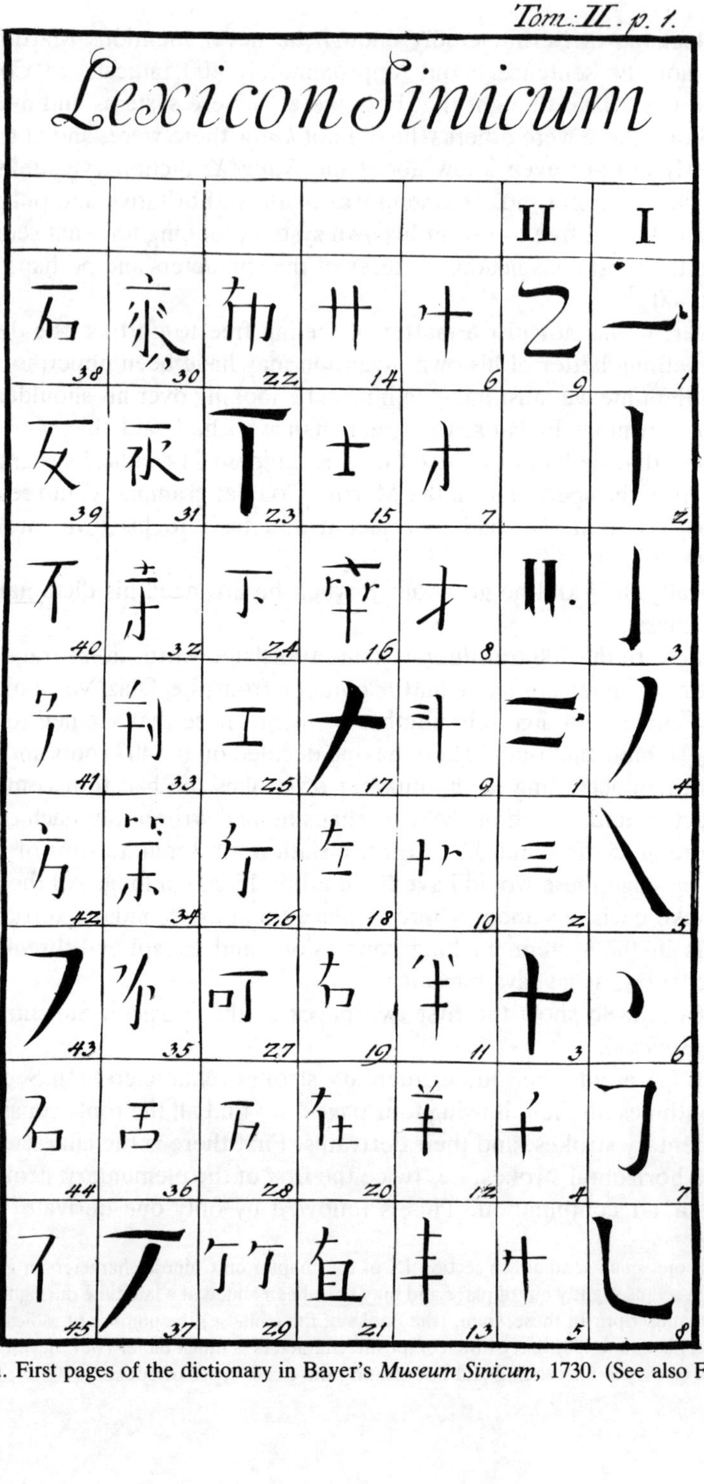

					II	I
石 38	枩 30	巾 22	廿 14	十 6	乙 9	一 1
反 39	永 31	丁 23	士 15	才 7	丨	丨 2
不 40	寺 32	下 24	卒 16	才 8	III.	丿 3
勹 41	刋 33	工 25	大 17	斗 9	二 1	丶 4
方 42	枽 34	彳 26	左 18	卄 10	三 2	丶 5
乀 43	竹 35	可 27	右 19	羊 11	十 3	丶 6
石 44	吾 36	万 28	在 20	羊 12	十 4	乛 7
乙 45	丁 37	竹 29	宜 21	丰 13	卄 5	乚 8

Fig. 8a. First pages of the dictionary in Bayer's *Museum Sinicum*, 1730. (See also Fig. 8b.)

Tom: II. p. 3. 4.

Fig. 8b.

three such strokes. Then we find the combination of the first and the second of the elementary strokes, a 1-2 combination, a cross.

Disregarding for the moment the derivates printed with smaller characters, we see eight more combinations of the elementary strokes on these two plates. However, inspection of them reveals that they are not 1-3, 1-4, 1-5 etc. combinations, but 1-4, 1-2, 1-4, 1-4, 1-2, 1-2, 1-6 and 1-6 combinations, the repetitions being caused by the strokes being *located* differently in relation to each other.[27]

However, this is not according to the *Ars combinatoria* which Bayer speaks about in so many places. It has no space relations, it is not a topology, it does not admit of doublets and two symbols can only form one pair, xy = yx. Nine symbols can form a total of 36 two-symbol combinations. Bayer has 37 characters in his second class, made up of combinations of the nine elementary strokes. He arrived at that number by the repetitions exemplified above, together with a number of omissions due to the fact that no character consisting of 1-3 or 1-4 etc. combinations existed in the character lists he worked with.

Now, if we examine the 'tertiary' and higher classes, the derivates arranged under the 37 secondary roots, we find only an approximation to a system, just as Bayer had said in his description of the method. Looking at the small derivates following the boldfaced root in the form of a cross, we find 13 of them, vaguely, but far from strictly according to the number of extra strokes.

Bayer's way of selecting his radicals and arranging their derivates leads to a great number of double or treble entries, e.g. we find the character for sheep, *yang,* as a derivate of the cross-formed second class character – No. 12 on our Fig. 2a – but it also occurs as one of the six-strokes radicals. In both cases the list of transliterations and translations has *yang, ovis*. However, as there is no *list* of the 407 radicals such redundancy may actually have been helpful to the reader groping for a certain character. Bayer refers to the redundancy himself, as we have seen: 'The characters thus formed as branches from their roots are also given in (higher) class(es) as roots'.

As to the quality of the Chinese characters here and everywhere else in the *Museum Sinicum:* it is obviously very poor and we shall see that most of the criticism directed against it concentrated on this fact. Some of them are hard to recognize, e.g. No. 30, *shu,* glutinous millet – Bayer took that from one of the rough characters in the 331 radical list mentioned above. No. 34, *song,* 'the name of a dynasty', can not be read without the transliteration and translation given. A few of the characters are simply wrong, such as No. 33, *li,*

27 Strictly speaking the number of possible combinations of the nine elementary strokes is 511. Bayer could have looked up that figure in Table I of Leibniz's *De Arte Combinatoria.* The number of possible combinations of these 511 characters is written with 1163 digits; it would fill half of a page if printed on the lines of the present book.

profit, where two strokes are missing, and No. 40 (and the identical No. 45), where the fourth stroke was mysteriously omitted.[28]

Finally about the transliterations and translations.

As mentioned above, the number on the plates refer to the 107-page list that gives the pronunciation and the meaning of each of the characters. Going through a number of them and allowing for some misprints – *ten* for *teu*, *tum* for *fum*, etc. – the transliterations are mostly reasonably correct, and so are the translations, but there are a number of errors. However, enough of this: we are looking at a very primitive attempt to construct a home-made Chinese dictionary. Bayer himself says this again and again. It was only meant to show the way and to incite others to go on and do it better than he was able to do, but also better than the Chinese did it. Undoubtedly it was a useful and stimulating exercise for his contemporaries and those immediately succeeding them to go through the whole of this dictionary, delighting in each of its mistakes, but it would be a waste of time for us to do so here.

This must suffice as a presentation of Bayer's lexicographic theory and practice. He started from the idea of a combinatory system, but the reality of the word-lists he was working with did not fit such a frame, and moreover he got tired of trying to live up to his own ideals – 'the European expectation of accuracy'. He felt that if only he had had the entire set of 80,000 characters at his disposal, and if he had been able to muster the strength required, he would have arrived at *the true system*. Now he had shown the way, leaving it to others, more gifted and with greater facilities, to complete his work.[29]

---

28 We know that the characters of the Diaz Vocabulary in Berlin, from which he took a number of his examples, were very fine. However, they were written with the Kai Shu or Official Script, not with the Sung Ban, the characters of printed texts, which are never used by the Chinese when writing. Those he had in his notebooks were his own copies of the characters of missionaries or of Christian Mentzel. Another reason for the poor quality of the characters in the *Museum Sinicum*, which he was to adduce in his defence against Fourmont's attack in the last days of his life, was the incompetence of the engravers of the St Petersburg Academy Press (see p. xxx).

29 In principle, of course, there is nothing wrong with a 'home made' radical system like that of Bayer's. For more than 300 years and until recently European students of the Chinese language have been accustomed to the 214-radical system, introduced by Mei Yingzi in his *Zi Hui* dictionary in 1615 and made *quasi* obligatory with the publication of the *Kang Xi* dictionary in 1716. But before that time, from the old *Shuowen Jiezi* and onwards, there had been numerous different systems, some with less than one hundred and some with more than five hundred radicals. – The first Chinese dictionary to be published in Europe, the *Dictionnaire chinois, français, latin*, edited by Deguignes in Paris in 1813, was a 214-radical dictionary, and so were most of the following ones, with a few exceptions, such as J.A. Golcalves' *Diccionario China-Portuguez*, Macao, 1833, in which the characters are arranged under 129 radicals of his own invention. Antonio Montucci (see Note 14 above) had planned to publish one or more enormous Chinese-Latin dictionaries and said that he intended to use two or three times as many radicals as in the Kang Xi dictionary. He mentions Bayer's name in one place, but does not refer to a possible similarity between his ideas and those of Bayer. – The

THE GRAMMAR

Book 1 of the 'Grammatica Sinica', entitled 'On the Chinese Language', is the grammar proper. It starts with the statement that Chinese is partly the popular languages (dialects) spoken in the provinces and partly the language which has been refined by the learned. This language, called *Guan Hua,* or Mandarin by us, is cultivated at the court and among the erudites.

The script, he says, is neither alphabetic nor syllabic, the characters being mental pictures of things and ideas. The Chinese learn to pronounce them by listening to the teacher reading a text. On the other hand, the written language can be understood and explained even by persons who know practically nothing about the spoken language. This is the Xavier idea (see p. 44), but Bayer adds, somewhat inconsistently, that it is good to know *something* at least about the pronunciation, and that therefore he will 'comment on the spoken language, in so far as it would seem to be useful for those who want to translate a Chinese text'.

There follows a list of the 353 syllables of the Chinese language, 'as pronounced in Spanish and Portuguese'. Le Comte, he says, gave it according to French orthography, Thomas Hyde to English, and he himself had used a German transliteration at some places in his *De Eclipsi Sinica* – but now he has changed his mind. Actually, he says, it is nearly impossible to express these sounds with our letters, so different are they from the European way of speaking. Therefore let us stick to the Portuguese and Spanish forms, because they are the ones we encounter in the writings of the missionaries.

He then proceeds to discuss the tones, shows the Jesuits' notation of them, as also used in 'the Dominican Francesco Diaz's beautiful dictionary, which I studied in Berlin', and tries – unsuccessfully, as was to be expected – to

---

Russian sinologist V.P. Vasil'ev invented a 24-radical system for his *Graphic System of Chinese Characters: An Attempt at a first Chinese-Russian Dictionary* (St Petersburg, 1867, in Russian). This system is still adhered to in I.M. Ošanin's great Chinese-Russian Dictionary (Moscow, 1959), currently used in the USSR. – After the introduction of simplified characters in the Peoples' Republic of China the number of radicals was reduced to 186 or 187. – The modern Chinese electronic typewriter, the SINOTRONIC CS 4000, a character processor made in Peking, is not built on the 214 radical system. The advertising booklet says: 'Some would consider radicals in Chinese characters to be fundamentals. But radicals are incomplete, their numbers are too many, and there is no standard agreement on decomposition of characters into radicals. From the geometrical point of view any Chinese character can be decomposed into dots and lines. The minimal set of dots and lines consists of the following five kinds: dots, horizontals, verticals, positively-sloped and negatively-sloped lines, irrespective of length'. The booklet shows these elements – they are T.S. Bayer's 'roots' no. 1, 2, 4, 5, and 6! (I am grateful to Professor Søren Egerod for calling my attention to this new invention). – *Li's Chinese Dictionary,* the *Li Shi Zhongwen Zidian,* published in Hongkong in 1980, is based on the same five 'radicals', but in this work they are combine to form 1,171 (mainly) phonetic units.

describe their phonetic values. He also prints parts of a system of 'double tones' from the Chin ceu Grammar (see p. 129), but gives up after a few lines.

Bayer was fully aware of the importance of the tones: 'A syllable pronounced with a different tone means something different', but he had decided to omit the tone marks (*accentus*) because, as he says, 'I am writing for those who want to read Chinese, not to speak it' (p. 15). We shall see that in a later work and in his defence against Fourmont's harsh criticism, written a few days before he died, he was to advance other arguments for neglecting the tone marks. Here in the *Museum Sinicum,* he had to give an approximate transliteration. Otherwise he would have been forced to print the text with strings of Chinese characters. Prémare's Grammar, the *Notitia Linguae Sinicae,* could be printed in that way, but only by Chinese printers, and only in Malacca, and not till 1831. Also, even giving each of his transliterated Chinese words its appropriate tone mark might have been too burdensome a task for his St Petersburg printers!

The grammar that follows these preliminary sections is based on the system of Latin grammars: substantives and adjectives with their declinations, pronouns, the conjugations of the verbs, adverbs and prepositions, etc.

These 40 pages with their categories and paradigms may be surprising to the unprepared modern reader. But in Bayer's time, and for a century after him, there was no other way of presenting the structure of a language. Prémare, who wrote his admirable *Notitia* . . . in Canton, while Bayer was toiling with his primitive work in St Petersburg, also used the Latin grammar frame, although most of his book deals with the particles. Another Chinese grammar was arranged in the same manner, namely that of the Augustinians Juan Rodriguez and José Villanueva; it was ready to be printed in 1785, but actually never appeared.[30]

So here a few lines may suffice to show Bayer's insight – or rather that of his Jesuit sources – into some important pecularities of the Chinese language.

Right at the beginning, and several times later, the reader learns the strange fact that nearly all the words or characters of the Chinese language can function like what he is used to calling substantives, adjectives or even verbs. This is connected with the fact, he learns, that all Chinese words are monosyllables and indeclinable: there is a word *za* and its character meaning 'to mix', but it may also mean 'mixed' or 'mixture'. This example occurs as *ça* on page 1 of Diaz's alphabetically arranged vocabulary! A number of important characters seem to be half way between our adverbs and prepositions. How could such a language function at all? The reader is told about the great importance of the word order and about the great number of particles that

---

30 See Knud Lundbæk: 'Une grammaire espagnole de la langue chinoise au XVIIIe siècle', in *Actes du IIe Colloque International de Sinologie,* Paris, 1980, pp. 259-69.

structure the meaning of the phrases and sentences, serving as our voices and tenses of verbs and the cases of our substantives. One particular feature, the Chinese measure words, is illustrated by 39 examples.

All the transliterated words in the text have raised numerals, referring to the characters on eight engraved plates. There is a total of 809 characters here, forming 437 words or short phrases, to exemplify the grammatical system of the Chinese language.[31]

Book II of the Chinese Grammar is entitled 'On Chinese Literature' and starts with a chapter on paper, brushes, ink and inkstones, referring for the way the Chinese handle the brush to the picture in Kircher's *China . . . illustrata* and to the portrait of Confucius in *Confucius Sinarum Philosophus*. Then follows a section, which must have been interesting at the time, about the technique of book printing in China, the forms of books and their subdivisions, the running titles printed on the outer margin of the double pages, so that 'one has to put one's hand in between the two leaves to read them', also about authors' names, places of publication and 'year of printing'. As examples he quotes from the title pages of a Mencius edition and two medical works he had seen in the Königsberg Library.[32]

Chapter 2 of Book II of the Grammar ends with a short but copiously illustrated section about two kinds of Chinese script, which he calls the correct style (*zheng zi*) and the straw or grass script (*cao zi*). One of the finest examples of the correct style is taken from a missionary pamphlet.[33] There are two plates of characters in grass script, taken from an unnamed big book with pictures of the Emperor's hunting expeditions. It has a seal at the end, and Bayer informs his reader that the Chinese have special dictionaries for seal characters – he had never seen one himself.

The last chapter of the Chinese Grammar is entitled 'On Eloquence'. Bayer admits that he knows very little about eloquence among the Chinese and

---

[31] The system breaks down between nos. 72 and 90. The careful reader would have been able to see through it, but it does not look nice. This kind may have been what Abel Rémusat referred to in his indulgent note on Bayer, 'who did not lack an elementary knowledge of Chinese and who could have published works of greater utility to the beginner (there is a misprint here: commerçant for commençant) if he had hurried less to havè them printed' (*Mélanges asiatiques* (1826), Vol. II, p. 70).

[32] There is one curious error in one of them, the Pulse Classic, which he had mentioned in the Preface, when discussing Boym's medical works (see p. 58). He had no means of recognizing the characters for *wang, shu* and *ho* as the name of the author, and thus wrote '. . . the king, et cetera.'

[33] This is Giulio Aleni's *The true Origin of all Things (Wan You Zhen Yuan)*, Peking 1628 and 1694. The Chinese title is the variant mentioned by Pfister, p. 132. Bayer notes that the same words were inscribed on the tablet which the Kang Xi emperor gave to the Jesuits for their new church in Peking in 1711.

actually all he does is to emphasize and praise the terse and brief style of their philosophers. The last pages are about Chinese poetry. He prints Nicolas Fréret's translation of a poem from the *Book of Songs,* and another by Arcadius Huang about a willow tree. There are no Chinese characters with these two translations. And then he adds two poems from the *Great Learning,* with Chinese characters, transliterations and translations, without mentioning that they are the small pieces he had already printed in his *De Eclipsi Sinica.*[34]

ON THE CHIN CEU (ZHANGZHOU) DIALECT

In the Preface we heard about a Spanish manuscript grammar of the Chin ceu (Zhangzhou) dialect which Bayer had copied in Berlin, and about his work with rearranging it in St Petersburg, with the help of a Spaniard named Bernardo Ribera. In the *Museum Sinicum* it forms the third and last part of the 'Grammatica Linguae Sinicae'. Bayer included it, as he included everything else he had at his disposal, but he felt it was important as an example of a language or dialect in which the sounds and the tonal system were very different from those of the standard Mandarin.[35]

It begins with an attempt to describe the ten 'modes' in which the five tones are expressed in that dialect, and the missionaries' notation of them. Then follows a grammar, seventy pages with numerous examples, arranged according to the system of Latin grammars, exactly as in his Mandarin grammar.

Finally Bayer's reader found the Lord's Prayer, the Apostolic Creed, Ave Maria and Salve, transliterations and word for word translations, but without the characters. This must have been of interest to Bayer himself and also to his readers, among other things because it showed the missionary technique

---

34 Bayer says that the poem translated and transliterated by Arcadius Huang is from a Chinese novel he began to translate. Bayer took it from Fréret's short article printed in 1717 (see Note 156 to Preface). – Fourmont was to mention it – 'a certain *fabula,* the kind of works called *romans* in French' – in his *Linguae Sinicae . . . Grammatica . . .* (1742), p. 501, but without giving the title of the novel. Actually the poem is taken from chapter 6 of a novel from the Ming period named *Yu Jiao Li,* a French translation of which was published with the title *Les deux cousines* by Abel Rémusat in 1822 and again by Stanislaf Julien, politely criticizing Rémusat's bad translation, in 1864. – Prémare's *Notitia Linguae Sinicae* contains a note in the Pars Prima about the Bishop of Rosalia, who had been so excited by the *Yu Jiao Li* that he had arranged its phrases in a kind of dictionary. This bishop was the man who brought Arcadius Huang to France . . . Perhaps someone will some day take a closer look at the story about the translation of this novel.

35 I owe to Professor Søren Egerod the identification of the language shown in this chapter with a southern Min (South Fukienese) dialect, having features in common with both the Amoy and the Chaozhou dialects. – The Lord's Prayer in the Chin ceu dialect had been printed in an anynomous letter inserted in the *Histoire critique de la république des lettres,* Vol. III, pp. 272-6, 1713. See Note 67 to the Preface.

used outside the Jesuit order: all the Spanish religious names and terms are presented with approximately similar Chinese sounds, e.g. *Dio si* for *Dios, Si pi ri to san ta* for *Espiritu Santo, Cu lut* for *Cruz, Galacia* for *Gracia,* etc. Bayer knew, of course, that this way of evangelization was a bone of contention between the Jesuits and the other missionaries, but he does not comment on it here – we shall see him doing so – cautiously – in the chapter on the *Xiao Er Lun* (p. 139).

THE CHRESTOMATHY

An introductory textbook of a language usually comprises a grammar, a vocabulary and a chrestomathy, i.e. a number of small texts for practice. In the *Museum Sinicum* we find three texts that may be regarded as a chrestomathy – a *Life of Confucius,* the first chapter of the *Great Learning* and a piece from a book called *Xiao Er Lun,* about Chinese mythology. They are given in Chinese characters, in transliteration, and in translation and as such should be helpful in practising what was learned from the grammar and from the vocabulary. Moreover, in most chrestomathies texts are selected that will cast light on some aspects of the civilization expressing itself in the language under study. The texts which Bayer presents can be said to do this – a biography of the greatest personality in Chinese history, a part of one of the basic Classics, the *Four Books,* and a piece that deals with the ideas of the Chinese about their earliest history.

However, in composing his chrestomathy Bayer had hardly any choice. These three pieces were all there was at his disposal, except for the Nestorian Stele. Undoubtedly he would have wished to include that, or part of it – in later years he implored the Peking Jesuits to send him a Chinese edition of it – but he had good reasons at the time for avoiding it. He knew that the Chinese text printed in Kircher's *China . . . illustrata* was corrupt and many of its characters were unreadable. Moreover, although of the greatest interest, this subject may have seemed to Bayer to be a hackneyed one, having passed through the hands of Kircher and Andreas Müller.

The texts Bayer presented were not new but hard to obtain, one of them – the *Xiao Er Lun* – having being printed more than 30 years ago in a German book. Of another one – the *Life of Confucius* – the Latin translation was available but the Chinese text had appeared with it only in a book printed in the East, of which only very few copies existed in Europe. The same was true of the *Great Learning.* The *Life of Confucius* and the part of the *Great Learning,* with Bayer's notes and commentaries, are quite short, but the one on Chinese mythology swelled under his hands to a long treatise, in fact, except for the Preface, this text is the longest in the *Museum Sinicum.*

The Life of Confucius

The first of these three pieces is called 'The Life of Confucius from the Goa edition of the works of Confucius'. Actually the text comprises the Life of Confucius printed in Intorcetta's *Sinarum Scientia Politico-Moralis* (Canton and Goa, 1669) as well as that which appeared in the *Confucius Sinarum Philosophus* (Paris, 1687), and points out the omissions and additions in the latter one.

Bayer does not say where he studied the 'Goa edition' and it is not even clear that he ever saw it. It was not in the Royal Library in Berlin, but he knew that there was a copy of it in the Imperial Library in Vienna. The Latin translation was no problem, for he had the *Confucius Sinarum Philosophus* and that of the Goa edition had been published in Peter Lambeck's Catalogue of Manuscripts in the Vienna Library as well as in Thévenot's *Voyages*.[36] But where did he get his Chinese characters?

There is an engraved plate with 63 names or terms (128 characters), corresponding to the 63 raised numerals of the text. They are even worse than those on the rest of the plates in the *Museum Sinicum,* and there are some odd mistakes, e.g. Zhong Ni, Confucius's courtesy name appearing as Ni Zhong. Bayer may have obtained a transcript, possibly made in Vienna – perhaps for himself but more probably for Christian Mentzel.[37]

In contrast to the other two pieces, Bayer abstained from furnishing this one with his own commentaries. For that reason, among others, it is not necessary to discuss this text here. Suffice it to say that besides giving a Confucius biography from Chinese sources, it presents the Jesuits' conception of the cult of Confucius as a civic rite, devoid of idolatry. This is particularly so in the long section included when the *Life of Confucius* was printed in the *Confucius Sinarum Philosophus*. Bayer dealt with these problems in his *De Eclipsi Sinica* but he does not take them up here.[38] As it stands, with its

---

36 At the end of the Life of Confucius Bayer inserted a small xylograph showing a Chinese seal, noting that this is the name of Intorcetta, S.J. He must have had it from a copy of the xylograph at the end of Intorcetta's *Sinarum Scientia Politico-Moralis*. But something had gone wrong. He translates the four characters of the seal as *Yinduoze Hui* but it is actually *Yinduoze Yin*, Intorcetta's seal. He got it mixed up with the characters and transliterations on the title page of Intorcetta's work: *Yinduoze Yesu Hui*, Intorcetta, of the Society of Jesus.
37 In the *Confucius Sinarum Philosophus* the 63 names or terms are marked out, not with raised numerals as in other parts of the work, but being printed with Roman type in contrast to the *italics* of the rest of this text. In Intorcetta's *Sinarum Scientia Politica-Politica* the Chinese characters are inserted in the text, on the lines.
38 The text refers to the belief of Chinese converts that Confucius, when speaking about a 'holy man in the West', was prophesying the coming of the Saviour. In later years Bayer returned to that point in his correspondence with the Peking Jesuits. – It also contains a variant of the words about adoring Heaven, loving your neighbour and knowing or controlling yourself – as in the *Innocentia Victrix* – but Bayer did comment on it here. (See p. 34).

precise indications of the parts existing or missing in the Goa edition and in the Paris work, this section of the *Museum Sinicum* may be valuable even today, saving us the trouble of digging out the *Confucius Sinarum Philosophus* and Lambeck's huge *Catalogue* for comparison![39] As a chrestomathy, an aid for readers who wanted to learn Chinese, it was not very helpful, among other things because the tables present only a selection of characters for personal and geographical names and dates, not a complete text.

The Great Learning

The second piece is an annotated translation of the first part of the famous *Da Xue*, the *Great Learning*, the first of the Confucian *Four Books*.[40] Bayer had seen the Chinese text, with transliterations and translations, among Mentzel's papers in the Royal Library in Berlin, but apparently had not had time to copy it out. Later on, probably in 1722, he asked Lacroze to transcribe it for him. In a letter dated 22 August, 'in the dead of the night, shortly before dawn', but without year or place, he writes:

'I would be very grateful to you if you would send me, as soon as possible, a copy of the first six pages of the *Confucius Sinarum Philosophus* from Ment-

---

39 There is one omission: Bayer forgot to note that the penultimate paragraph about the Yong Le emperor is only found in the *Confucius Sinarum Philosophus*.

40 *The Four Books*, comprising the *Great Learning*, the *Doctrine of the Mean*, the *Analects* and the *Mencius*, have been the basic Confucian texts since Zhu Xi (1130-1200) collected and edited them together from various Classics. There are numerous translations of the *Four Books*, the most commonly used still being James Legge's in his *The Chinese Classics*, Vol. I (1861) with many reprints. The first presentation of the *Four Books*, or rather of the first three of them, is found in the *Confucius Sinarum Philosophus* (see Note 36 to the Preface), but actually the beginning of the *Great Learning* in Michele Ruggieri's translation had been printed in Europe nearly a hundred years before (see Note 25 to the Preface). – Supposedly at the time when Bayer wrote his *Museum Sinicum* he had never seen a copy of the *Four Books*. He never exposes the structure or the content of the *Great Learning* or that of the *Four Books* in general. Mentzel had owned a copy of it, but it was not among the Mentzeliana in Bayer's time, for Mentzel had sent it as a present to the Emperor Leopold in Vienna in 1688 together with a transcription of the characters, with transliterations and translations, of the first of them, the *Great Learning*. The manuscript in the Oesterreichische Nationalbibliothek, (Sin. 290) has an interesting title: 'Thai Hio. Confuzii Philosophi Sinensium primarii Ta-Hio, i.e. Magnae Scientiae . . . translatus in sermonem latinum a R.P. Philippo Coupletio S.J., textum vero sinicum, sive characteres et voces Sinensium manu licet invalida adposui Christianus Menzelius M.D. . . . 1688, aetatis meae 66'. The fact that Mentzel suffered from Parkinson's disease in his old days was often mentioned at the time in reference to the quality of his Chinese characters. – See also Eva Kraft's article about Mentzel's presents for the Emperor (Note 125 to Preface). – As late as in 1735 Bayer asked his Jesuit friends in Peking to send him a 'Confucius', i.e. the *Four Books*, to compare with his *Confucius Sinarum Philosophus*.

zel's Chinese excerpts, until "atque haec est ipsumet Confucii Sinarum oraculi doctrina . . .".'[41] Lacroze copied it out and sent it to him in a letter dated 1 May 1723.[42]

Bayer included the Chinese text, and a transliteration with a word for word translation, adding also a fluent translation – 'an impartial one (meaning different from that of the Jesuits!), what I imagine Confucius would have said if he had spoken Latin'.

Here are a few examples of this translation:

The Nature of the Great Doctrine, i.e. philosophy, is to illuminate virtue (*de*); it is to regard the people in a responsible way; it is to persist in the highest goodness (*zhi shan*) . . . Things (*res omnia*) have beginnings and ends; works (*opera, officia, negotia*) have beginnings and ends . . . to perfect the intelligence is to penetrate everything.

In his notes he criticizes the Jesuits' translation in several places. The Chinese word *de,* which he renders as virtue, was translated in the *Confucius Sinarum Philosophus* as 'rational nature'. It is easy to understand, he says, why they did this, but what they wanted (to put into it) – namely the Christian idea of *lumen naturale* – is not in Confucius' text. For the Chinese *Zhi shan* Bayer gives 'the highest goodness', objecting to the Jesuits introducing 'the European disputations about the Highest Goodness (Summum Bonum)'.

He mentions a much-discussed anti-Jesuit work, 'Minorelli's book about the erros of Jouvenci', but only in connection with the problem of the authorship of Confucius, not referring to the Rites Controversy. He was to return to that book in his correspondence with the Peking Jesuits in later years. (See p. 158).

The notes explain a number of characters he had looked up in Diaz's Vocabulary and the Martini-Couplet Grammar. He also demonstrates his sinological abilities in a digression about names and titles of emperors, where he writes: 'In the *Zizhi Tongjian,* i.e. the official Annals of the Chinese Empire ('L.193') Tai Zong, who is celebrated with this name on the Nestorian Stele, is called . . . (a nine character epithet)'.[43]

This indication of his acquaintance with the great Chinese vocabulary and with the huge 'Annales Sinici' may have impressed his readers. Presumably, however, it was one of the few things he could do when he handled the history book in the Royal Library in Berlin in 1716. He may well have brought with

---

41 Lacroze Correspondence, II, p. 277. The first chapter of the *Great Learning* actually occupies pp. 1 to 6 of the Scientia Sinica Liber Primus in the *Confucius Sinarum Philosophus,* ending with the 'atque haec' clause.
42 Lacroze Correspondence, III, pp. 58ff.
43 Bayer had already mentioned this in his *De Eclipsi Sinica.*

him from Königsberg his little 'Glossarium Sinicum' with its complete transcription of the Stele text from Kircher's *China . . . illustrata,* including the name Tai Zong (character No. 39 in column 8). Knowing from Boym's paraphrased translation in Kircher's book that this emperor was on the throne in A.D. 636, he was able to locate him in the 'Annals'.

Finally about an amusing mistake:

In a note (p. 250) he repeats the Ode on the Yellow Bird from the second chapter of the *Great Learning,* referring to the Chinese text of it which he gave in the Grammar Chapter (see p. 129). He thinks it was 'a kind of Chinese Phoenix', a picture of which he had found in a Chinese book on natural history, and asks the reader to contemplate the figure that adorns the last page of the *Museum Sinicum*. It is indeed the famous Phoenix, but it is not the Yellow Bird, which, according to Chinese commentators, is an oriole.[44]

Xiao Er Lun

A part of a book called *Xiao Er Lun* (*The Child's Book*), a popular illustrated primer, had been printed by Mentzel in his *Kurtze Chinesische Chronologia* (1696). (See p. 81). Bayer reprinted the text and used it for an extended discussion of the earliest history of China. He presented it in four engraved plates with 230 characters.[45]

---

44 The bird is shown with two Chinese characters, nearly correct, for *Feng-Huang,* the mythological Phoenix that appears when a Sage is born. He may have thought that this was the Yellow Bird because of the similarity between the character for yellow and a part of the character for *Huang* in *Feng-Huang.*

45 See Note 141 to the Preface. – Bayer describes the *Xiao Er Lun* according to Mentzel's description: it is a small book, illustrated with small primitive pictures, containing the rudiments of Chinese history, a map of the stars, geography (Mentzel had written 'map with the provinces'), something about nature, about measures and weights, coins and public institutions and religious ceremonies. Mentzel had included two xylographic plates with the first part of the beginning of Chinese 'history' from this book. This is the text that Bayer reproduces and discusses in his long article about the early history of China. – Mentzel had thought that his *Xiao Er Lun* was the Children's Classic, the *Xiao Xue,* but Bayer realized that that could not be the case. It must have been much smaller than this Classic, published, as he knew, in a Latin translation by Noël in 1711, as part of his *Sinensis Imperii Libri Classici Sex.* He did not comment on the likelihood that a Chinese Classic could *look* like the book Menzel described – he had seen too few Chinese books! – Bayer tried unsuccessfully to get more information about the book. In a letter to Lacroze, shortly after returning to Königsberg, in October 1717, he wrote: 'I would dearly like to know if the *Xiao Er Lun* is in the Royal Library or from whence Mentzel had it'. Lacroze answered two weeks later, saying that this book was not among the Chinese books that came to the Royal Library after Mentzel's death. 'I remember', he says, 'that fourteen or fifteen years ago (that was one or two years after Mentzel's death) a young man, his son, came to me with it and asked me to buy it. At the

This text which is the first part of a 'General Record of Emperors and Kings' tells us that in the beginning there was Water, which divided to form the things. Then appeared three 'Ruling families', called the Celestial, the Terrestrial and the Human, each of them with nine to thirteen 'brothers', ruling for between 18,000 and 45,000 years. These were followed by the Fruit Ruler and the Fire Ruler, who taught the art of agriculture and that of cooking and smelting. Then came the three Huang – the August Emperors – Fu Xi, Nü Gua and Shen Nong, and finally five or six emperors who appear here only as names. The first and the third of the Huang are characterized as follows: Fu Xi, with his serpent body and human head taught music and invented the Eight Gua, and Shen Nong, an Ox's head on a human body wrote a book on medicine. Nothing is said in the text about the second Huang, but it was known already from Andreas Müller's translation of Al-Baidawi's *History of China* that Nü Gua was a woman.

This short text, which Mentzel had found in his Children's book and which Bayer worked so hard on, is a brief formulation of one among many Chinese stories about the earliest days of the world.[46]

Mentzel's translation had been short with a limited number of comments. Bayer follows him in most places, the exceptions being mostly disagreements about the 'theological' interpretation of certain words and phrases.

Bayer's comments comprise a 65-page treatise entitled 'Commentarii Originum Sinicarum'. The first two characters, meaning 'the oldest times', are discussed over six pages, and there are another six pages of commentaries to the four water-words, the whole text brimming over with remarks and

time, however, I was not at all interested in that kind of thing, and afterwards I do not know what happened to the book or to the young man' (*Lacroze Correspondence*, I, p. 26 and III, p. 34.) – In the Glasgow University Library – not among the Bayeriana – I found two nearly identical, badly printed Chinese primers that fit the description of Mentzel (Hunter books, p. 396, No. 21 and 23.) The titles are not *Xiao Er Lun*, but *Za Zi* and *Za Zi Daquan*, Miscellaneous Characters. However, one of them had the celestial map and the map of China showing the provinces, both contain the small pieces mentioned by Mentzel, including the stamp-size primitive pictures of people, animals, household utensils, etc. and both of them have the text that Mentzel, and later Bayer, printed about the 'earliest times of the world'. (Hunter books, p. 396, Nos. 21 and 23.) – See Knud Lundbæk: 'Dr. Mentzels kinesiske Børnebog', in *Danmark-Kina*, December, 1982. – Evelyn S. Rawski has recently called attention to these hitherto neglected books prepared for use by poor and middle-class people's children in her important study *Education and Popular Literacy in Ch'ing China*, Ann Arbor, 1979. They were known, however, already in the first part of the nineteenth century. In *The Chinese Repository* (1841), Vol. X, pp. 613-18, there is an anonymous description of a *Za Zi*. This book is not the same as any of the two books in the Glasgow University Library, but a very similar work.

46 Some years later the European reader was informed about these stories in great detail in *Le Chou-King, un des livres sacrés des chinois* . . ., traduit par le feu P. Gaubil . . . revu . . . par M. de Guignes (1770) The mythology is contained in the nearly 100 page long 'Discours préliminaire' by Joseph Prémare, S.J.

quotations from Al-Baidawi, Mendoza and Martini, as well as from Hesiod, Thales of Miletus, Anaximander, Anaxagoras, Ovid, Diogenes Laertius, Lactantius Firmanus, and from 'the divine Moses'. The most interesting parts of it contain his reflections about the historical events he believed were described in the humble Chinese text he had before him, and his 'etymological' speculations about two of its characters, the name Nü Gua.

Working with the *Xiao Er Lun* text, Bayer came to the conclusion that the story told in it about the earliest times of the world might well be a corruption of the true story contained in the Bible, in the first chapters of the Genesis.

This sort of speculation had been indulged in by many of the missionaries in China throughout the seventeenth century, e.g. by Martini whose works were well known to Bayer. The greatest problem was how to accommodate the traditional chronology of the Chinese with that of the Old Testament; it was easier done using the Septuagint with its much longer time intervals than on the basis of the Masoretic text. Martini had come to the conclusion that the Chinese civilization had existed before the Flood, but many other missionaries believed that the Chinese people must have originated from the Noah family. After the Flood one of Noah's sons, perhaps Ham, had migrated towards the East, carrying with him memories about the old Hebrew traditions. The old emperors and culture heroes of the Chinese historical works were regarded by many missionaries and also by European scholars including Athanasius Kircher as corrupted reminiscenses of Old Testament patriarchs.

Bayer came to his personal view by his reflections about the true meaning of the characters of this little text.

As to the four characters with the water radical at the beginning of the text, he looked up the right-hand part of them in a dictionary – probably the Diaz Vocabulary – and translated them as 'coming', 'flowing', 'pacific' and 'composite' water. He felt that they must have to do with the primordial Tohuwabohu, the 'emptiness and desolation' of the Genesis, not with the Flood as Mentzel had thought. As to the Celestial, the Terrestrial and the Human Rulers, all he could do was to remind his readers that God created first Heaven, then Earth and finally Man. His scoop was when he recognized what he thought was a compatibility between the story told in his Chinese children's book and that told in the Bible.

The Human Rulers were nine 'brothers'. The list of Huang and Emperors comprises nine, from Fu Xi to Huang Di (who is not in the Chinese text shown in Mentzel's book, but comes just after it). The name of the ninth of the emperors may be another name for Huang Di. However, with Nü Gua we arrive again at the figure nine. Now, in the Old Testament there are nine patriarchs from Adam to Noah. 'So we may well compare the Chinese series of the first Rulers with the first ones recorded in our Holy Scripture'.

When it came to identifying Noah more closely with Huang Di, Bayer showed that the traditional years of life of Huang Di – 2697 to 2599 B.C. – fall within the life span of Noah, as calculated by Bishop Ussher. It is true that Huang Di lived only 100 years, as against the 950 years of life of Noah, and that the time of the Flood – again according to Ussher – occurred 250 years after the death of Huang Di. However, such things need not disturb us, he says, we cannot expect precision in dating these remote events.[47]

And now to Bayer's 'etymological' speculations about the name Niu Kua (Nü Gua). He had read in the *Kurtze Chinesische Chronologia* about Mentzel's studies of this name. In the *Zi Hui* dictionary Mentzel had found and translated some entries according to which Nü Gua was a woman of ancient times. She was Fu Xi's sister and had invented many things. This interested Bayer, who did not have the *Zi Hui* at his disposal in St Petersburg and, anyhow, probably would not have been able to use it; but what interested him even more was Mentzel's remarks about the right part of the character for Kua (Gua). Bayer took the matter up in his own way. The sound of the word struck him and made him exclaim: 'Kua – that is exactly the same sound as the Hebrew word for Eve – Chaua!' Then he presents his analysis of the double word Niu Kua.

Niu is a very common word and means female, a virgin or a woman. But if we regard the two elements composing *Kua,* the next character, then, according to Mentzel, we can find the following explanation of the right hand part of it in the *Zi Hui* dictionary: '*Kua keu kuai po chim ye*'. Mentzel then says: '*Kua* means bite, as when one eats from a tree or the fruit of a tree, the tree to which this woman came by a secret path, which was neither just nor right'.

Here you see, here is the bite, here is the tree, here is the woman from whom our wickedness originated! In this place again I must say that I am very sorry that Mentzel did not include the characters from the *Zi Hui* dictionary, but I am rather sure I know what they are. There cannot be anything about a tree, and nothing at all about a woman coming by a secret path. Undoubtedly, *Kua keu kuai* were the characters for 'Kua', 'mouth' and 'bite'. *Po chim* must be 'not right', i.e. illicit, a sin. And *ye* seems to be just the final particle.

In other words, this is how we should understand this sentence: the right part of the character for Kua means bite of the mouth, but also sin. For it is composed of the following simple elements: *Nui (Nei),* inside, *Kium (Jiong),* vacuity, and *Keu (Kou),* mouth. Inside the hollow mouth . . . inside the mouth . . . what else is that but the bite? Therefore, Kua means the woman who bit and also the woman who sinned.

---

47 Bishop Ussher's chronology was widely accepted at the time, but Des Vignoles, in the book mentioned in Note 147 to the Preface, was to say that he knew about 200 different ones, placing the time of the creation of the world with differences of up to 3,000 years.

This is a good example of the ideas we have seen Bayer explaining about the nature, the *system,* of the Chinese characters. The right part of the character he has before him consists of nine strokes. It can be dissected, giving a two-, a three- and a four-stroke character, each of which means something. Together they give the meaning of that part of the character; together with the woman radical to the left it shows the complete and unquestionable meaning of the whole character: Eve.

However, apart from ideas about a *system* underlying the Chinese characters, such an analysis may seem ridiculous, especially coming from a person who knew as little Chinese as Bayer did. But etymological speculations based on the similarity of sounds – such as Kua and Chaua – were within an accepted philological tradition of his day. And there was a long tradition in the Cabalistic studies of the Renaissance for taking apart Hebrew words and letters, searching for the mystical secrets they were supposed to contain. Athanasius Kircher in the seventeenth century still thought and wrote within this framework.[48] But there is one strange thing about Bayer, sitting in St Petersburg in the 1720s, etymologizing Chinese characters in search of a Biblical name.

At that time, during the first part of the eighteenth century, there was a group of Jesuits in China, the so-called Figurists, who included just that technique among their proposals for a renewal and strenghtening of the missionary work among the Chinese. The Figurists, who had a profound knowledge of the Chinese language and of Chinese literature, were convinced that many Chinese characters did contain vestiges of Old Testament wisdom, and also pointed to persons and events in the New Testament. In all probability Bayer was unaware of this fact, and nearly everybody in Europe was, for the works of the Figurists were suppressed and hardly anything of it was allowed to be published. But that part of 'Chinese Figurism' had its root in European Hermetic-Cabalistic traditions, especially in the writings of Kircher, well known to Bayer.[49]

---

48 Frances A. Yates ranges Kircher among the *Retardataires after Causabon's explosion of the Hermes Trismegistus myth in 1614 (Giordano Bruno and the Hermetic Tradition,* London, 1964). – However, such speculations were aired far into the nineteenth century. Chevalier de Paravey argued in great length his 'discoveries' that certain Chinese culture heroes were identical with Biblical patriarchs, gravely confuting 'the hypothesis of the learned Bayer' (*Annales de philosophie chrétienne,* 1837, pp. 115-34).

49 The ideas of the Figurists became known in the nineteenth century when G. Pauthier published the 'Lettre inédite du P. Prémare sur le monothéisme des chinois' in *Annales de philosophie chrétienne,* III (5. serie). p. 128 ff., 1861. – Another Figurist work of Prémare's, the *Vestiges des principeaux dogmes chrétiens, tirés des anciens livres chinois . . .* was published by A. Bonnety and P. Perny in 1878. It contains a sympathetic *breve,* written for it by Pope Leo XIII. *Tempora mutantur!* – There are many modern works dealing with the Chinese Figurists, especially from the last years: Virgile Pinot: *La Chine et la formation de l'esprit philosophique en Françe* (1932) and his *Documents inédits* (1932). Paul A. Rule: K'ung-Tzu or

Finally there is one more point worthy of note. In composing this intricate text about the earliest days of the world according to the Chinese, Bayer wove into it his general opinion about the Jesuits who had been the 'first to bring the Gospel to China', and about the bitter Rites Controversy that raged at the time.

It seems that the Jesuits are right when they refer to the testimony of the oldest Chinese works, claiming that the old kings worshipped under the open sky and implored the help of *Tian*. But *Tian* is the name of God among the Chinese philosophers; this we know from many places in Al-Baidawi the Persian's *China History,* written 450 years ago . . . As this is also what the Jesuits affirm from their studies of the Historical works of the Chinese, how can it then be said that the old Chinese were atheists? . . . Today, of course, it is true that they are idolatrous and atheists, but that is another matter . . .

Bayer even enters into the heated discussion about the name to be used for God by the China missionaries.

Why are the Jesuits wrong when they use the Chinese word *Tian Zhu,* the Lord of Heaven, for God? The Dominicans do the same. There may be a Chinese idol called by that name, but the missionaries have only to define their use of the term. Is it not much better than to speak of 'Deus', as some missionaries do in Japan, introducing a rather strange syllable which has no meaning to the natives? I cannot see why it should be more dangerous to use the term *Tian Zhu,* or just *Tian* . . . I do not claim this to be a settled matter, but as long as the entire controversy has not been clarified, I do think we ought to leave out any prejudice and stop slandering these people and all their forefathers for their impiety . . .

Bayer concludes these reflections as follows:

But now I expect a tempest to arise . . . many serious persons will feel it to be absurd that a notion about the Creation should have prevailed among such depraved people, who do not know the name of God . . . some will reject the whole Chinese

---

Confucius? Thesis, Canberra University, 1972. David Mungello: *Leibniz and Confucianism – the Search for Accors.* (1977), and his article 'The reconciliation of Neo-Confucianism with Christianity in the writings of Joseph de Prémare, S.J.' in *Philosophy East and West,* 26, 1976, pp. 389-410. John W. Witek: *Controversial Ideas in China and in Europe: A Bibliography of Jean-François Foucquet, S.J. (1665-1741)* (1982). Claudia von Collani: *Die Figuristen in der Chinamission* (1981), 'Chinese Figurists in the Eyes of European Contemporaries', in *China Mission Studies (1550-1800) Bulletin,* IV, 1982, pp. 12-23, and *P. Joachim Bouvet S. J. – Sein Leben und sein Werke* (1985). – Together with Jean Alexis Gollet, the three Jesuits mentioned in these titles are the ones usually discussed as China Figurists, but there were more that were influenced by these ideas. The last letter from Koegler and Pereira to Bayer, of 1736, where they tell him that the first of the hexagrams does not mean 'material heaven' but Heaven, has a strong Figurist flavour (see p. 168).

chronology because they think it is at variance with the Old Testament . . . However, I know that I am not qualified to determine these matters . . .

Comparing these remarks with the author's comments upon the Jesuits in his *De Eclipsi Sinica,* it appears that he had carefully reconsidered the matter and had come to another conclusion. We shall see, however, in the chapter on his correspondence with the Peking Jesuits in the last years of his life, that he did not go all the way; he still had his doubts about it. On the other hand it is not difficult to imagine what happened when these lines were read by his old friend Lacroze in the Royal Library in Berlin. The concluding excuse about not being qualified to determine these matters may not have satisfied the fiery anti-Jesuit. At any rate Bayer never heard from him after that.

ADDENDUM ON TIME, WEIGHTS AND MEASURES

The last part of Volume II of the *Museum Sinicum* contains information about time words, measures and weight, taken as Bayer had said in the Preface, from Golius, Thomas Hyde and Noël. Here again he presents the characters and their pronunciation.

There is a short chapter on the time system of the Chinese – days, hours and minutes, also months, years, the 60 years cycle and the Great Year of 129,600 years. Then follow chapters on weights, including the weight 'in Chinese' of French and Spanish coins, and on measures, with detailed information about the difference between important units, such as the *Li,* approximately a third of a mile, and of *Mu,* about one-sixth of an acre, at various times of history in different provinces, and about smaller units as used by different professions – tailors, carpenters, etc. Bayer included this detailed information from Noël's *Observationes mathematicae* . . . (see p. 96) – 'because it is available to very few persons'.

At the very end of his book, Bayer explains how to read a small booklet about solar and lunar eclipses. He prints a part of Ferdinand Verbiest's Chinese-Latin report of a solar eclipse in 1669 (*Typus eclipsis solis anno 1669* . . . , Peking, 1669), containing information about the degree of the eclipse in various provinces, giving their names and characters. 'Thus, you can easily read these booklets – there are many of them in Europe, and I am sitting here with one describing a lunar eclipse in the year 1721.'

Fig. 9. The St Petersburg Academy of Sciences and the Kunstkammer.

Fig. 10. The Library of the St Petersburg Academy.

UT qualiscunque induſtriae noſtrae ſpecimina quae hoc tertio volumine comprehenduntur, ante quam in publicum prodirent, TIBI, AVGVSTA, offerremus, et ſi opusculorum prohibebat exilitas, incredibilis tuae erga collegium noſtrum benigni-

Fig. 11. Page 1 of the Dedication to Empress Anne, from the *Commentarii Academiae Scientiarum Imperialis Petropolitaneae*, Vol. III, 1732. Upper part: The Russian Empire – the double-headed eagle looks towards Western Europe and to the East. Lower part: Through the initial a view of the Academy and the Kunstkammer from the Admiralty side of the Neva.

Fig. 12. The origin of hte Chinese characters according to Martino Martini. From his *Sinicae Historia Decas prima*, 1658. Odd numbers 1-11 in the first column: 'original forms'; even numbers in the third column: 'modern forms'.

Die erste Tafel der Chinesischen Chronologiæ, von dem vermeinten Anfang der Welt mit ihren ersten fünff Käysern/ die so viel tausend Jahr sollen regieret haben.

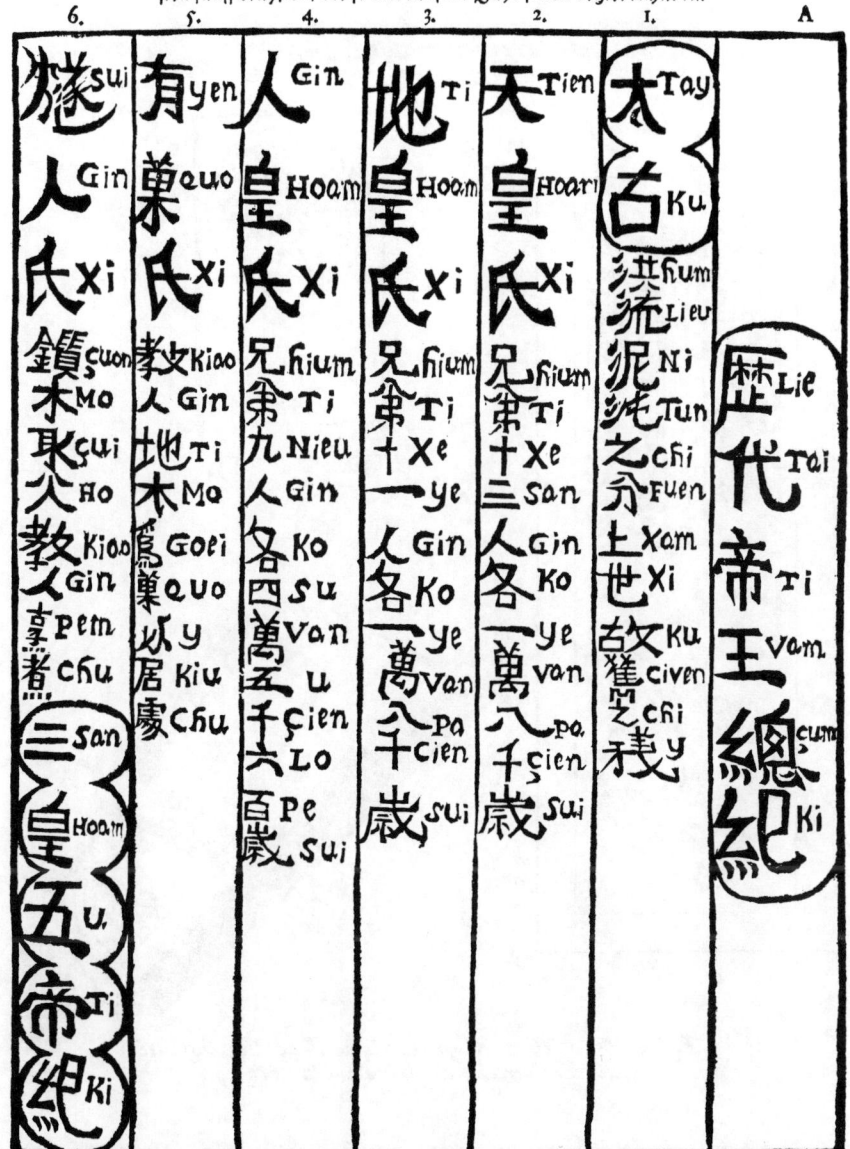

6.	5.	4.	3.	2.	1.	A
燧 Sui 人 Gin 氏 Xi 鑚 Cuon 木 Mo 取 Cui 火 Ho 教 Kiao 人 Gin 烹 Pem 者 Chu 三 San 皇 Hoam 五 U 帝 Ti 紀 Ki	有 Yen 巢 Quo 氏 Xi 教 Kiao 人 Gin 地 Ti 木 Mo 爲 Goei 巢 Quo 以 Y 居 Kiu 處 Chu	人 Gin 皇 Hoam 氏 Xi 兄 Hium 弟 Ti 九 Nieu 人 Gin 各 Ko 四 Su 萬 Van 五 U 千 Cien 六 Lo 百 Pe 歲 Sui	地 Ti 皇 Hoam 氏 Xi 兄 Hium 弟 Ti 十 Xe 一 Ye 人 Gin 各 Ko 一 Ye 萬 Van 八 Pa 千 Cien 歲 Sui	天 Tien 皇 Hoam 氏 Xi 兄 Hium 弟 Ti 十 Xe 三 San 人 Gin 各 Ko 一 Ye 萬 Van 八 Pa 千 Cien 歲 Sui	太 Tay 古 Ku 洪 Hum 流 Lieu 泥 Ni 沌 Tun 之 Chi 分 Fuen 上 Xam 世 Xi 故 Ku 略 Civen 之 Chi 矣 Y	歷 Lie 代 Tai 帝 Ti 王 Vam 總 Cum 紀 Ki

Fig. 13. Mentzel's *Xiao Er Lun*, the first of two plates. From Christian Mentzel: *Kurze Chinesische Chronologia*, 1696.

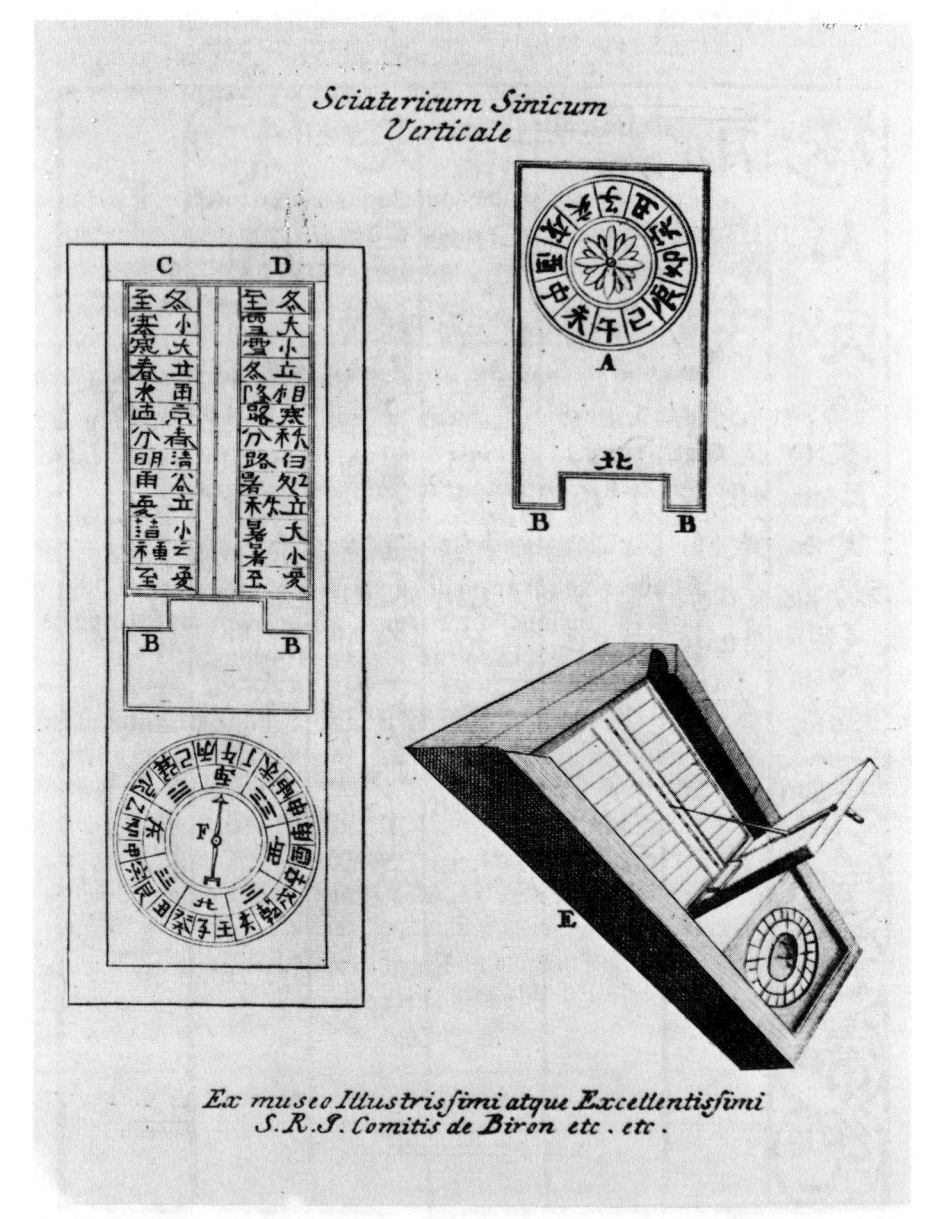

Fig. 14. Count Biron's Chinese sundial, from Bayer's *De Horis Sinicis*, 1735.

PART III
AFTER THE *MUSEUM SINICUM*

PRELIMINARY

In the Preface to the *Museum Sinicum*, and on many other pages within it we see Bayer writing with great modesty about his work, freely admitting its imperfections and weaknesses. That did not prevent him, of course, from being happy and feeling elated as the book materialized.

On 1 December 1730 he writes to his great friend Johann Mathias Gesner in Leipzig:

Museum Sinicum, two volumes, is being printed. I do not want to boast, but I can say that here I have written more about the Chinese language and Chinese literature than all those many people who have dealt with these problems during the last two hundred years. I hear you say: 'I salute you, Father of Sinology!' and I am pleased to hear it . . .

However, after a few more humorous phrases he breaks off: 'But enough and more than enough of such nonsense!'[1]

The title page of the *Museum Sinicum* gives 1730 as the year of publication, but actually it did not come off the press till the beginning of the next year.[2] Shortly afterwards things began to happen in rapid succession, entrenching Bayer for the rest of his life in the field of Chinese studies.

We have seen in the Preface to the *Museum Sinicum* that just as this book was about to appear Bayer was expecting two Chinese lexica, the *Zi Hui* and the *Hai Pian*, together with a Chinese-Latin dictionary, which were on their way from Moscow. The last-named work had been composed by the learned Dominique Parrenin, Jesuit missionary in Peking, and was a gift from him to Count Sawa Raguzinskij-Vladislavich, for whom he had acted as interpreter during the Kiakhta negotiations. On the Count's return to Russia Count Ostermann asked him to lend Parrenin's dictionary to Bayer to copy.[3] During the months of August and September Bayer copied the 562 quarto pages – it took him less than six weeks.[4] In September 1731 he sent his *Museum Sinicum*

---

1 Johann Mathias Gesner (1691-1761), German classisist and influential educationist. In 1732 he was head of the Thomas School in Leipzig, from 1734 Professor of Rhetorics and Poetry in Göttingen, founder of the famous Göttingen University Library. There are a number of high-spirited letters from Bayer to him in the *Sylloge*. The one quoted here is in Vol. I, p. 31.
2 Letter to the Danish historian Hans Gram, Copenhagen, dated 4 August 1731. Royal Library, Copenhagen.
3 It was probably in the same way that he obtained the two Chinese lexica. They came to him through Count Ostermann (Letter to J. Chr. Wolff, 31 July 1732. Wolff Correspondence Sup.Ep. 114). – For Sawa Raguzinskij-Vladislavich, see Note 15 to 'Bayer's Life'. In the correspondence he is always called only by his patronymic Vladislavich.
4 *Patris Dominici Parrenini, S.J. Lexicon Sinico-Latinum*, 4° (Hunter MS 224). – In spite of the title there is a considerable admixture of French and Spanish words and phrases. – On the fly-leaf there are the following lines: 'This was originally composed for Count Sawa Vladislavich,

with a letter to the Jesuit fathers in Peking. Two years later, he received letters from them. This was the beginning of a correspondence which was to last until Bayer's death. It gave him confidence that now he would be able to extend his knowledge of the Chinese language and encouraged him to work on in that difficult field. The learned Jesuits were just over there; caravans passed to and fro; he was not alone!

However, already in 1732, before hearing from the Peking Jesuits, Bayer had started on a great sinological project: the huge Chinese-Latin dictionary we are going to hear about in a later chapter.

On 5 October 1732 he wrote to Bishop Benzelius in Linköping:

Now I will tell you what I am working on: Chinese matters! When the *Museum Sinicum* came out I hardly thought that I should come to deal with these matters, except occasionally. Now for nearly one year I have been occupied with them. I have undertaken to write a Chinese dictionary, composed in a very accurate way and containing *all the words of the language* [My italics]. It was nearly against my will, but Count Ostermann asked me to do it and afterwards urged me and subsidized my work. People in Germany also pressed me to do so, e.g. Count Pada of Creutzenstein. I did not know him before, but he is not ignorant of Chinese. Would it not be a shame, he wrote, if I, a German, should let the French reap the laurels in that field? Thus urged on I bravely shouldered the enormous burden. Why not? The Greeks got into Troy by trying, everything is done by trying, as the old woman of Alexandria says in Theocritus's Bucolics . . .[5]

A few months before, on 29 June, he had written in a more humorous way to his friend Gesner: 'Good-bye Muses! My heart, deserting Greece and Rome, is set on the Barbarians!'[6]

And then Bayer met the Chinese! A large embassy from the Emperor of China – the second one after the conclusion of the treaty of Kiakhta – was in St Petersburg from 27 April to 9 July 1732.[7] In the letter to Benzelius men-

---

Ambassador Plenipotentiary from European Russia to the Court of Peking, by his most humble and devoted servant Parrenin, S.J. of the China mission'. Underneath we find: 'T.S. Bayer of Königsberg copied it from the original manuscript'. The first and the last pages carry the words 'Begun 17 August, old style, 1731', and 'Finished 23 September 1731, respectively. – The original is in the Vatican Library (Borgia Cinese 424). Antonio Montucci (see Note 15 to Chinese Language) sold that and several other manuscript dictionaries to that library in his old days. He had bought it from Julius Klaproth, the noted orientalist, who had obtained it from Count Jean Potoçki (1750-1815), Polish savant and voyager, the protector of Julius Klaproth, with whom he travelled on the unsuccessful embassy to China in 1805.

5 Benzelius Correspondence No. 298. – Leopold Maximilian Pada von Creutzenstein, Bohemian nobleman.
6 Sylloge, Vol. III, p. 29.
7 It was described in G.F. Müller's *Sammlung Russischer Geschichte*, I, pp. 34-74, St Petersburg, 1732. – The ambassador visited the Academy Press on 7 July and admired the machin-

tioned above he related an incident with the Chinese ambassador in St Petersburg:

> I was often in the company with them . . . they were sure I had been in China. We wrote Chinese characters, and with my pen I produced by far the most elegant ones. Then the ambassador challenged me on the Chinese brush. I was not completely beaten, although it was the first time I had seen and used a brush. At this they all exclaimed that no doubt I must have been in China . . .

The last part of the present book will deal with Bayer's sinological studies from 1731 till his death in 1738. Until then his sources of information about the Chinese language had been the tiny notes about it in Jesuit books printed in Europe and Mentzel's papers in the Royal Library of Berlin, including letters written by China Jesuits in the seventeenth century. Now he established personal contact with some of the most eminent Jesuit missionaries in Peking. They accepted him and helped him with their stimulating letters, the dictionaries he got from them, and the Chinese works they sent him. Bayer, pioneer sinologist in Europe, was a pupil of the Jesuit sinologists in China, indirectly at first, then through direct and friendly human contact.

He entered into sinology with a number of preconceived ideas about the nature of the Chinese language and especially about the Chinese writing system. At the very end he learned from his Jesuit friends in Peking that he was wrong. The tragedy of his professional life is that he did not have time to assimilate and digest this correction of his ideas and to proceed from there to new discoveries.

The following – before entering upon a discussion of Bayer's later works – is a presentation of the Peking correspondence with some excerpts and comments, but leaving the strictly linguistic parts of it to the chapter on his big Chinese-Latin dictionary. This presentation is far from complete and it is to be hoped that the entire correspondence, kept in the Hunter Collections of the Glasgow University Library, will be published together with the parts of his other letters – printed and unprinted – dealing with Chinese matters, including the ones kept in the Archive of the Academy of Sciences in Leningrad.

---

ery producing a fine xylograph of his name in Manchurian script. Müller included it, together with the name of the Yong Zheng emperor, his Bogdichanian Majesty, in Chinese, on an engraved plate.

7
CORRESPONDENCE WITH THE PEKING JESUITS

In the summer of the year 1731 Bayer was busily engaged in copying Parrenin's great Chinese-Latin dictionary, which he had borrowed from Count Sawa Raguzinskij-Vladislavich. In the midst of these exciting labours he wrote a letter to the Jesuit missionaries in Peking and sent it together with a copy of his *Museum Sinicum*.

Unfortunately this letter is not among the copies preserved in the Glasgow University Library. We know, however, from the answers he received that it was dated 12 September 1731, and that it was addressed to the Jesuits in Peking, without names, probably because Bayer did not know them. From the answers we can also guess some of the things Bayer had been writing to them about – his old problem about the Paschal Eclipse in the 'Chinese Annals', and the new one that had occupied him while writing the *Museum Sinicum*, the system of the Chinese characters. He had also asked for certain Chinese books, including one with the text of the Nestorian Stele.

In Peking it must have been decided that he should be answered by Antoine Gaubil and Dominique Parrenin of the French house, and by Ignatius Koegler, André Pereira, and Karl Slaviček of the Portuguese house. They wrote three letters to him late in the summer of 1732; Bayer received them one year later[8]

---

8 The Peking correspondence in the Glasgow University Library is marked A 1-9, 12-15, 17-18 (letter to Bayer) and B 1-14 (letters from Bayer). Bayer published parts of A 1, 3 and 7, and B 1 (his second letter) under the title 'T.S. Bayeri Commercium Sinicum' in the *Miscellanea Berolinensia*, Vol 5, pp. 185-92, 1737. – Parts of Gaubil's letters are to be found as Nos. 117-19, 144, 155, 175-6 and 182 in Renée Simon (Ed.): *Le P. Antoine Gaubil, S.J.: Correspondance de Peking, 1722-59*, Geneve, 1970. This collection also contains several letters to Delisle, one of which includes a complete list of the Peking Jesuits, those of the Portuguese as well as those of the French House. Bayer took a copy of it (Glasgow Bayeriana C 2).

Antoine Gaubil (1689-1759), French Jesuit missionary, in China 1722-59, erudite mathematician and astronomer. He wrote many works in French about the history of Chinese astronomy, and on the history of the Mongol dynasty, and translated several of the Chinese Classics, e.g. the *Book of History*, the *Book of Rites* and the *Book of Changes*, sending many of them to France to be published there. Some of his astronomical studies were published by Souciet in his *Observations mathematiques, astronomiques . . .* I-III (1729-32). His translation of the *Book of History (Le Chou-King)* was published in Paris after his death, in 1770. In Europe he was probably the best known among the China Jesuits, both for his published works and for his voluminous correspondence with many European scientists and men of letters. He was honorary member of the Imperial Academy of Sciences of St Petersburg.

Dominique Parrenin (1665-1741), French Jesuit missionary, active at the court in Peking from 1698 till his death, excellent linguist, equally well versed in Chinese and Manchu. During his 40 years in Peking he acted as interpreter for missionaries, ambassadors and merchants. Highly esteemed by the Kang Hsi as well as by the Yong Zheng emperor. Principal of the Imperial College of Interpreters in Peking. He baptized several members of the

Gaubil's first letter (A1) contains a few remarks about his *Museum Sinicum* – 'admired by all of us for the great labour it must have cost him, and for its usefulness'.

There are general comments on the Chinese time system and on the much discussed Paschal Eclipse in the 'Chinese Annals', with a necessary emendation of the text, etc. However, the main aim of Gaubil was to inform Bayer about the great number of useful works about China sent to Paris by the French Jesuits: Prémare's *Notitia Linguae Sinicae,* sent from Canton to Fourmont, de Mailla's huge China History, Gaubil's own works on Chinese astronomy, and his History of the Mongol dynasty. Parrenin and others, he says, are preparing a Latin-Chinese dictionary and Slaviček is working on something about Chinese music . . . if only people in France would have all these things printed . . .⁹

Parrenin tells him in his letter (A2) that he has studied the erudite Preface to the *Museum Sinicum* with great pleasure. As to the text itself, he has only had time to give it a cursory reading because he was kept busy with his many duties. He cannot, therefore, judge it properly. 'I can say, however, that I never expected a scholar outside China – however learned – to be able to write so much about the Chinese language, demonstrating such insight, such profound study and such diligence for public utility'.

He is pleased to hear that Bayer has obtained his Chinese-Latin dictionary and the two Chinese lexica, the *Hai Pian* and the *Zi Hui,* from Count Sawa Raguzinskij-Vladislavich and speaks about a Latin-Chinese dictionary he is preparing for the Imperial College of Interpreters in Peking, organized by the Emperor four years ago, and of which he is the principal. He sends him two things he has asked for – editions of the Five Classics and a picture of the

---

Sunu (Sourniama) family, Manchus of the imperial clan. See Auguste Demoment: 'Un savant missionaire: Le Père Dominique Parrenin', in *Mémoires de l'Académie des Sciences, Belles-lettres et Arts d Besançon,* Tome 175, 1962-3, pp. 225-43.

Ignatius Koegler (1680-1746), German Jesuit missionary, in Peking 1716-46 as President of the Tribunal of Mathematics. Published numerous works on mathematics and astronomy in Chinese, among them two large astronomical ones and a Celestial Map – the one he sent a copy of to Bayer.

André Pereira (Andrew Jackson) (1689 or 1690-1743). Portuguese Jesuit missionary of English descent, in China 1716-43. Vice-President of the Tribunal of Mathematics in Peking from 1727.

Karl Slaviček (1678-1735), Bohemian Jesuit missionary, in China 1716-35, most of the time at the court in Peking. Astronomer, musician and a fine Latinist. He is said to have been of a melancholy temperament.

9 Prémare had sent his *Notitia Lingua Sinicae* to Étienne Fourmont in 1728. It was not published till a century later, (Malacca, 1831). For a history of the manuscript and the editions see the long note in the *Bibliotheca Sinica,* col. 1664-9. – For Gaubil's works mentioned here see Pfister pp. 676-86. – Slaviček's works on Chinese music were never published, see Pfister p. 656.

mythological Qilin animal, explaining that it is represented differently by different artists. He includes a map of the world, made for the use of the Chinese by earlier missionaries, and some Chinese pictures to adorn his rooms.[10]

Bayer had asked if they were interested in the St Petersburg Academy *Commentarii* and Parrenin says that they would be happy to have them. They would put them in their library along with those of the Académie francaise. He ends his letter by enumerating, as did Gaubil, the many treatises and translations they have sent to Paris, adding that he has heard that de Mailla's History of China is being printed now.

The long letter from Koegler, Pereira and Slaviček (A3) must have worried Bayer. It too starts by praising his labours and ardour in the composition of the *Museum Sinicum,* but warns him that an understanding of the Chinese language cannot be obtained without a competent teacher. Bayer seems to have asked to be their pupil, but they reply that they cannot undertake that task. They refer him to Prémare's *Notitia Linguae Sinicae,* 'printed we hear, by order of the King, in Paris'.

As to the problem that vexed Bayer all his life, the system of the Chinese characters, he got no help. 'The construction and analysis of the Chinese characters, their meaning and harmony, the combinations and uses from which the laconism and the force of the language derive, are worthy of study, not only by the Chinese, but also by European scholars. However, it is like an ocean, it cannot be transmitted through the rivulets and channels of a correspondence . . .' They add that the syntax of the Chinese language cannot be learned from dictionaries and also that, unfortunately, the Chinese do not write the characters as they are printed.

With this letter they sent Bayer a little religious book by Father Verbiest, written in the popular style. This is the kind of book, they say, which newcomers to China study here, because it is clearly written and because it deals with Christian matters. To engage in unknown matters, among so many

---

10 The mythological Quilin or Lin animal, 'the mildest of animals', was supposed to appear when the world was ruled by an excellent prince. It is mentioned in one sentence: 'In the spring, hunters in the West captured a Lin' – just at the end of the *Spring and Autumn Annals,* thought to have been written by Confucius. The apocryphical 'Family Sayings of Confucius' describes the Sage weeping at the sight of the Quilin, sighing: 'Why has it come? Why has it come?'. There is a long story about it in Martino Martini's History of China which Bayer knew. It is about a certain Chinese philosopher, turned Christian, who interpreted the Quilin passage as a prophecy by Confucius, alluding to the Agnus Dei and the birth or the death of Christ (*Sinicae Historiae Decas Prima,* Liber IV, Kingu). – Bayer had mentioned the Quilin problem in a letter to Lacroze as early as 1716 (Lacroze Correspondence I, pp. 6-7 and III, p. 16), and in a letter to Gaubil in 1735 (see below) where he enumerated the articles or chapters of a forthcoming book, he included one of the Quilin. There is a draft of such a chapter among the Glasgow Bayeriana, a 50-page text entitled 'Historia Ecclesiarum Orientis'.

homonyms and without a teacher, is not only a waste of one's time but even dangerous. The Chinese themselves have difficulties; the (classical) works are never published without learned commentaries. They also included a little book about music, as he had asked them to do, a Chinese calender and a celestial map.

Two weeks after receiving these letters, in November, 1733, Bayer sent separate answers to Koegler, Parrenin, Pereira, Gaubil and Slaviček, all of them filled with gratitude and expressions of satisfaction. He was now in contact with the only Europeans who knew Chinese. He seems to do his best to keep their attention, flattering them with a description of a meeting in the Academy, admitting the weakness of his *Museum Sinicum* and insisting on his dire need for help, while at the same time exhibiting his historical and astronomical erudition and his acquaintance with many languages.

In the letter to Koegler, whom he addresses as President of the Astronomical Tribunal (B1), he relates how their letters were received solemnly at a meeting in the Academy, read and applauded by Count Ostermann and the new president, Baron Keyserling, and the other academicians. He adds some information about the state of the Academy, the munificence of Empress Anna, etc. Then follows a long discussion about the surprising similarity between the 19-year period discovered by the Greek astronomer Meton in the fourth century B.C. and a Chinese cycle described by François Noël in his *Observationes mathematicae . . .* printed in Prague in 1710.[11]

Bayer chose Pereira for his reply to the criticism – apparent and between the lines – in the collective letter from Koegler, Pereira and Slaviček (B2). Humbly he admits that the quality of the characters in the *Museum Sinicum* is very bad and that there are 'numerous errors on every page of it'. However, he consoles himself by pointing to his undaunted spirit and hard work; anyhow his *Museum Sinicum* has made it easier for other scholars to proceed further. Moreover, it took only a short time for the book to be nearly sold out, and now he is contemplating a much enlarged and ameliorated edition of it.

Referring to the little tract by Verbiest which they sent him for study, he diverges into the problems of missionary techniques. He quotes a sentence from Navarrete's *Tratados historicos . . .* , criticizing Ricci's accommodation methods. Bayer defends it with many examples from the history of the Christian church.

In the letter to Slaviček (B3) he speaks about the Nestorian Stele text, printed incorrectly in Kircher's *China . . . illustrata*. He would very much like to have a Chinese edition of it, 'for it deserves to be elucidated and defended'.

---

11 The 19-year cycle relates the integral numbers of the months and years, 19 solar years being very close to 235 lunar months.

Apparently he had already asked for that in his first letter and was disappointed by the reply from the three Jesuits: it is hard to find and anyhow it needs expounding.

The letter to Gaubil (B5) is very long and full of erudition. Referring to the many works Gaubil had told him had been sent to Paris, Bayer remarks that none of them have been printed except Souciet's work, the first volume of which he has found. Du Halde's book is being printed now, but Bayer is afraid he will not see it because of the war with France.[12]

He tells Gaubil about a certain handwritten Turkish genealogy, kept in St Petersburg. He has tried to translate it, but could not do it properly because of the many admixtures of Mongol expressions. However, in this work Bayer has read that the Indians spoke of China as 'Sin'. From there he proceeds to a long discussion about the name of China in Arabic, Persian, Turkish, Mongolian and even Tamil, with numerous quotations in these scripts.

This is followed, among many other learned divagations, by his speculations about a passage in Couplet's *Chronologia* (p. 39), where he has read about the western expedition of the famous Han dynasty general Ban Chao in the last decades of the first century A.D. Could this have been the Alanic expedition at the time of Vespasian, mentioned by Josephus? Could the Alanes have been a miswriting for Chinese? He even thinks he has numismatic support for such a hypothesis, a coin he has described in his book *Historia Osrhoëna et Edessena . . . ex numis illustrata . . .* , St Petersburg, 1734.

At the end of this letter he tells Gaubil that Minorelli's little anti-Jesuit book, which he has, was actually written by the famous Maigrot. 'If this is all that can be said against the Chinese rites and the Jesuits' name for God, then I cannot agree with him'. But Bayer adds, as he has done and as he will do again: 'The only thing that upsets me is the authority of Father Longobardi'.[13]

---

12 Jean Baptiste Du Halde (1674-1743): French Jesuit. He compiled the vast *Description géographique, historique, chronologique, politique de l'Empire de la Chine et de la Tartarie chinoise*, I-IV (1735), based on information he had obtained from the China Jesuits.

13 Niccolo Longobardi (Longobardo) (1565-1654), Italian Jesuit missionary, in China from 1597 till his death, the successor of Matteo Ricci as Superior of the China mission, 1610. He rejected Ricci's accommodation practice and initiated the famous Rites and Terms controversy, insisting that the ancient Chinese had been atheists. He expressed his opinions in a report composed about 1624, entitled 'Brevis relatio super controversias de Xangti aliisque nominibus et terminis sinicis . . . directa ad Patres residentiarum Chinae, ut ab eis videatur . . .'. (See Pasquale d'Elia (Ed.): *Fonti Ricciane* (1942-9), Vol. I p. 132.) – Navarrete published this text in his anti-Jesuit *Tratados historicos . . .* (1676) (see Note 31 to Preface). – In connection with the violent Sorbonne disputations about the Jesuits' methods of evangelization in China, this internal document was printed again in Paris in 1701 under the misleading title *Traité sur quelques points de la religion des chinois*. – Leibniz commented on this edition in his important 'Lettre sur la philosophie chinoise', printed in Kortholt's collection of Leibniz letters (see Note 4 to 'The Chinese Language'), Vol. II, 1735. See also Olivier Roy: *Leibniz et la Chine* (1972) and Knud Lundbæk: 'Notes sur l'image du Néo-Confucianisme dans la

There is another letter to Gaubil (B7), written three days later. Bayer had forgotten to tell him about Des Vignoles' and Kirch's papers in Volume IV of the *Miscellanea Berolinensia,* dealing with the Paschal Eclipse. Sending him a copy of these articles Bayer reminds him that he himself dealt with that problem in 1718, without giving the title of his Eclipse book, but summarizing his arguments against the identity of the solar eclipse in the 'Chinese Annals' and the 'darkness over Golgatha' in the year A.D. 33.

In his letter to Parrenin (B4) Bayer thanks him again for the Chinese-Latin dictionary: 'Without that I would have had to give up my Chinese studies'. Now, however, he has been living, so to speak, inside it, spending all his time and energy on producing one of his own. His presentation and discussion of the principles he is following in that work will be dealt with in the chapter on his big Chinese-Latin dictionary.

One year later, in November 1734, a caravan was getting ready to leave for Peking, and Bayer took the opportunity to write a new series of letters to the Peking Jesuits.

The letter to Gaubil (B7) contains an interesting passage from one which Souciet, in Paris, had recently sent him:

Nobody has worked harder on the Chinese language than Fourmont, and nobody has been more sumptuously endowed than he – the King has given him more than 30,000 livres – and yet those who have lived in China and learned the language there maintain that he is wasting his time. Outside China and without Chinese teachers it is simply impossible to learn to speak or read Chinese, even just a little bit. This is why they do not send us anything that could help us to understand the language.[14]

Strangely enough, at this point Bayer does not take the opportunity to ask for details about Prémare's *Notitia Linguae Sinicae.*

In this letter there is also a note about H.W. Gerdes, a London clergyman.

---

littérature européenne du 17e à la fin du 19e siècle', in *Actes du IIIe Colloque internationale de Sinologie* (1983), pp. 131-76. – Bayer knew about the text printed in Navarrete's book. He mentions Leibniz's 'Lettre sur la philosophie chinoise' in a footnote to his last work, the article on the *Spring and Autumn Annals,* but he does not comment on Leibniz's comments.

14 In 1734, was Souciet unaware of the fact that in 1730 Fourmont had received the manuscript of the *Notitia Linguae Sinicae* from Prémare, at that time in exile in Canton? Had Fourmont kept it secret? Koegler and his fellows in the Portuguese House in Peking knew that Prémare had sent it off and even believed, as mentioned above, that it had been printed in Paris. More important, however, is the fact that Prémare did *not* share the general opinion held by many Jesuits and expressed by Souciet in his letter. In 1733 he wrote angrily to Fourmont from his final exile in Macao: 'I never dreamed that you would be the only one to read it. I composed it for future missionaries and for all the European scholars who desire information, as you do, about Chinese antiquities'. (See Henri Cordier: 'Fragments d'une histoire des études chinoises au XVIIIe siècle, in *Centenaire de l'Ecole des Langues orientales vivantes 1795-1895* (1895), pp. 223-93).

Bayer is helping him with a new edition of Chamberlayne's multilingual *Lord's Prayer*. This Gerdes was the man who acquired Bayer's Chinese books and all his sinological manuscripts shortly after his death – only four years later.[15]

Bayer also tells Gaubil that he is sending him the *Acta Medicorum Berolinensum* where he will find something that might interest him: the biography of Christian Mentzel. Finally, it appears from this letter that Bayer has had a look at the *Spring and Autumn Annals* which was going to occupy him so much at the end of his life. For he asks Gaubil about the last words in it – the sentence about the Qilin animal.

In his letter to Koegler, Pereira and Slaviček, and in another written shortly afterwards to the first two of them (B8), he asks, among other things, for their comments on the 19-year cycle he wrote about in an earlier letter, and tells them about his problems with translating the text of the celestial map which he had received from them. He asks them to send him a 'Confucius' – probably meaning the *Four Books* – to compare with his copy of the *Confucius Sinarum Philosophus*. He also tells him that he is sending them Wolff's *Cosmographia generalis*.

In writing to Parrenin (B12) Bayer thanks him for various gifts that have just arrived in St Petersburg: Verbiest's map of the world, the Chinese pictures – a mandarin with his daughter and concubines, Bayer supposes – he is going to hang them on his wall. He also thanks him for the picture of the Qilin animal he had asked for in his first letter.

Bayer announces that the Imperial Academy has decided to send the Peking Jesuits a complete set of its publications. He himself is sending three volumes of the *Miscellanea Berolinensia* and copies of Wolff's *Psychologia* and his *Ontologia*. Once again he asks for a book with the text of the Nestorian Stele. And, perhaps with the intention of showing the Peking Jesuits that he might be able to do something with this text, Bayer had included in his former letter (B4) four pages of Chinese about the word *sheng* (holy), extracted from the *Zi Hui* dictionary, with his own transliteration and translations. It did impress his Peking correspondents, as we are going to see, but he did not get the Stele text, for reasons which will also become clear in the following.[16, 17]

15 For Gerdes, see Appendix. Apparently the book was never published.
16 Bayer wrote his *Zi Hui* extracts with a brush – for the first time, he says, since the few characters he wrote in the company of the Chinese ambassador in the Academy in 1732. (See p. 153). These characters are not elegant, but infinitely better than those of his printed works, all the way from the *Museum Sinicum* to the last articles in the *Commentarii*. This shows that he was right when he said, several times, e.g. in his final letter to the *Bibliothèque Germanique*, that the miserable appearance of his Chinese characters was due – at least to some extent – to the incompetence of his engravers.
17 For Wolff, see Note 12 to 'The Chinese Language'. The three works must have been his

Bayer's letter to Slaviček (B10) is a friendly and humorous one, telling him about a Tibetan 'idol' he possesses – actually a small part of a mandala – and of the opinion expressed about it by visiting Mongols and Japanese. He includes a poem in 'Indian', transliterated and translated, and says that he would like to meet him if and when he returns to Bohemia – then he could teach him to sing Chinese songs . . .[18]

In January 1735, very shortly after these letters had been dispatched from St Petersburg, Bayer received new letters from Peking. Now the matter was clinched – a serious correspondence had been established, based on mutual interests and erudite enthusiasm, and marked by respectful friendliness.

Gaubil thanks him for his long and learned letter (A4). He is obviously impressed by Bayer's vast oriental erudition, and pleased to read the exposition of the name of China in various languages. He compliments him for the 'stupendous progress he has made in Chinese'. He wants to help him with his studies of Chinese chronology and asks him which 'Chinese Annals' it is that he is using, quoting a number of the common ones.

As to Minorelli's book, Gaubil says that he did not know that it had been written by Maigrot – 'as you advance in your Chinese studies you will see that the Chinese knowledge of this bishop was far below what some people pretend it to be'.

Most of the letter is filled with astronomical discussions about planetary conjunctions in Chinese works and the misunderstandings of European astronomers. There is also a page about the so-called Paschal Eclipse – 'There are still some people who believe in Grelon's and Gabiani's postulates; therefore I have written extensively to Europe about it'.

Commenting in general upon Des Vignoles' and Kirch's astronomical papers, copies of which Bayer had sent him, Gaubil deplores the hostile way in which the first of these scholars speaks about the Jesuits, incited no doubt by their enemies. On the other hand he is pleased to hear what Kirch has written

Cosmologia generalis (1732), the *Psychologia empirica* (1731) or the *Psychologia rationalis* (1732), and the *Philosophia prima sive Ontologia* (1729), all of them printed in Frankfurt-on-Main. Surprisingly Bayer never mentions his sinophile *De Sapientia Sinensium Oratio*. He can hardly have been ignorant of it but he may not have seen it. The book was published again recently as *Christian Wolff: Oratio de Sinarum philosophia practica,* with an introduction and a German translation by Michael Albrecht, Hamburg 1985.

18 'Idolum Tanguticum, Sinicum, Mungalicum, Calmucicum, Japanicum ex Septem Palatu direptum . . .' (Hunter MS No. 246) is a fine bound manuscript, including a 23.5 by 18 cm. extremely well-preserved piece of a tanka or mandala showing a blue Lamaist deity sitting on a tiger skin, brandishing his sword. There is a Tibetan text on the back of it. It is stated that it is a gift from Baron de Rehbinder, perhaps Friherre Henrik Johan Rehbinder (1684-1746) who was prisoner of war in Tobolsk from 1709 to 1722 and who is said to have been an educated person. (See C.M.V Rehbinder: *Ätten Rehbinder genom åtta Sekler* (1925), p. 229) – The manuscript itself contains Bayer's interviews with visiting Kalmucks, Japanese and Indians to whom he had showed the picture.

about them and asks Bayer to let him know.

In another letter, written two days later (A5), Gaubil comments on the peoples that are said to have come from Scythia and Sarmatia. The Chinese historical works speak about such tribes originating from north of the Great Wall. 'Please inform me; I know how well versed you are in the history of all nations. I want to compare the notions of the Chinese with European ideas about the Scythians, Alanes, Burgundians, etc.'

The letter from Slaviček (A6), signing himself as 'Minimus e minima Societate' – an allusion to a word by Loyola – in his fine handwriting, is encouraging: 'Now you may be able to reap the fruits of your earlier labours'. As to Bayer's desire to produce a better translation of the Nestorian Stele text, however, Slaviček warns him again that this will be very difficult. It has been done and can be done again, but 'a really correct and exact translation is difficult if not impossible, such is the excellence of its ancient, inimitable, majestic and profound style'.

Most of the letter, however, is filled with melancholy reflections about his failing health, his disgust of 'the climate of this court and of this Empire'. He wishes to go home to Prague and would like to meet Bayer there, but he feels that his end is drawing near. Sick as he is – he died one year later – he takes the trouble to copy out in fine Chinese characters a whole page of comments about the character *sheng* (holy) from the *Pin Zi Jian* dictionary and the *Gang Jian Bu*, a *Supplement to the Chinese History*.[19]

The letter from Koegler and Pereira (A7) also discusses the Paschal Eclipse, stating that very few among the China Jesuits believe in that story, but some do. They take up Bayer's suggestion about the Metonic cycle and a similar one in Chinese literature: it may well derive from the West, but they know of no evidence for this. They are sending Bayer two works he had requested, Matteo Ricci's *Tianzhu Shiyi* (both volumes), the Chinese edition of Couplet's *Catalogus Patrum S.J.*, adding the *Shengjiao Xinzheng*, and the *Tianshen Huike*, an estimated catechism written by François Brancati.[20]

Parrenin's long letter, with enclosures (A8), is the most important as far as we are concerned in the present book, and it must have been the one that Bayer read with the greatest satisfaction. It was now clear that Parrenin had

---

19 *Pin Zi Jian*, a Qing dynasty dictionary arranged according to the finals (Courant No. 4650-52). – *Gang Jian Bu*, an addition to Zhu Xi's history work, the *Tongjian Gangmu*, written by Yuan Jing of the Yuan dynasty.

20 *Tianzhu Shiyi*, see Note 4 to '*De Eclipsi Sinica*'. – Bayer wrote on the cover of it 'This is the book that caused such quarrels between the Jesuits and the Dominicans' (Hunter Books, p. 396 No. 10). – Couplet's *Catalogue* had been mentioned by Bayer already in the Preface to the *Museum Sinicum* (see Note 138 to the Preface). The Chinese title means *Trustworthy Testimony about the Christian Religion*. – Brancati's cathecism was printed in Peking in 1661 and often reprinted. Pfister translates the title as *Leçons pour la congregation des Anges* and says that its style is very simple and easy to read (p. 229).

taken on the role of a teacher, as Bayer had hoped he would; there is one page in the letter which Bayer must have remembered all his life, a compliment not on his vast erudition in general, but on his Chinese, and on a concrete instance. Bayer had sent him four pages of Chinese text – 85 characters – and his translation of them: the entry on *sheng* (holy) in the *Zhi Hui* dictionary, asking him to correct it for him.

Parrenin wrote:

I am not surprised that you are proficient in European sciences and languages, for you have pursued these studies since you were a child. But who would have believed that when you entered the rugged paths of the forest of Chinese characters, deprived of any intercourse with Chinese people, and practically without help, you would have extricated yourself with such ease – future generations will wonder at it! That this is true is clear from your translation from the *Zui Hui* dictionary. I return your pages with some small emendations.

Parrenin included a parallel set of four pages on which he had a Chinese write the same characters, giving Bayer the opportunity to compare and to learn from observing the differences. The emendations, mostly comments, are indeed few.

Parrenin also included a copy of an eight-line Chinese poem, each half of which is written on scrolls beside a large picture of the Nativity. It is in seal characters, but Parrenin also supplies transcriptions in ordinary characters with transliterations, as well as the text written in 'running hand' and in grass script. He adds a few explanations to some of the difficult characters – 'This is all you need to make a fine translation of it with the help of dictionaries. You may send it to me on some occasion, if you want'. Also as teaching material he sends Bayer a poem written by a visiting literatus who had admired the books and scrolls in his studio. It is a *Dui Zi*, he explains, 'the kind of poems exchanged between bachelor literati. If you yourself are a bachelor, you may hang it on your wall'.[21]

In this letter Parrenin also tells Bayer comfortingly that very few Chinese literati know more than 3,000 characters; that is enough for reading and writing. However, he cannot help including four pages with obsolete characters, as preserved in the *Hai Pian* and the *Pian Hai* dictionaries, complete with pronunciation according to the *fan qie* technique and explanations![22]

Finally Parrenin comes back to the Latin-Chinese dictionary he mentioned

---

21 Parrenin translates the poem as follows: 'During the day I work in my room with my books and pictures / in the evening I sit at my window, conversing with the moon and the breeze'.
22 There are several kinds of Chinese dictionaries or encyclopedias called *Hai Pian* (see p. 198).
 – *Pian Hai*, a dictionary arranged according to initials and tones, was first composed during the Jin dynasty (1115-1234) and appeared in modified editions many times afterwards. Courant No. 4632-33.

in his last letter. He is now sending Bayer a copy of it made by Father Chalier, although he doubts that it will be of any use to him. There is also some exact information about the Chinese language, but that is better dealt with in the chapter on the big Chinese-Latin dictionary.

Parrenin ends this long, rich and friendly letter with the following words: 'I omit several things, these dog-days the heat in Peking is so intense that it seems as if the air were burning'.

Bayer responded to these letters immediately. On 11 January 1735, only a few days after he had received his letter, he wrote to Gaubil (B11). He thanks him profusely for the kind and erudite letter, telling him that the letters of the Peking Jesuits were applauded at a meeting in the Academy, and that the President ordered all the correspondence – their letters as well as his own – to be copied and inserted into the acts of the Academy.

Reflecting on Gaubil's words about the usefulness of his lucubrations about medieval travellers in China and on the name of China in his earlier letter, Bayer states that he has pursued this study and will send him two articles about it, including one about the Chinese in Tibet. Then follows a list of articles dealing with the Christian church in the Far East that he had began to work on at the age of twenty. There is one on the prophecies of Christ in ancient Chinese literature, such as the Qilin passage at the end of *Spring and Autumn Annals,* and the passage about the holy man in the West, noted already in the Preface to Ricci's *Tianzhu Shiyi,* one on the three Magi from the East, demonstrating that they come from a country north of India, one about St Thomas, defending him against Lacroze and Tollius, one on the Catholic faith in the Far East, one on the Nestorians, who suppressed it, one about the Nestorian Stele, defending it against Maigrot, one on Cathay being outside China, one about Prester John, showing that this name was a common one for a series of kings, one on the state of the Christian religion in Genghis Khan's time, one on Christian vestiges in the Tibetan religion, and finally one about the early history of the Jesuits in China, the religious books published by them there, and about the Rites Controversy.[23] Bayer says that he agrees with them in their accommodation policies, but with a caveat: Longobardi! He had said so before, but here he states the problem quite clearly:

---

23 The 'Holy man in the West' is not mentioned in Ricci's preface to his 'catechism' but in the preface written by one of his magistrate friends Feng Ying-jing (see d'Elia's *Fonti Ricciane* – Note 13 above), Vol. II, pp. 162-3 and 292-301). – St Thomas: Lacroze had written to Bayer in 1723 that the idea of St Thomas preaching the Gospel to the Indians was a ridiculous one, believed by the ignorant people on the Coromandel coast and spread by vicious Jesuits. Bayer had sent him an indignant reply to this postulate (Lacroze Correspondence, I, p. 49 and III, pp. 62-4.) – Tollius: probably Tollandus, i.e. John Toland (1670-1722), the controversial Irish author of *Christianity not Mysterious* (1696) and other works that gave great offence.

I must admit that when I examined (Longobardi's text in) Navarrete's book in Berlin some years ago, it disturbed me, and it will continue to disturb me until I read it again. This will enable me to see more clearly what is right and wrong; that is only fair.[24]

This tabulation of so many learned studies of Church history may have impressed Gaubil, who knew from his earlier letters about Bayer's erudition in Asian matters. Bayer, who had written vaguely to Lacroze about such a project in his young days, probably meant it seriously. However, he never got time to produce that ambitious work.

Bayer continues with a long discussion about the term *Da Qin* in the Nestorian Stele text – does it really mean the Roman Empire? Then come three whole pages complying with Gaubil's request about the history of the Scythians – Bayer refers Gaubil to his article in Volume IV of the St Petersburg *Commentarii* – as well as that of the Goths, the Swedes, the Masagetes, Alani . . . Huns and Hungarians . . . the Turks and the Germans . . . 'These are things I have reflected on very much, but not yet put on paper'.

This extraordinary letter is followed by a postscriptum full of quotations in Greek, Coptic and Sanskrit: Is the Indian unicorn the same as the Chinese Qilin animal? etc., etc.

Bayer answered Parrenin's long and interesting letter with an equally long and excited letter written a week after he wrote to Gaubil, on 16 January 1735 (B13).

'What shall I say? You overwhelm me with your generosity and affectionate kindness! I can hardly believe it . . .'

He thanks him – and Father Chalier – warmly for the beautiful dictionary; certainly it will be extremely useful to him. Not that he dreams of translating from Latin to Chinese, but it gives him so much insight into the language and he can insert many of its passages in his own dictionary. He also thanks Parrenin for his remarks about his *Zi Hui* exercise, 'as becomes a pupil to thank his excellent teacher'.[25]

About his own situation he says that he has had to stay away from Chinese studies for more than a year because of other duties. Now, however, he has ceded his chair in Greek and Roman Antiquities to another scholar and taken

---

24 In a letter dated 26 January 1717 Lacroze tells Bayer about a copy of Navarete's book, which he had received recently from Lisbon.
25 This handwritten dictionary is in the Glasgow University Library (Hunter MS No 392): *Petri Daneti Lexicon Latinum Sinice conversum in usum Gymnasii Pekinensis a R.P. Dominico Parrenino S.J. Missionario Pekinensi* (1734), 877 pages. It is beautifully written with transliterations, mostly in the French way. – Pierre Danet, died 1709, worked with other French scholars on editions *ad usum Delphini*, e.g. the Latin-French dictionary (1691). – Valentin Chalier (1697-1747), French Jesuit missionary, in China from 1728, working at the Imperial court.

on the chair of Oriental Antiquities, hoping thus to be able to work more steadily in this very important field.[26]

Referring – without directly mentioning it – to Parrenin's question about his marital state, he informs him that he is happily married and has four daughters. 'If I had been a bachelor, I would have come over to you, if possible'. In this connection he says that he cannot look forward to a successor in his new chair. Apparently he had tried to persuade some young persons to follow in his footsteps, but they had run away, much to his regret. 'I myself shall never desert this field of study, I am deeply convinced of its utility both for history and for our own lives'.[27]

Most of the letter deals with his burning problem of getting to grips with the system of the Chinese characters. Now, confronted with the page of seal characters and their normal style equivalents which Parrenin had sent him, he feels that his favourite idea of Chinese as a *philosophical language* is threatening to collapse. This part of the letter will be discussed in the chapter on his big dictionary.

Six months later in a short letter dated 12 May 1736 (B14) – it was to be his last letter to his Peking friends – he tells Parrenin he is sending his *De Horis Sinicis* (1735); it is for Parrenin, Koegler and Gaubil.

'You will tell me where I have erred, where I did not explain myself properly, putting me on the right track'.

He has received the collection of Chinese coins which Parrenin sent to Count Ostermann, and which he has asked Bayer to explain. He is sending Parrenin some of his comments; the rest will follow: 'I am the pupil; you are the teacher'. He also says that he has written an article about these coins and sent it to the *Miscellanea Berolinensia*, adding that the Berlin Academy has asked him to submit other studies related to China.[28] 'Therefore I am working on an article about Couplet's *Catalogus Patrum S.J.* . . . – I wish you could send me a supplement bringing the record up to the present. I am noting carefully the Chinese names of your predecessors as well as the Chinese titles of their works'.

He has received Verbiest's map of the world and translated the texts on it. He includes a small part of his translation – the insert about Judea, the Holy Land. Here, however, as bad luck would have it, he has misread one Chinese character for another very similar one. Parrenin corrected it in a letter written

---

26 Another scholar: J.G. Lotter, see p. 20.
27 In a late letter to Johannes Christoph Wolff, dated 5 May 1737, Bayer wrote that he had tried in vain to stimulate scholars in London and Berlin to take up the study of Chinese – that is why he cherishes Count Pada of Creutzenstein who is very interested in such studies. (Wolff Correspondence, Sup.Ep. 122.)
28 P.S. Bayer (sic): 'De Re numaria sinorum', in *Miscellanea Berolinensia*, Vol. V, 1737, pp. 175-84.

in December 1736. Bayer received it on 17 June 1737, but did not get time to change the translation, as is clear from the Verbiest article in the *Miscellanea Berolinensia,* where it was printed in 1740 – two years after Bayer's death.[29]

It took nearly two years before Bayer's many letters – the four he wrote in January 1735 and the last one, written in May 1736 – arrived in Peking. The Jesuits answered him with three letters written 27-29 December 1736. They came by special courier and Bayer received them on 28 June in the next year.

Parrenin wrote to him, on 29 December 1736 (A14) that he had received his letters, including the last one. Most of them come, he says, with Lorenz Lange's caravan via Siberia (as was the case with most of the earlier ones). Parrenin begins his letter with glimpses of the present situation in Peking. On earlier occasions Lange had prudently avoided visiting the Jesuits there and letters had been handed over by intermediaries. Now he had been received by the Emperor, who had given him presents and issued the permit for a permanent Russian travelling station in Peking. With his new status he can now visit them and in fact they are expecting him at any moment. Parrenin continues for a whole page in an informal and friendly vein with remarks about the various ways of sending letters from Peking to St Petersburg. Only on the last page does he come to Bayer's problem: 'I shall answer two of your questions so that this letter will not be completely useless to you'.

First he comments on the translation of the little phrase about Judea on Verbiest's map of the world, which Bayer had sent him, correcting his 'little error'. Then he gives a precise explanation of how the first and the last years of the reign of an emperor are indicated, also reminding him that the emperors' 'names' are not personal names. He ends with a sentence in French adding: 'I suppose you know French, that language which is current among scholars because so very many books are printed in it'. Earlier in his letter he had acknowledged receipt of Bayer's *De Horis Sinicis,* his description of the coins in Count Ostermann's collection, and the translation from the Turkish genealogy, but he does not comment on them.

All in all this was a disappointing letter for Bayer to read, after the last exuberant one and Bayer must have blushed at his 'little error', a howler he could have avoided by looking up the character in his own dictionary in the *Museum Sinicum* (V, 173)!

The short letter from Koegler and Pereira (A17) is friendly and complimentary, the heading of it including a greeting in Chinese. They thank him for sending his *De Horis Sinicis,* making an important comment on it. Bayer had translated *qian,* the name of the first trigram in the *Book of Changes,* the *Yi Jing,* as 'material heaven' (*coelum materiale*). To this they respond as follows:

---

[29] 'De Ferdinandi Verbistii S.J. scriptis, præcipue vero de ejus Globo Terestri Sinoco', in *Miscellanea Berolinensia,* Vol. VI, 1740, pp. 180-92.

You should not restrict the meaning of *qian* to the material heaven, it means Heaven in a general sense (*coelum absolute denotat*). The present Emperor has given his reign the (symbolic) title of Qian Long which may be translated as 'Support of Heaven' (*coeli adjutorium*).

Together with this letter Koegler and Pareira sent Bayer two books of *Yi Jing* commentaries with the traditional figures, composed by a certain Te P'ei (De pei) of the imperial family, a Christian, having been baptized by Father Koegler.[30] This must have made quite an impression on Bayer who already possessed a *Yi Jing* edition with the figures of the Lo and Ho Maps and the two arrangements of the 64 hexagrams. We shall return to that matter in the chapter on the *De Horis Sinicis*.

Koegler and Pereira told Bayer that Slaviček had died in the previous August. Referring to Bayer's last letter to him with the copy of the Indian song, to his humorous remarks about singing Chinese songs together when they met in Bohemia – but probably also to Bayer's note in the Preface to his *Museum Sinicum,* on John Webb's book about Chinese as the primordial language, they write:

Our pious hope is that he is now in the country of the Blessed, singing Chinese and Indian songs, accompanied by celestial harmonies. He invites us sweetly, both us and you who offered to visit him in Bohemia, to join him where he is now . . . And what if the primordial language in Paradise was Chinese – as some have thought and as it is permissible to conjecture – is it then not possible to imagine that the Blessed Ones converse with each other in that language? How will you rejoice, dear Sir, if you shall find that the language which you are studying so assiduously now is the principal language in Heaven?

The two short letters from Gaubil that came to St Petersburg at the same time (A15) had no poetry in them. They deal mostly with astronomical problems, and here the writer mentions the *De Horis Sinicis,* complimenting Bayer on his progress in this kind of sinological studies. He also remarks that he has heard that Du Halde's *Description geographique . . . de l'Empire de la Chine* (1735) has arrived in Canton. In his last letter, as we shall see, Parrenin was to mention this work in connection with Bayer's studies.

In May 1737 the Peking Jesuits were packing boxes with books for Bayer and for the Imperial Academy. The two accompanying letters, dated 16 and

---

30 The title of the book – one book in two volumes – is *Yi Tu Jie,* Explication of the Yi Jing figures, by De Pei (1688-1752). There are two prefaces, by Li Fu (1675-1750) and by Gan Rulai (1684-1739) both dated 1736. All three are mentioned in A.W. Hummel: *Eminent Chinese of the Ch'ing Period* (1943), on pp. 714, 455-7 and 456, respectively. They strongly recommend the use of the traditional Ho Map and the Lo Figure in the study of the *Book of Changes,* the *Yi Jing.* (Hunter Books, p. 396, No. 44).

17 May, are the last ones in the Glasgow collection and they may well have been the last ones to have been written for Bayer by the Jesuits in Peking.

Bayer received these letters on 31 January, 1738. He did not get time to reply to them, but he wrote a piece based on one of them, the *Explicatio Sigilli* presently to be discussed.

This time the letter from Koegler and Pereira (A17) was somewhat official in tone and quite precise. They thanked him for his interesting and extremely erudite articles in the *Commentarii,* especially that on the Scythians, as well as for Wolff's *Cosmologia* and for the two volumes of the *Acta medica Berolinensis.* They included a list of Chinese books they were sending to him, religious tracts, but also the *Kang Xi Zidian* – Bayer probably saw this dictionary now for the first time in his life – and a number of unspecified books, Chinese Quolibets, they call them.[31] There is nearly a whole page with explanations of the system of Chinese personal names and titles, and answers to questions about the celestial map. They try to explain to Bayer why the entry on Ruggieri and Ricci in Couplet's *Chronologia* looks odd, and enter upon a small learned discussion with him about an eclipse predicted by Thales in 601 B.C. and apparently equivalent indications in the 'Chinese Annals'.

Parrenin's letter (A18) is informal and personal, as usual. Here, as in his early letters, he excuses himself and regrets that his days are filled with the affairs of the mission and his work at court as Chinese-Manchu-Latin interpreter.

He sent Bayer two religious tracts, a book on the four Chinese scripts, a new calender, and 'the first part of the *Lun Yu* or *Confucian Analects* in Latin translation – I do not have the second part'. He explains the different kinds of Chinese script, once again, and discusses briefly how to write Chinese and Manchu proper names in Latin. There is a short section on Du Halde's great work – 'When we get it here I may have more to tell you' – and a long one on the system of Chinese characters, intending finally to extricate Bayer from his fantasies about a philosophical language. We shall come back to that later.

Parrenin ends his letter, praying that God may protect Bayer and his beloved family and lead them on the right path to eternal life.

Finally about the *Explicatio Sigilli,* the explication of the Dalai Lama's seal.

There is one small section of Parrenin's last letter that cannot be understood, except for a piece called *Explicatio Sigilli,* which is also kept among the Bayeriana in Glasgow together with the seal itself. It was written a week after Bayer had read Parrenin's letter.[32]

Four years before, Count Ostermann had sent Bayer a diploma with the Dalai Lama's big red square seal, for translation. Bayer had copied it, but was

---

31 The Kang Xi dictionary, see Note 36.
32 Glasgow University Library, Bayer MS A. 26.

unable to read its Chinese, Mongolian and Tibetan text. He must have sent a copy of the Chinese part of it to Parrenin, for in his last letter this missionary had included a transcription of the Chinese seal characters into ordinary Chinese and had added a translation of a few difficult expressions. 'With the help of these', he wrote, 'you can easily translate the whole text'.

The *Explicatio Sigilli* is a four-page manuscript, apparently a draft of a letter from Bayer to Count Ostermann, his high protector:

I wished to satisfy my benefactor and therefore I sent a copy of the Chinese text of the seal to Father Parrenin in Peking. In his letter of 17 May, 1737 he sent me the Chinese text in the usual characters, with some comments, and suggested that I should translate it – I am his pupil. So I did, as well as I could, and here it is.

Then follows the text, but only in transliteration, with the Latin translations, noting carefully the two expressions he had from his teacher, and one that he cannot read.

The last lines of the draft letter read as follows:

My errors, whatever they are, may be due to the medicine. St Petersburg, 7 February 1738. T. S. B.

8

DE HORIS SINICIS

In 1735 Bayer published his third book about Chinese matters, the *De Horis Sinicis et Cyclo Horario Commentationes* . . ., a small but grand book, printed by the St Petersburg Academy Press. It is a remarkable and complicated text which must have cost him much labour. It demonstrated how far he had progressed in his knowledge of the Chinese language and of Chinese matters in general, and it is especially interesting for the light it throws on his acquaintance with the *Book of Changes,* the *Yi Jing,* and with *Yi Jing* lore.

There is a long dedication to Count Biron, one of his Russian patrons, and the book itself is in the form of a letter to the old Berlin scholar Adolphe Des Vignoles, calling him the 'Chief Chronologist of the Century'.

Bayer starts with excusing himself for not having quoted Des Vignoles as he ought to have done in his *Museum Sinicum,* but he did not know a certain article of his, printed in the *Bibliothèque Germanique* in 1722. These petty questions of priority need not detain us here. He repeats his earlier discussion about the hours and days of the Chinese. As to the months, he insists that what he wrote in the *Museum Sinicum* is in accordance with the information he has now found in the *Hai Pian* dictionary: months *can* be written simply with the duodecimal system characters. It is true, however, that in the calendars they are denoted differently.

A large part of the text deals with a Chinese sundial that belonged to Count Biron.[33] It is shown in a fine engraving and described in great detail, starting with the twelve characters for the (double) hours on the movable slab carrying the sundial itself. The instrument was equipped with a magnetic compass, surrounded by two rings of symbols. Bayer explains the eight symbols of the inner ring, and also the complicated system of the 24 characters of the outer ring. As to the double characters of the horizontal plate, the 24 fortnightly periods, he refers to his discussion of them in his *Museum Sinicum.* It is not clear whether he has understood the idea of the *movable* sundial that can be adjusted to the latitude of the observer.[34]

In explaining these intricate matters, Bayer refers to the *Book of Changes,* the *Yi Jing.* Speaking about the inner ring of the compass, he says that four of its eight symbols are the Chinese characters for North, South, East and West, and then he goes on as follows:

---

33 Ernst Johann Biron (1690-1772), Count of Courland, Grand Chamberlain and great favourite of Empress Anne.
34 It is quite similar to the portable sundial shown in Joseph Needham: *Science and Civilisation in China,* Vol. III (1959), fig. 134, and discussed on pp. 310 and 405.

The four other sections show four of the *Ba Gua,* the eight trigrams. The Chinese believe they were invented by Fu Xi, the first man, who copied them from the back of a dragon . . . These trigrams are combined, two by two, to form the 64 hexagrams *according to the Art of Combination* (my italics). They are shown and explained in the *Yi Jing.* Each of the trigrams has a special name. I show them here in the following list, taken from the *Yi Jing.*

The list gives the trigrams with their names in Chinese characters, the transliterations and the translations, from the first one consisting of three whole lines, the *Qian,* which Bayer translated as 'material heaven', to the last one, consisting of three broken lines, the *Kun,* meaning 'earth'.

This system is called the *Tai Ji,* the Great Circle or the Great Pole, but the same name is applied to the whole of the system of the 64 hexagrams. There is much more to say about this system, which I have decided to omit here, except for one thing: these eight trigrams are usually shown in an octagonal ring, each of them referring to one of the eight corners of the world. In the *Yi Jing* this figure is called the *Ba Gua Fangwei,* the eight corners of the world. Similarly the 64 hexagrams, disposed in a perfect circle, is called *Liu shi si Gua Fangwei,* the 64 corners of the world. However, Fu Xi arranged the trigrams in a different way from that used by King Wen. I shall not say more about that . . .

Bayer does not state clearly where he got all this from, but probably he took most of it from a *Yi Jing* edition called *Kui Bi Yi Jing,* which he had obtained from somewhere, and on the cover of which he had written 'Ye Kim, Liber prima/secunda'. This book contains all the traditional *Yi Jing* figures, including the two different arrangements of the trigrams and the hexagrams. Bayer refers in a footnote to 'Ye Kim, 1.c. p. 3 and p. 6', but elsewhere he does not mention this book, either in his works or in his correspondence with the Peking Jesuits.[35] However, as we have seen in the chapter on this correspondence, Koegler and Pereira on obtaining a copy of his *De Horis Sinicis* took the opportunity of sending him a small book with *Yi Jing* commentaries which also contained these figures, correcting his translation of the *Qian* trigram. (See p. 168).

35 Glasgow University Library. Hunter Books, p. 396, No. 38. – Fangwei means localization or direction. The sequence of trigrams shown here are in accordance with the 'Prior to Heaven' or 'Fu Xi' arrangement, invented by the great Song philosopher Shao Yong and presented in his *Supreme Principle Governing the World.* The square and circular hexagram figure which Leibniz received from Bouvet was also arranged according to Shao Yong's system (see p. 83). This is the one that *can* be read as a binary system. The King Wen arrangement is the one shown in the *Confucius Sinarum Philosophus* and that which is found in the usual editions of the *Book of Changes* (the *Zhou Jing).* It contains no system, or at most tiny bits of a system, such as successive mirror presentations of the hexagrams. Both are shown and discussed in Legge's *The I Ching – the Book of Changes,* London, 1899. Kui and Bi: two constellations traditionally preseding over literature .

One wonders what he meant by speaking about the 64 hexagrams arranged *according to the Ars Combinatoria*. He does not say if this applies to the Fu Xi arrangement, which is, indeed, composed according to a combinatory system, or to the King Wen arrangement – the one we know from the many modern editions of the *Book of Changes* – which is not. Also, did it occur to him that Leibniz, the idol of his younger days, got his idea about the identity of his binary arithmetics and the hexagrams from the Fu Xi arrangement of them? He does not say so.

The last part of the book is an appendix containing the Chinese calendars for the years 1723 to 1734, which he had received with a letter from the three Peking Jesuits – Koegler, Pereira and Slaviček, written in 1732. At the end of the book he refers to some remarks about intercalated months in his *Museum Sinicum,* saying that now he is able to explain it more clearly. 'Let me quote *verbatim* what I have been told by . . .', followed by the names of the above-mentioned three Fathers.

The problem of Central Asian peoples using zodiac symbols similar to those of the Chinese, discussed in the *Museum Sinicum,* is enlarged upon and Bayer includes fine tables showing the duodecimal term system in Mongolian, 'Kalmuck', Manchu, Tibetan – and Persian script.

The initial 'Q' on page 1 contains a miniature picture of two Chinese, and under the text of the last page there is a vignette showing two Chinese children riding on some mythological animal, a kind of *chinoiserie* that Bayer usually did not indulge in. He may have felt that they were appropriate in a book dedicated to Count Biron.

9
ARTICLES IN THE *COMMENTARII* OF THE ST PETERSBURG ACADEMY

'ON THE ZI HUI DICTIONARY'

Volume IV of the *Comentarii Academiae Scientiarum Imperialis Petropolitanae,* printed in 1739, but containing works presented in 1733, includes a 25-page article by Bayer entitled 'De Lexico Çu gvey' *(Zi Hui)*. Its presentation in the Academy is not mentioned in G. F. Müller's *Materiali* and perhaps it was never formally presented. At any rate, the article cannot have been finished before 10 January 1735, for it contains information which Bayer received on that day from Father Parrenin in Peking, and Bayer says so himself.[36]

The article is carelessly printed with several typographical errors; it is clear that Bayer did not see it go to press before he died. There are also errors of his own that he would have corrected if he had had time to see the galley proofs – characters which are upside down, one common character read correctly on one page, incorrectly on another, etc. All the same, this paper must be regarded as an important contribution to budding sinology and it must have been useful to eighteenth century scholars starting out in this field. The China trade was growing and it was not too difficult to obtain a copy of this standard dictionary from Canton. Bayer's article would have been helpful in the first attempts to come to grips with the *Zi Hui,* or with the similar but larger *Zheng Zi Tong* dictionary.

It contains a detailed exposition of the arrangement and the contents of this dictionary, illustrated with numerous examples in Chinese characters. And now, for the first time, the characters were not shown on separate engraved plates, but included in the text, and the transliterated syllables carry their appropriate tone marks.

Bayer says that he has seen three copies of the *Zi Hui* dictionary – one of them is his own; he gives no indication of the whereabouts of the other two. He states the year of publication of one of these two – 1724 – but tells us that they are practically identical, page for page; only the prefaces are different.[37]

---

36 The *Zi Hui* dictionary was composed by Mei Yingzuo of the Ming dynasty and first published in 1615. He dismissed the old Shuo Wen systems, based on 540 Seal character radicals, and produced a 214-radical dictionary of the regular style characters, which became very popular. The *Zheng Zi Tong* was a greatly enlarged version of it. The next to follow was the *Kang Xi* dictionary (*Kang Xi Zidian*), an expurgated and ameliorated *Zheng Zi Tong,* with a preface by the Emperor. This 214-radical dictionary became the standard work for the net 200 years. – The history of the Chinese dictionaries is presented in a recent work entitled *Zhong-wen Zidian Shi Lüe* by Liu Yequi, Peking 1983.

37 The *Zi Hui* in the Glasgow University Library (Hunter Books, p. 396, No. 66), with a few

They are printed in 14 'codicillae', i.e. *juan*. The first of these volumes has the preface, an index, and various small pieces, part of the last one deals with phonetics. Thus the dictionary itself comprises *juan* number two to thirteen.[38]

Bayer gives a precise description of the first *juan*. After the Preface comes the *Mulu* or Index, a list of radicals. The radicals follow each other in 17 sections which he calls 'classes', but these simply comprise the radicals written with one stroke, followed by those written with two strokes, etc. up to the 17 stroke radicals. The number of radicals is 214 and the characters classified under each of these are given; *Zi Hui* dictionary contains 38,095 characters.

As for the 214 radicals there is an interesting footnote that may have been added at the last minute. Bayer says that he took it from one of Leibniz's letters to Lacroze, printed in the *Epistola ad diversos* . . ., Vol. I, 1734. Here Leibniz wrote that a certain Augustinian missionary, by name Cima, had informed him that 'the fundamental characters are supposed to be about 400, the rest being combinations of these'. But Bayer only writes, 'In reality there are more radicals than in this dictionary'. It was grist to his mill, but he did not enlarge upon it here.[39a]

The five following small sections of the first volume of the dictionary are described and the number of pages in each of them is indicated. The first one, the *Yun Bi*, or the movement of the brush, teaches the order in which the individual strokes of a number of characters have to be made. The next section is called *Cong Gu*. Bayer translates it as 'simple old characters', but his examples and the way he explains them show that he understood it to be a list of ordinary or 'vulgar' forms of certain characters. Then follow two sections with old obsolete characters and their modern equivalents. There is one example for each of these sections, with characters, transliterations and translations.

The next section is called *Jian Zi*. Here one finds the different shapes of the radicals when they occur alone or at various places in the composed characters. Bayer emphasizes – as he did in his *Museum Sinicum* – the importance of knowing these variant forms, presenting no less than 39 examples with explanations, e.g. '*Ren:* Man, second form in composites and always to the left'. Finally there is a list of the characters arranged in 32 'classes', but as with the radicals, these simply comprise all the characters according to the number of

words from Bayer's hand on the cover, is the 1724 edition mentioned, not the one he says he owns himself.
38 Among the twelve editions of the *Zi Hui* dictionary in the Bibliothèque nationale in Paris there is one – Courant No. 4446-47 – that has the phonetic section in the last juan. In the other ones, as in the copy in the Royal Library of Copenhagen, this is found in juan two.
39a The letter to Lacroze is dated 8 October 1707. It is to be found on pp. 377-8 of the first volume of the Kortholt collection of Leibniz's letters. Oddly enough, Bayer does not mention here that he had seen the same statement about 400 radicals in one of Couplet's letters to Mentzel which he copied in Berlin (see p. 121).

strokes, from one to 32. He notes that the individual characters are marked here as being radicals, or are referred to as specified radicals. This is a very useful table, he says, for often the assignment of a character to a certain radical is difficult to decide.

Bayer then proceeds to describe the dictionary itself. All the characters are arranged under their radicals. First there is the radical itself with its explanation. Then come the composed characters assigned to this radical, in groups according to the number of extra strokes. This number is shown in white inside a black circle. Unfortunately, however, characters with more than 15 extra strokes are jumbled together at the end. Even more inconvenient is the fact that characters in which the radical occurs to the right or left, at the top or below, or even in the midst of other elements, are mixed together without any order. This makes it very tiring to use the dictionary. 'The Chinese do not bother about that matter, but in the dictionary that I am composing this defect will be corrected. I arrange them according to the place of the radical in the composite characters, in sub-groups, which I call sections'. These brave phrases are followed by one clear example of the difficulty in deciding under which radical 'it has pleased the Chinese to enter a certain character.'[39b]

Bayer then explains the Chinese way of indicating the pronunciation of words by the 'cut apart method' *(fan qie)* and the sound/rhyme method, giving three reasonably correct examples. If a character has more than one meaning or pronunciation, this is shown by a small circle in the text.

The article concludes with a long section about an important feature of Chinese lexica: the many citations illustrating the use and the meaning of the characters. But before embarking on that project, he makes it clear that the series of citations he gives here is not presented only to give the reader an impression of the appearance of a page of a dictionary, but first of all to discuss his ideas about the system of the Chinese characters. As always, his problem is that he does not know what to do with the simplest ones:

> If you look at (some of) these quotations you will see another artifice, which consists of reducing a character to its simpler elements thereby showing the meaning of it. Obviously the nine primary elements – for there are so many – represent certain ideas which the inventor of the characters wanted to combine in the second class (that with characters of two strokes) to define (certain) things – that is clear enough.

What *is* clear, however, is that here Bayer is trying to convince himself and his reader about something which he obviously does not find clear at all! The next sentence says, 'This appears most clearly in the higher classes', i.e. the

---

[39b] In his big Chinese-Latin dictionary Bayer did arrange the characters according to the place of the radical in them. In our days this arrangement is used in the 'Encyclopedic Dictionary of the Chinese Language', the *Zhongwen Da Cidian,* Taipei, 1962-8.

characters listed under radicals with many strokes. And from there on, of course, it is plain sailing:

> For whenever a complex of strokes occurs which in themselves mean bird, fish, plant, water, dog, fire, gold, precious stone, etc., then the character of which they are a part means something having to do with bird, fish, etc., indicating a connection or a property, or sometimes suggesting a figurative expression. But this is not always so with these complexes, and it is not as easy with the characters made up of only a few strokes . . .

Bayer adds that unfortunately Li Si, who reformed the Chinese script in 240 B.C., did not elucidate the meaning of the simplest characters.

For the double purpose of showing a page of the *Zi Hui* dictionary and of bringing home his idea of the combinatory 'artifice', Bayer chose the character that had haunted him since his first contact with Chinese matters, namely *sheng*, i.e. holy, wise or perfect. This was a central word in the short passage in the 'Chinese Annals' about the 'Chinese Eclipse', which Andreas Müller had presented in 1684, and which Bayer himself had discussed already in his *De Eclipsi Sinica* of 1718.

Over seven pages he copies the whole entry on that character in the *Zi Hui* dictionary, adding once again all the transliterations and translations of each of the characters. As mentioned above, he had sent this translation to Parrenin, who had returned it with compliments and a few suggestions. Bayer included them here, acknowledging the help he had received from Peking.

The quotations in the *sheng* entry are from the *Book of History*, one of the five Classics; the *Kong Shi Zhuang*, a work about Confucius' family; the *Shi Fa*, a small Song dynasty treatise about posthumous names and titles; the old *Shuo Wen* dictionary *(Shuo Wen Jie Zi)* from the first century A.D.; and the *Tong Lun*, comments on the Classics.[40]

It was the two last works that interested Bayer, because of the systematic 'artifice' he had found in them.

The *Shuo Wen* dictionary says that the character for *sheng* is composed of an element of 'ear' and one for 'offering to a superior'. According to the *Tong Lun*, the word means penetrating and understanding. The 'ear' element does not mean the ear but the mind that penetrates and understands the properties of the myriad things in the same way as the ear penetrates and understands the sounds.

This seemed to confirm Bayer in the 'etymological' ideas he had aired when he analysed the Nü Gua term in his *Museum Sinicum*, but his teacher in

---

40 *Kong Shi Zhuan* is probably an abbreviation of *Kong Shi Zuting Cuangji*, Extended Records of the Kong family Ancestral Hall, a work from the Jin dynasty (1115-1235). – *Tong Lun* is an unspecified reference to the comments traditionally printed in the editions of the Classics.

Peking had warned him against this kind of analysis, so he adds:

> I want to quote, however, what Father Parrenin writes to me about such subtleties. He says that the explanations found in the dictionaries are arbitrary and therefore the authors differ, their opinions not being based on any fundamental principle. Some write the character for 'king' instead of that (very similar) for 'offering to a superior', and then speculate, or rather rave, about the etymology of this character, insisting that it means 'the king of the ear and the mouth', i.e. the wise man who knows when to listen and when to speak.[41]

Bayer inserted this explanation, 'as the pupil inserts the words of his teacher' – although it must have worried him to see and to admit this negation of one of the elements of his belief about the 'rationality' of the Chinese language. It was nothing, however, when compared to the reaction of his Jesuit friends to his basic idea about the combinatory system of the *strokes* of the Chinese script. This came too late for him to include it in his works and anyway it is difficult to imagine what he would have done with it.

Finally Bayer describes the fourteenth and last volume of the *Zi Hui* dictionary, containing a large section on phonetics, especially about the tones, with many tables.

He gives the Chinese titles of this section and its subsections, but refrains from a detailed discussion, especially of the tones: 'I did not find it worthwhile to explore that matter'. Instead he refers the reader to what he wrote about the tones in his *Museum Sinicum*. As we saw above, however, his discussion of the tones of the Chinese words in that book is very meagre indeed. The fact is, of course, that Bayer was quite unable to make sense of this chapter. He may have realized that this was exactly the point where he was sure to be beaten by Fourmont, the Parisian sinologist he admired so much, for he knew that he had been helped by Arcadius Huang, the young Chinese who worked with him in his Bibliothèque nationale.[42]

Finally, as if to console himself and to justify his neglect of the study of the tonal system, he adds a paragraph from the letter he had received from Parrenin in Peking. It runs as follows:

> The four tone marks which the Europeans put over Chinese words are really useless. The characters themselves do not indicate the tones and the Chinese just learn them from practice. Moreover, when they speak, the tones are nearly inaudible. You might have noticed that yourself when you heard the members of the Chinese embassy

---

41 The character written with the 'king' element is to be found in the larger *Zheng Zi Tong* dictionary which Bayer had. There it is called a 'vulgar' variant, but the story about when to listen and when to speak is not there.

42 Fourmont dealt with it in Chapter 10 ('On tonic dictionaries') of his *Meditationes Sinicae* (1737).

speaking Chinese. The ambassador, the great Ogegin, is an Eastern Tartar (Manchu), but he was born in Peking and has an excellent knowledge of the Chinese language and literature. Would you say that he sings or whistles, as the English do? If a European speaking Chinese arranges his sentences correctly, i.e. if he does not invert them, then he will always be understood, even if he pronounces the words with the wrong tones. But if he alters the order of the words, then he will not be understood, for then it is simply not Chinese.[43]

Bayer could not have known at the time when he included these lines in his article how important they were going to be for him at the end of his life.

'ON THE SPRING AND AUTUMN ANNALS'

Bayer's last major sinological work was the 60-page article about the 'Chun Çieu of Confucius', the *Spring and Autumn Annals,* printed in Volume VII of the St Petersburg *Commentarii* in 1740, two years after his death. As usual, Chinese words are given here in transliteration – now, as in the *Zi Hui* article, with tone marks – but nearly all the characters are shown on engraved plates as in the *Museum Sinicum*. There is a total of 934.

The *Spring and Autumn Annals* – the *Chun qiu* – is one of the thirteen Classics of old Chinese literature. It was thought to have been written by Confucius and was regarded with the greatest veneration by Chinese scholars from Dong Zhongshu in the early Han period to those of Bayer's own time. It is a small book dealing with the history of Lu from the year 722 to 481 B.C. The state of Lu, in present-day southern Shandong, was one of the nearly independent vassal states of the Zhou Empire and the birthplace of Confucius, who lived, according to tradition, in the latter part of that period. The book reports in brief annalistic style, the events of the years of the fourteen successive dukes of Lu, with some reference to the relationship between that state and the neighbouring ones.

Bayer had access to two editions of the *Spring and Autumn Annals,* one in the Imperial Library, the other one was his own copy, a present from Father Parrenin in Peking.[44]

---

43 This paragraph must have been added after he gave the paper in the Academy, for the letter is dated 30 July 1734. For the Chinese embassy in St Petersburg in 1732, see p. 152. – Prémare stated a similar view, though more cautiously, in his *Notitia Lingua Sinicae,* Pars prima, Caput primum, Articulus secundus: 'If you pronounce some words with a wrong tone the Chinese will know that you are a foreigner, but as long as the arrangements of the parts of speech in your sentences is correct they will have no difficulty in understanding you'.

44 The edition in the Glasgow University Library (Hunter Books, p. 396, No. 74) is in eight volumes with copious historical and phonetical commentaries. – Bayer had written on the cover of the first of them: 'Chun Cieu. Spring and Autumn. The fifth of the Classics. Confucius used these terms for the history of the wars that raged in his time, because the events of

Bayer's article on the *Spring and Autumn Annals* has even more errors than the *Zi Hui* article. Bayer had died and the office proofs were badly read. Some of the errors are due to the compositor's misreading of the manuscript, e.g. the Han dynasty occurring several times as the 'Hia' dynasty.

The article begins with a long discussion about the definition of a Classic or 'Sacred Book' and a listing of them. Bayer says that the *Spring and Autumn Annals* is regarded as the most sacred among them all.[45] He speaks of the fate of these ancient works through history, the burning of the books under the Qin Shi Huang emperor in the second century B.C. and the recovery of many of them, though damaged, during the Han dynasty (206 B.C. to A.D. 220), all the way inserting passages comparing situations in China with those of classical Europe.

Bayer gives translations of a few passages from the Preface, among others one that deals with the five vassal titles from *Gong* to *Nan*, calling them by the equivalent Roman terms from *Reguli* to *Praecedes*. These are followed by complete chronologies of the dukes who ruled over the twelve most important of the 120 or 124 vassal states of the period, including years of rule which he had calculated from the cyclical years contained in the commentaries of his edition of the work. Scanning these barren leaves – ten pages of names and numbers – we must keep in mind that the art of pure chronology was highly estimated in Bayer's days. It was connected with theology because of the problems of Biblical chronology, and it was related to the new sciences because of its exactitude.

In the next paragraphs Bayer discusses the Spring-Summer-Autumn-Winter concept of the Annals and the occurence of 'empty entries', sentences saying only e.g. 'It was the third month of Spring'. He quotes, from Martino Martini's *Sinicae Historiae Decas Prima,* the story about the finding of the damaged Confucian texts, written on bark or hide, inside the wall of an old house, shortly after the fall of the Qin dynasty. Bayer criticizes Couplet for his moral and lyrical explanation of the title of the work which he had given in the Proëmialis Declaratio to the *Confucius Sinarum Philosophus*. It is clear that he failed to grasp the meaning of Couplet's words presenting the Chinese idea of a virtuous spring-like beginning, followed by a vicious fall-like end of

each year is divided into those of the spring and those of the autumn, as in Thucydides'. – His *History of the Peloponnesian War* is divided into successive 'Summers' and 'Winters'.

45 In explaining the term 'Classic' he mentions the Jesuits' discussion about the status of the *Xingli daquan shu,* the Neo-Confucian anthology, this being regarded as more or less a 'Classic' by the Chinese literati and by the missionaries. Neither Longobardi, nor Antonio de S. Marie nor Navarrete nor other opponents of the Jesuits deny, he says, that it was published under imperial auspices in 1415. Bayer refers in a footnote to the second volume (1735) of Kortholt's edition of Leibniz's *Epistolae ad diversos,* containing the texts of Longobardi and Sainte Marie, as well as Leibniz's reflections about them – the 'Lettre à Mons. de Remond sur la philosophie chinoise' – but he does not comment upon these problems.

dynasties and ruling families – a concept that was familiar to and had become second nature to the more than half sinicized China Jesuits.[46]

Bayer notes that in this work the Zhou emperor is never mentioned by name, or reign title, but only as the Heavenly King. He explains and exemplifies correctly the different terms used for the death of an emperor, a prince or a commoner.

Finally, before coming to his translation, he returns to his old favourite, the Chinese eclipses, referring to Gaubil's works, as published by Souciet in Paris, but not to the letters he had received from him. He remarks that many of the solar eclipses mentioned in the *Spring and Autumn Annals* are stated to have occurred 'at New Moon'. They must do so, of necessity, as we know, but these ancient astronomers just noted down, and rightly, what they saw in the heavens. He concludes by mentioning once more the 'Paschal Eclipse' in the year A.D. 33, the one he had written his first little sinological work about when he was 24 years old. Now he says that in the *Mirror of History* – the 'Chinese Annals' – it is stated to have occurred in the last part of the lunar period – 'but Gaubil has corrected and explained that error'.[47]

Bayer's translation from the *Spring and Autumn Annals* may be read together with one of the two modern translations, that of Legge (1872) or that of Couvreur (1914), but, of course, such a comparison is neither just nor meaningful.[48]

The reader knows by now about Bayer's understanding of the Chinese language when he composed his *Museum Sinicum* in the late 1720s. He himself felt that in the following years, after entering into correspondence with the Jesuit Fathers in Peking, and after having worked with many Chinese books, he had learned a great deal more, and he had demonstrated his new insight in the *Zi Hui* article. However, the fact that his knowledge of that language was still very limited, to put it mildly, becomes glaringly apparent on perusal of his *Chun qiu* translation, even without comparing it to Legge's rendering.

Legge's translation of this work, together with the long *Zuo Zhuan* commentary, came as Volume 5 of his great translations of the Chinese Classics, beginning with the *Four Books* in 1861. This translation, covering more than 900 pages, is an immense work of erudition, performed by a modern sinologist steeped in the language of the classics, and working for 30 years in Hong Kong, surrounded by Chinese scholar-assistants. As in his editions of the other Classics, he adds to this translation learned notes many times longer,

---

46 *Confucius Sinarum Philosophus*, p. XIX.
47 In the transliteration he retains the word *hui*, the last day of the month, but the corresponding character in the engraved plate is *shuo*, the first day!
48 James Legge: *The Chinese Classics*, Vol. V: *The Ch'un Ts'ew, with the Tso Chuen*, Hongkong and London, 1872, p. 3. – S. Couvreur: *Tchóuen Ts'iou et Tso Tchouan*, Ho Kien Fu, 1914.

drawing from his vast experience with the commentaries of all ages. To compare Bayer's and Legge's translation of the *Spring and Autumn Annals* is like comparing the mathematical understanding of a primary school boy with that of an eminent old professor of mathematics.

Before starting his translation Bayer says:

> If we examine what it is that is described in this book, we may enjoy the simplicity of the ancient writer, but we look in vain for wisdom, eloquence or any other form of greatness or refinement.

In his edition, he says, there are magnificent Prefaces by famous men of letters, but their opinions are nothing but expressions of their awe of Confucius. To him the *Chun qiu* text appeared more like the private jottings of persons noting down memorable events, such as eclipses, accessions to the throne, births, deaths, etc. He also compares it to the old laconic annals of the Greeks and Romans.

> I have translated a part of it to make it possible for the reader to form his own opinion of the negative estimate I have offered here. I have kept on with this work in spite of the meagreness and tediousness of the text and the waste of my time, which might have been more profitably employed otherwise. I have even gone to the point of perusing some other parts of the book, looking for better things – but in vain.

This estimate – so different from that of the Jesuits – was new at the time and must have contributed to the general ideas about Chinese wisdom, dealing as it does with the most hallowed among their Classics. It does not really matter, in this respect, that Bayer's translations are often wrong. They are right in the sense that they reveal the insipidity of the *Spring and Autumn Annals*. As a matter of fact, his judgement is nearly the same as that of the learned Legge, writing more than a hundred years later. In his Preface Legge has this to say:

> When we look into the *Chun qiu* we experience immediately an intense feeling of disappointment. Instead of a history of events woven artistically together, we find a congerie of the briefest possible intimations of matters in which the court and the state of Lu were more or less concerned . . . without the slightest tincture of literary ability in the composition, or the slightest indication of judicial opinion on the part of the writer.

Generally it may be said that Bayer was able to read and passably translate a great deal, perhaps more than half, of the sentences. He used the explanatory notes under the text, generally correctly. And he found the pronunciation of the characters and gave it, usually with the correct tone mark. But there are a great number of more or less understandable and excusable mistakes, demonstrating clearly that a translation of this text was far beyond his powers. In many instances his translations go haywire because he takes personal names for words and vice versa. Sometimes one wonders at his mistakes with common words – e.g. *sha,* to kill, translated as 'to condemn'.

In several places when we compare his translation with that of Legge, it is clear that Legge has introduced information from various commentaries into his rendering of the phrase. 'Great rain and snow', as Bayer writes correctly, appears in Legge's translation as 'great rain with thunder and lightning and a great fall of snow'. Similarly, when Bayer writes 'Princess X retired to Y', Legge says that she went to the harem of Y. In some cases it is easy to see why Bayer could not translate the text. Where Legge, who knew what it was all about, wrote 'For the first time he (the Duke) exhibited (only) six rows of pantomime', followed by a long footnote, Bayer had to restrict himself to 'He began to offer six birds' wings' (*yu*), adding that this sentence seems to refer to some Chinese ritual about which he had no information. On the other hand he scored a success with the one-word entry about *ming,* an unusual word meaning a certain kind of insect pest. The note in his text here is nearly identical with that in Legge's footnote.

There is no reason to go into detail about the successes and failures of Bayer's translation. He made the wrong choice when he decided to concentrate on the *Spring and Autumn Annals.* He may have been led by his ambition to be the first in Europe to publish a translation from a Chinese Classic and he must have selected this one because he knew it was regarded by the Chinese as the finest among the Confucian texts. Another reason for his choice may have been the treacherous appearance of simplicity, the shortness of the sentences.

It is interesting that Abel Rémusat, writing in 1810, said only that Bayer's characters were 'more correct (than those of the *Museum Sinicum*) but not more elegant'. He did not say a word about the quality of the translation. He knew much more Chinese, of course, than Bayer, but European sinology was still so feeble at his time that a good translation of the *Chun Qiu* was impossible.[49]

---

49 *Notices et Extraits des Manuscrits de la Bibliothèque du Roy,* X (1818), pp. 292-3 (the text had been composed in 1810). – In the Preface to his *Élémens de la grammaire chinoise* (1822), p. XXX, Rémusat gave a list of the few Chinese texts with translations which were available at the time and which should be used by the students. Among them we find Bayer's translation of 'a fragment of the *Spring and Autumn Annals*', with a correct reference to the volume and the page numbers of the St Petersburg *Commentarii.* He does not remark upon the quality of the transliteration. – Le Roux de Deshauterayes (1724-95) one of Fourmont's pupils, made a partial translation of the *Spring and Autumn Annals,* but it was never published. The manuscript is in the Bibliotheque nationale in Paris. Rémusat owned a transcription of it (Biblioteca

It would have been so much wiser for Bayer to have chosen the *Analects*. The translation of that work in the *Confucius Sinarum Philosophus* was obviously a long-winded and untrustworthy paraphrase. Taking advantage of the raised numerals in the first part of the *Analects,* corresponding to the absent Chinese characters, and collating words so marked with his Chinese edition, he might perhaps have been able to give a better translation of some of the interesting stories which it contains, but first and foremost – he might have learned some more Chinese.

Finally, by presenting this pearl of Chinese history writing and suggesting its triteness, Bayer contributed to the general debunking of the Chinese civilization which was under way in the middle years of the eighteenth century. Montesquieu dismissed the idea of the Chinese Empire as an ideal state in his *Esprit des lois* (1748) and Johann Jacob Brucker ridiculed Chinese philosophy in his *Historia Philosophiae critica* (1742-4). The time for the great onslaught was approaching – Pauw's vicious attacks on everything Chinese in his *Recherches philosophiques sur les Egyptiens et les Chinois* was devoured and enjoyed by lay and learned when it appeared in Berlin in 1773.

Sinica, Col. 1385). – Bayer never mentions the *Zuo Zhuan,* the magnificent Han dynasty 'commentary' to the *Spring and Autumn Annals* – he may not have been aware of its existence.

10
SMALLER ARTICLES IN THE
MISCELLANEA BEROLINENSIA

In 1736-7 Bayer offered two contributions to the *Miscellanea Berolinensia* of the Berlin Academy of Science. One of them was an article about Chinese coins: 'De Re Numaria Sinorum', the other one was a sample of his Peking correspondence: 'Commercium Sinicum'. Shortly afterwards he must have sent the editors a third article, dealing with a famous China Jesuit of the seventeenth century: 'Verdinandi Verbiestii S.J. Scriptis, praecipue vero de ejus Globo Terrestri Sinico'.

The article entitled 'Commercium Sinicum' contains extracts from four letters, one of his own and three from his correspondents in Peking from the years 1732-4. Bayer omitted personal remarks, including the Jesuits' polite praise of him. He added no comments. This article must have been read with considerable interest, for apart from the famous *Lettres édifiantes et curieuses* very little of this kind had been printed in Europe. However, these extracts need not detain us here; the letters themselves have been presented in the chapter on Bayer's Peking correspondence.

The article on Chinese coins is interesting especially because it shows Bayer collaborating with an academician working in a field quite different from his own – J.G. Leutmann, Professor of Mechanics and Optics.

Numismatics was a highly respected part of the scientific study of the past in Bayer's time, and he published several papers in that field, e.g. on Roman coins found in Prussia. His article on Chinese coins was the first of its kind to be published in Europe. It is an abbreviation of a report he had prepared for his high protector, Count Ostermann, who had received a collection of coins from Parrenin in Peking, each one of them packed separately in its own cardboard box, labelled with the name of the emperor under whom it was issued. Bayer studied them with the help of his *Zi Hui* dictionary and Parrenin's Chinese-Latin dictionary. In this article the coins are described in chronological order and shown on engraved plates.[50]

The oldest coin is said to be from the time of Gao Di, the founder of the Han dynasty in the second century B.C. The inscription, which is in seal characters, reads 'U xi' (*wu zhu*), five Zhu. Bayer has looked up the modern character for the word *zhu* in the *Zi Hui* dictionary and gives the volume (*juan*) and leaf number where it is to be found. He has read the text correctly

---

50 Bayer says that he has copied the faces of the coins for Count Ostermann and arranged them after the successive dynasties and emperors. Actually he composed a small book about these coins for the Count, entitled *Numophylacium Sinicum* . . . Anno 1735. His own transcript of it is kept among the Bayeriana in the Glasgow University Library (Hunter MSS, No. 395). In the margin of the title page Bayer wrote 'De Re Numaria'.

and gives the significant characters on the engraved plate.[51] The more recent coins date from the Tang, Song and Ming dynasties, the series ending with a coin issued by the present emperor, Yong Zheng (1723-36).

One of the coins is of gold, but Bayer says that this is not a real coin. It is a commemorative coin given by the Emperor to members of his household on his birthday. The rest of them are copper alloys – brass or nickel ('Packtung' or 'Chinese Silver'). Some of them look like gold but the touchstone reveals that the alloy does not contain gold. On some of them there seems to be a fine foil of gold, as if painted on, but in the obrussa, the vessel in which the test of cupellation is performed, this layer evaporates.[52] Bayer says that these experiments were carried out by a colleague of his, his great friend Johannes Georg Leutmann, the excellent scientist, who had shown his kindness to him on so many other occasions.[53]

Finally a few words about the article about Verbiest and his world map, printed in 1740, three years after Bayer's death.

It begins with a list of twelve of Verbiest's Chinese works about astronomy and about the Christian religion. On the three engraved plates Bayer showed the characters of their titles; he took them from the Chinese edition of Couplet's *Catalogus Patrum S.J.* . . ., which he had obtained from Peking, adding his own transliterations and translations of them. These characters are much better than those of his St Petersburg works and, except for the omissions of two small clauses, the transliterations and translations are correct.[54]

The rest of the paper deals with one of Verbiest's works, the *Kunyu Quan Tu*, a map of the world on two huge sheets. Bayer describes it with its many lateral decorations, pictures of animals unknown in China, and remarks upon the fact that the meridians start from Peking. He gives the Chinese names,

---

51 Joseph Needham's *Science and Civilisation of China,* Vol. V, Part II, Fig. 1324,2 shows a 'Wu chu coin', identical with that in Bayer's Tabula V.

52 In Needham's work, quoted in the previous Note, there is a long and very interesting discussion of the procedures called tinting or tingeing of metal surfaces to make them look like gold (Vol. V, Part II, p. 251ff.).

53 Johannes Georg Leutmann (1667-1736), German scientist. In 1724 he had published a technological work on clocks, fire pumps and other pumps. (*Trfolium utile,* Wittenburg 1724). When he came to the Academy in 1726, the same year as Bayer, he was nearly 30 years older than most of the other members. From 1727 Professor of Mechanics and Optics. He was a specialist in the assaying of metals and invented a very sensitive balance for that purpose. He was called to the Imperial Mint in Moscow and worked there for a short time. G.F. Müller says about him that he was cheerful, full of jokes and completely indifferent to the quarrels of his vociferous colleagues – a man after Bayer's own heart! (*Materiali,* pp. 56-57).

54 Ferdinand Verbiest (1623-88), Belgian Jesuit missionary, in China from 1658 till his death, astronomer and very influential President of the Tribunal of Mathematics at the Imperial court. He published a great number of works in Chinese, dealing with the Christian religion, with astronomy and with the founding of canons. His map, the *Kunyu Quan Tu,* is described by Pfister, p. 355.

with the characters, of many European countries and cities noted on the map: 'Loma' (Rome), 'Yatenie' (Athens), 'Gelhmanyya' (Germany), 'Pomelaniya' (Pomerania), etc. Beside the names, Bayer translated the small insert about Judea: 'God (*Tianzhu*) was incarnated here, therefore it is called the Holy Land', and it was here that he made his 'little error' by misreading the character for *gu*, 'therefore' (see p. 166).

In connection with the presentation of the many place-names, he made some remarks about a fact that may have interested and amused his readers. To write a non-Chinese word in Chinese characters one can choose between several homonyms for the individual syllables. In doing so there is a choice between characters which in their normal use denote or allude to something good or beautiful, or the writer may choose characters that normally mean something ugly or otherwise unacceptable. This kind of game has been played by the Chinese through the ages.

Bayer wrote:

The name France (Francia) on the map seems to suggest an expression of contempt, consciously or unconsciously introduced, for '*Fae lam çy ya*' means 'girlish and cringing opposition to men and masters, afterwards followed by compulsory respect'. This offended the French missionaries who changed it to '*Fa lam çi ya*', which may be read as 'Laws and rules of men, with majesty and gravity'.

This may be stretching it a bit, but actually in Chinese eyes the one form looks as depreciatory as the other one looks complimentary.

Finally Bayer mentions two other maps he knew about. One of them had been brought to Italy many centuries ago by the Venetian Nicolaus de Comitibus (?) and was kept in the St Michael Monastery on the island of Murano outside Venice. Andreas Müller had obtained a copy of it, which was now in the public library of Stettin, from whence Bayer had got a copy of it through the good graces of Mauclair. The other one is a Japanese map in Hans Sloane's collection – Bayer had obtained a copy through Mortimer. These maps are not mentioned elsewhere in Bayer's printed or unprinted works.[55]

---

55 Nicolaus de Comitibus: Perhaps Bayer meant Niccolo, the father of Marco Polo. – Mauclair: probably Paul Emilius de Mauclair, see Note 74. – Sir Hans Sloane (1660-1753), British physician and great collector, member, later president of the Royal Society. – Cromwell Mortimer, died 1752, English physician. Acting secretary to the Royal Society from 1730, a great friend of Sir Hans Sloane.

There is in the Sloane collection of the British Library a manuscript entitled '*Specimen Lexici Sinensis* by Gottlieb Siegfried Bayer, professor at St Petersburg, 1734'. (Sloane 3960), nine folio pages copied by Bayer from his big dictionary (see p. 197). It includes the two pages carrying the character *yi* (change), with notes on the *Book of Changes*. See also note 27.

11
THE BIG CHINESE DICTIONARY

From 1731 till his death Bayer was working on an enormous Chinese-Latin dictionary. This was known, of course, to his fellow academicians and it was discussed at meetings in the Academy. Bayer speaks about his dictionary project in letters to Bishop Benzelius in Sweden and to the Jesuits in Peking, but the Benzelius correspondance only became available after Alvar Erikson had published it in 1979, and the Peking correspondence has not been published till in the present book. In 1741, three years after Bayer's death a 'Mémoire historique sur la vie et les ouvrages de Mr. Bayer' appeared in the *Bibliothèque Germanique* (Vol. L, pp. 99-113). This article was based mainly on information which Bayer himself had sent to the editor in 1737. It contains a bibliography of printed works and works to be printed, but here we find no mention of the big dictionary. The following year, however, the existence of his work was made known to the public when I.L. Uhl published the first volume of the *Thesaurus Epistolicus Lacrozianus* (1742). In the last of Bayer's letters to Lacroze, written in 1736, he speaks of a large Chinese-Latin dictionary he has compiled, 'several volumes in Royal Folio'.

The next mention of it was in 1767. When the Oxford orientalist Gregory Sharpe published his *Syntagma dissertationum quas olim . . . Thomas Hyde separatim edidit,* he added a long 'Appendix de Lingua Sinica . . .' In this appendix he included a footnote with a 'Catalogue of the writings of T.S. Bayer' (See p. 219). It contains an entry about the big dictionary:

Clavis Sinica. Bayer worked hard on the compilation of a Chinese lexicon from several Chinese dictionaries and arranged it in thirty classes (?) to make it easy to find a Chinese character. One copy of this work is in the Library of the St Petersburg Academy, another one is owned by his daughter, who is married to Mr. Carius, superintendent of the Prussian fortresses in Tettenborn . . . I believe that it could be acquired for a small sum of money.

The copy in the Academy of Sciences is mentioned in two lines on p. 119 in B. Dorn's *Das Asiatische Museum d. K. Akademie der Wissenschaften zu S.Pb.* (1846). Here the title of the work is printed correctly and the number of volumes is said to be 23 – three were missing. In G.F. Müller's *Materiali –* when they finally were published in 1890 – the dictionary appears in the bibliography of Bayer's works as 'Lexicon Sinicum. 26 Bände Royal Folio'. In the second edition of Henri Cordier's *Bibliotheca Sinica* (1904-22) there are many Russian works and copious informations about handwritten Chinese-European dictionaries in many libraries and private collections. Here Bayer's big dictionary appears only in the form of a quote from Sharpe's book, mentioned above.

Finally, when we come to Franz Babinger's doctoral dissertation *Gottlieb Siegfried Bayer* (1915), we find the dictionary in the extended bibliography, quoted from G.F. Müller's *Materiali*. Babinger says that the other copy, the one which had belonged to Bayer's daughter, may be the 15 folio volume copy mentioned in A. Seraphim's *Handschrift-Katalog der Stadtbibliothek Königsberg i.P.* (1909).

Apparently, this work which Bayer toiled at for so many years has not been studied before; at any rate there is no information about it in the literature, including, I believe, that of Russia/USSR.

On the following pages we shall first look at the way Bayer discussed it in his correspondence. After that, the work itself, as it exists in the Archive of the Academy of Sciences in Leningrad, will be presented.

THE BIG DICTIONARY IN BAYER'S LETTERS

We know about the progression of Bayer's work with the dictionary from his printed and unprinted correspondence. In a letter of 5 October 1732, to bishop Benzelius in Linköping we see the big dictionary *in statu nascendi*. The first part of it is quoted above on p. 152. This is where we found the surprising phrase about 'containing all the words of the Chinese language'. Bayer proceeds as follows:

When I got started on my dictionary the work was not very hard. Now I regard it as a play in three acts: to arrange the characters according to the art of combination, to write it out for the Academy, and to make a copy for myself. The first volume *in folio* is completed, and I have a large part of the second one. I expect to spend two years on the project. If I go on like this it will be ten or more thick volumes.

I am using the *Zi Hui* and the *Hai Pian* dictionaries. Besides these I am also using a manuscript lexicon written by the Jesuit Parrenin. This, however, is arranged alphabetically, according to the pronunciation of the Chinese words: *ca, cai, cam, can, fa, fam, fe*, etc. The Chinese character of each word is given with extended translations, phrases and various chrestomathies. It contains about 12,000 characters and is much better than the Diaz Vocabulary in Berlin. All the same, I will try to get a transcript of it through Kirch and Count Pada of Creutzenstein.

I also have a Chinese work on natural history, called *Cao Gangmu*, in 40 books. The second volume consists of pictures of minerals, gold and silver mines, stones, plants, insects, fishes, birds and animals. How useful that will be for me – besides the names of plants, fish, etc. I can include pictures![56]

---

56 Benzelius Correspondence, No. 298. – Count Pada, see Note 5 to 'After the *Museum Sinicum*'. – Kirch, see Note 120 to the Preface. The fact that Bayer intended to use the *bona officia* of his astronomer friend in Berlin and Count Pada tells something about the estrangement between him and Lacroze after 1726. – *Cao Gangmu:* this must have been an edition of

In a letter to Johann Christoph Wolff in Hamburg, dated 8 April 1733, Bayer writes that he is on volume eight – the whole work will be about twelve volumes. He says that he is working at it day and night, trying to finish it by June because he wants to leave St Petersburg and return to Königsberg. He adds: 'Now I am disgusted with my *Museum Sinicum* and I regret having published it'. However, he consoles himself with the thought that this book has opened up the field of Chinese studies. It may incite other scholars to work on this language, and anyhow it is useful to persons who are completely ignorant of Chinese. We shall find Bayer expressing the same feelings about his *Museum Sinicum* a few years later, but this time taking comfort in other thoughts.[57]

A year later, in a letter to the bishop, dated 22 June 1734, Bayer writes: 'Because I am very busy my Chinese dictionary is proceeding at a slow pace, but it is proceeding: I am on volume 13'[58] At a meeting of the Academy in the winter he presented a number of volumes of it – perhaps the thirteen he had written to Benzelius about. G.F. Müller, the German historian at the Academy, wrote about it in his *Materials for a History of the Imperial Academy,* composed 30 years later:

> Professor Bayer has finished (?) his important work, the *Lexicon sinicum,* a manuscript of . . . volumes in folio. At a conference on 2 December it was decided that it should be printed. However, as more than 10,000 characters had to be cut in wood this project never materialized. After his death the manuscript came to the Imperial Library.[59]

Some time later Bayer wrote to Count Ostermann:

> I was moved, by the extraordinary grace of Your Excellency (the loan of count Sawa Raguzinskij-Vladislavich's copy of Parrenin's Chinese-Latin dictionary) to compose a complete Chinese Lexicon for the Academy. In doing so I have had to bear all the expenses, including giving free meals for the students who helped me with ruling the paper for three years. Moreover, the constant occupation with this work has endangered my health, especially my eyes. Till now I have given twenty volumes to the Academy and about three more will have to be made.[60]

Li Shizhen's famous Materia medica, the *Ben Cao Gangmu,* first published in 1593. Bayer mentioned it – calling it 'Cao Mo' – already in the grammar chapter of his *Museum Sinicum* (p. 84).

57 Wolff Correspondence, Sup.Ep. 114, fol. 134-5.
58 Benzelius Correspondence, No. 306.
59 For G.F. Müller's *Materiali,* see Note 12 to Introduction. The quote is to be found on p. 337 (December, 1734).
60 This letter is quoted by Babinger, p. 33, from a manuscript in Königsberg. No date is given. For Babinger, see Note 1 to Introduction.

Meanwhile, Bayer had written a letter to Parrenin in Peking about his great project. Parrenin replied to it in the summer of 1734. Bayer wrote back in January, and Parrenin wrote once more in May 1737. Bayer received this last letter shortly before his death.

These letters have been discussed in the chapter on the Peking correspondence, except for the parts dealing with the big dictionary, with Bayer's exposition of his general ideas about the Chinese writing system and with Parrenin's comments upon it. The part of the correspondence to which we are now turning was of the greatest importance for Bayer. Confronted with Parrenin's rejection of his theory about the Chinese characters forming a philosophical system, Bayer tried to hold on to his ideas, but it is clear that he felt the ground being cut from under his feet.

In his letter to Parrenin, dated 26 November 1733 (B4), Bayer tells him that by now he has been working on the Chinese language for more than two years, using his lexicon every hour of the day.

I will give you a short description of how I go about composing my own Chinese-Latin dictionary. Later on you will receive a fuller one with a specimen of the dictionary. I follow the fine order and disposition of the *Zi Hui* dictionary, the one I know best. [61] Its deficiencies are made up for by the excellent list of radicals at the end of the first volume. I add the pronunciation carefully so that no misunderstanding should be possible, and my explanations are both copious and erudite. However, as there are many more characters in the *Hai Pian* dictionary, I start from that, although in other respects it is inferior to the *Zi Hui*. Its radicals follow each other in a senseless way, but I arrange them neatly in separate groups. Then I add the composite characters from the *Hai Pian* and the *Zi Hui* dictionaries. As to the number of groups, I use 32 as in the *Zi Hui*, for I do not like the way in which some characters are placed under radicals where nobody would think of looking for them, or under more than one radical.

Giving an example of a composite character which he thinks is misplaced, Bayer says that it ought to have been placed either under one or under the other of its four composite elements – in the example given these turn out to be identical with the radicals 32 and 34, and upper as well as the lower part of radical 29 in the 214 radical system. Therefore, he says, there are a considerable number of radicals in his dictionary. Further down in the letter Bayer gives more details:

61 In a letter to J. Chr. Wolff, dated 8 April 1733 (see Note 57), Bayer writes: 'As to the method I use for composing the dictionary, I am doing my best. How it can be done is explained in my *Museum Sinicum,* I, p. 114 and on p. 92 of the Preface. However, working day and night on it now, I introduce much to increase the accuracy of the work, things that did not occur to me before'.

The composite characters are disposed in groups, the first being the (single) character by itself; the second consists of characters where it is placed to the right, the third those where it occurs to the left, etc. This will be of great help in finding the character one is looking for. In each of these groups the composite characters are arranged according to their 'capita', roughly in the same manner as in the *Zi Hui* and the *Hai Pian* dictionaries, leaving ample space for my explanations. For many of them I use the ones found in your lexicon, noting them as 'P' or 'P.Lex'. Sometimes I also take the explanation from the Diaz vocabulary in Berlin – it is very elegantly written but infinitely inferior to yours. In several instances I make my own translations and transliterations, but only when I am quite sure about it. – Till now I have completed 25 volumes in Royal Folio, each one of about 500 pages. I still have to make a fair copy of the characters in groups four to six.

Then follows a whole page about some really monstrous characters he has found in the *Hai Pian* dictionary, and examples of characters written upside down. What does that mean, he asks. On the next page he introduces Parrenin to his two pet subjects, the nine elementary characters and the characters as a *system:*

When I thought that I could see a particularly elegant composition of some characters, indicating the thing they meant – it was more often so with complex characters than with the simpler ones – I began to train myself in this wonderful field, working from the *Zi Hui* dictionary. It troubled me more than anything else that I did not know the nature and the significance of the nine elementary characters from which the other ones derive. When I heard from Assemani, an old friend of mine, now director of the Vatican Library, that there were people who knew Chinese among the dignitaries in Rome – Nicolai and Foucquet – I asked him to inquire about these elements. He wrote to me: 'I have asked them about the nine elementary characters you mentioned in your letter. They answered that they had no meaning in themselves, but that the other characters are made up of them'. I suppose they thought it too burdensome to answer or too unimportant. Therefore I have tried myself to find the meaning of them in the *Zi Hui* and the *Hai Pian,* but till now unsuccesfully.[62]

Parrenin replied to these declarations and speculations in his letter of 30 July 1734 (A 8):

Your method of composing a Chinese dictionary is excellent, but you should not waste your time on the simplest characters from which the other ones are formed. This is not done according to any law or rule, although *prima facie* some of them look as if it were.

---

[62] Bishop Giovanni Nicolai de Leonissa, OFM, in China 1684-99, died in Rome, 1737. – For Nicolai and Foucquet see Witek's recent book, mentioned in Note 49 to 'The Chinese Language'.

He follows up this thought in a paragraph where he combines it with a reply to Bayer's wondering about certain very strange characters he has found in some dictionaries.

Li Si, the minister of Qin Shi Huang Di, inaugurated a reform of the ancient characters, but he did not complete it. However, shortly after his death they were changed to the forms used today. Before the time of this famous minister the characters were not only deformed, but many writers took it upon themselves to add to them or subtract from them at their pleasure, even inventing new ones that you may well call monstrous, causing much confusion.[63] There are some of them in the *Hai Pian,* as you mention, and there are many in the *Pian Hai* – I am sending you some examples from it.[64]

Included in this letter there are four pages of obsolete characters, complete with dictionary entries. Underneath, Parrenin writes: 'Nobody has used these characters during the last many centuries. If they occur in a book the reader, even if he is a scholar, has to look them up in dictionaries.'.

Turning from these abnormalities Parrenin tells Bayer about the various kinds of script actually in use now – the seal characters for inscriptions and poetry, the Running Hand script and the Grass script – 'they are much used and differ profoundly from those which you see in the dictionaries. I include some samples on separate sheets.'

The separate sheets accompanying this letter have been discussed in the chapter on the Peking correspondence. The poem mentioned there is given in seal characters, standard script, Running Hand and Grass script. Under the specimen with Running Hand Premare writes: '*Sui Bi Shu* means written freely (*libero penicillo*). It is very common in letters and various notes'. Under the Grass script he notes: 'This is a cruder form used by merchants and when you are in a hurry'.

Finally, after answering a question about the small vertical strokes found all over in the dictionaries – they are just signs of repetition – Parrenin adds a long note about the tones of Chinese words. They are of slight importance because in normal speech they are nearly inaudible. We have seen that Bayer inserted this note in his article about the *Zi Hui* dictionary (p. 206) and he was to come back to it again in the last piece he wrote.

This letter was a shattering blow for Bayer. From his first acquaintance with Chinese characters in the books and manuscripts he studied in Berlin in

---

63 Li Si, died 208 B.C., said to have invented the lesser seal characters. – For 'monstrous characters', see Note 58 to Preface. Parrenin had sent a leaf or a scroll with the word *shou*, longevity, in 100 'old characters' to de Mairan in 1735 (Pfister, p. 514). – See Knud Lundbæk: 'Imaginary Ancient Chinese Characters', in *China Mission Studies (1550-1800) Bulletin*, V, pp. 5-23, 1983.
64 *Hai Pian* and *Pian Hai*, see Note 22 above.

1716 he had felt that they formed a *system,* and he had been supported in this conviction by what he had learned about the opinions of Leibniz, Fourmont and Bülffinger. He had worked for nearly 20 years on the assumption that this was so – it had not become entirely clear, but the fact that the Chinese writing system embodied a philosophical idea could not be doubted. Now this whole edifice seemed to crumble, dismissed in a few lines by his teacher, Father Parrenin in Peking.

Bayer expressed his despair in the letter he wrote to Parrenin on 16 January 1735 (B 13).

As to the laws of composition, I learned them first from Dr. Christian Mentzel's manuscripts and from Reverend Father Couplet's letters to him, which were very useful to me. Afterwards, by studying and comparing individual characters with each other, I came to understand that the inventors of this combinatory art had always aimed at a representation of things. We find it in the composite characters derived from the characters of horse, fish, and bird, and it also applies in other cases. Later on, working with the *Zi Hui* dictionary, this principle was often so obvious that I simply cannot doubt that this art was brought into play. I do not deny that this, as it were, nature of the characters is more apparent in the more complex ones, but I did not doubt that this philosophy had been at work all the way down to the simpler ones, and to the elementary characters in which indeed it had its origin. In some cases I feel my understanding is increasing, but in others I am still at a loss. However, this matter is of the utmost importance.

Bayer then turns to the seal characters he had found in Parrenin's letter – perhaps it was the first time he saw seal characters.

If then inventor of the Chinese characters, in defining such properties (*characteristica*), have followed some philosophical method, as it seems to me from innumerable examples that they must have done, if they have struck to the same principle in forming the simpler characters and even in the nine elementary ones from which the others derive, what shall we say then about the ancient seal characters, the forms of which we recognize in the new ones, but not the system and the nature of them? Truly, I do not know what to say about it. Were the old ones just fortuituous forms? If no ingenuity were at work in shaping them, from whence then did the artfulness of the new ones come? Were the books of Confucius written with these chaotic characters? And before that – if it was from before – the *Book of Changes?* . . . All these things have the highest consequence; I beg you, Reverend Father, to explain them to me!

In a letter dated 15 May 1737 (A 18), Parrenin acted once more, and for the last time, as Bayer's teacher, explaining to him the Dalai Lama's seal:

In the margin I have written the characters in the ordinary script, which you know. You can easily translate the text when I tell you the meaning of five of its characters, two of which mean Tibet and three which make up a personal name. *Ta Lay Lama* is a generic name, as when we say 'Summus Pontifex', the Pope.

Bayer used this information in the draft of a letter he wrote to Count Ostermann on 2 February and which we discussed in the chapter on the Peking correspondence. But Parrenin also returned to the vexed problem of the Chinese script as a philosophical system, now using authority, but adding his own remarks that once again confused the matter.

You should not speculate about an art or some rule according to which the ancient characters were formed, or whether they signify a relationship to things and were invented for that purpose – you are just wasting your time. I asked several literati about the matter, among them the famous Xu Yuanmeng, who is over 85 years old, imperial minister and responsible for history and the translation from Chinese to Manchu – he excels in both these languages. He answered me: 'Where did you get such an idea from?' I told him I had heard some Europeans discussing it among themselves. Then he said: 'I myself have wasted some time, beguiled by the *Tschim see* lexicon, in searching for certain rules according to which the characters should have been formed by a combination of their elements, i.e. from the various strokes of the brush, so that each character was a picture of a thing or had some relationship to it. But it was in vain. Except in a few cases, perhaps a hundred, I found nothing of the kind. No conclusion can be drawn on the matter'.[65]

The case should be closed, it seems, but Parrenin continues.

In the course of time the characters have been changed and augmented and therefore no certain rules can be found except that the Chinese have always used the same five elements to form the simple characters. The complex characters are formed by combining the simple ones. It should be noted, however, that when they want to indicate somthing related to wood, water, metal, reason etc. in complex characters, they usually put the sign of this concept on the left side of the character. The character for mouth also occurs at the lateral side of some characters. This must be enough for you today.

This letter must have baffled its recipient. It was a waste of time to look for rules or relationships to things, the best among the Chinese confirmed this. And yet there were rules: there were elementary characters and complex

---

65 Xu Yuanmeng (1655-1741). Parrenin writes Su Yven meng. I am grateful to Professor Yves Hervouet in Paris for having identified this man. Once Su is corrected to Xu, this Manchu dignitary can be found in A. Hummel's *Eminent Chinese of the Ch'ing Period* (p. 659) as the grandfather of the great statesman and general Shu-ho-te (1717-77). – The *Tchim ssee* lexicon is presumably the *Zheng Zi Tong* dictionary, known for its many fanciful 'etymologies', but the transliteration is odd – normally Parrenin writes *Chim cu*. However, this letter is not written by him, nor is it Bayer's copy; somebody else must have written it for Parrenin.

characters made out of them, and there were object-related parts of characters!

As to the five elementary characters given by Parrenin, Bayer must have wondered at them. He had seen the seven simple characters in Menzel's *Sylloge* and the six in the *Zi Hui* dictionary. He had read in his Semedo that there were nine and he himself had invented nine. The ones he found in Parrenin's letter were the first five of his nine elementary characters . . .

There is one more letter of Bayer's dealing with his big dictionary, a late one, dated 1 February 1736. It is addressed to his old friend Lacroze in Berlin.

The correspondence between Bayer and Lacroze seems to have stopped when Bayer moved to St Petersburg – there are two letters from Bayer written in 1726 and 1728, but no letters from Lacroze. Of course the Lacroze Correspondence may not be complete, but there is one letter in Uhl's *Sylloge nova Epistolarum* which shows that Lacroze actually had ceased to write to him.[66]

Bayer's letter to Lacroze of 1736 begins with some remarks that seem to indicate that he has written to him now and then in the course of the years. The first part of the letter deals with various numismatic matters, but this looks like a pretext to arrive at the last part, containing the information he wanted to give Lacroze about his Chinese studies, and especially about his present estimate of his earlier work in that field.

> The Chinese lexicon I have made totters under its own weight – it consists of several volumes in Royal Folio. Other business keeps me away from it and often I do not work on it for many days. Besides Parrenin's lexicon, which is infinitely better than that of Diaz, I received, two years ago, the Danet Lexicon, translated into Chinese and elegantly written on superb paper. Because of the goodwill of the Jesuits I am able to use this work when I want to know the Chinese character for a Latin word. Parrenin's Chinese-Latin dictionary is arranged like that of Diaz (namely alphabetically). I have included most of it in my own lexicon which is arranged like that of the *Museum Sinicum*. This work was very poor, but I do not regret that I wrote it. It was that work that opened the door to the wealth of information now available to me. At some time we should discuss if I ought to publish a revised edition of the *Museum Sinicum*.[67]

---

66 It is a letter to Philip Joseph Jariges (1707-79), secretary of the Berlin learned Society, dated 10 January 1737. He ends it in the following way: 'But tell me about Lacroze, whom I always regarded as my father – has he forgotten me these last twelve years?' (Sylloge, IV, VIII, pp. 4-7).

67 Lacroze Correspondence, I, pp. 60-2.

THE BIG DICTIONARY IN LENINGRAD

Bayer's Chinese dictionary, formerly kept in the Department of Manuscripts of the Oriental Institute of the Academy of Sciences, is now in the Archive of the Academy in Leningrad.[68] It consists of 23 huge volumes, each one containing between 110 and 376 pages. The title of the work is given on the first page of the first volume: *A Chinese lexicon compiled from old Chinese lexica and other books and dedicated to the St Petersburg Imperial Academy by T. S. B.*

Volumes I to VII contain the one to three-stroke radicals and their derivates. Volumes VIII to X are missing. Volumes XI to XXVI contain the remaining characters, arranged under radicals written with seven to twenty-two strokes. Each of the latter volumes – from volume XI onwards – has a separate title-page and indications about the number of the strokes in the radicals it contains, e.g. 'Volume XI containing the first part of Class VII' (the radicals written with seven strokes and their derivates). The missing volumes are probably the ones which Bayer wrote to Parrenin about in 1733, those with the four to six-stroke radicals which were not finished. Bayer may never have given them to the Academy.[69] As the existing 23 volumes contain about 50,000 characters on their 7,500 pages, the 26 volumes of the whole dictionary may be assumed to have contained nearly 60,000 characters.

The characters of the 23 volumes are arranged under 528 radicals; presumably the total number in the 26 volumes was about 600. These radicals are arranged in 'classes' according to the number of strokes in them, from one to twenty-two. Many of them appear with several variants. Under each of the radicals we find the derivates, from one or two to about 2,000. They are arranged in a number of sections according to the position of the radical in them: doublets (*character secum*), those with the radical at the right side, at the left side, on the top, at the bottom, in the middle, and 'crossing' (*intra se*). Within each of these sections the derivates are listed according to the number of extra strokes.

All this seems to correspond rather well to what Bayer says in the letters quoted above, and the surprising statement about 'all the words of the Chinese language' as well as the term used in the letter to Count Ostermann – 'a complete Chinese Lexicon' – seems to be justified by the inclusion of about 60,000 characters. In the letter to Parrenin late in 1733 Bayer does not men-

---

68 Archiv AAHCCCP, F. 783, Op.1. – Royal Folio, 27 by 43 cm. On the outside the volumes are renumbered from 1 to 23.
69 According to B. Dorn in his book *Asiatische Museum* . . . mentioned above, Volumes XI, XIII and XXVI are the missing ones, clearly a counting error. – Müller's '26 Bände' seems to indicate that at that time all the 26 volumes were in the Academy, but he may just have looked at the last one on the shelf which is marked 'Volume XXVI'.

tion the number of characters. From the way Bayer speaks about taking many translations from Parrenin's dictionary and some from Diaz's Vocabulary, a few being of his own invention, Parrenin must have thought that essentially what Bayer was doing was to take his, Parrenin's, alphabetical dictionary, and rearrange the characters according to the radical system he had invented for his *Museum Sinicum*.

However, an examination of the big dictionary in Leningrad reveals that Bayer had not disclosed to his correspondents the preliminary state of the great work. This enormous work is not a dictionary, ready to be printed, most of it is just the framework of a Chinese-Latin dictionary.

In his letter to Parrenin in 1733 (B4), Bayer had said that in working with his dictionary project he had relied primarily on the *Hai Pian* dictionary because it contained more characters than the *Zi Hui* dictionary, and also that he was 'leaving ample space for my explanations'. As a matter of fact, in the *Chinese lexicon compiled from old Chinese lexica and other books,* very few, certainly less than five per cent, of the characters are presented in transliteration and translation. The great majority carry only a reference to one of the Chinese dictionaries, usually *Hai Pian*. Leafing though these thousands of pages one finds on most of them six Chinese characters, three in the left and three in the right column; beneath each of them there is a line referring (mostly) to the *Hai Pian* dictionary, e.g. '*Hai Pian,* vol. 6, p. 3, 1.9'; below this line follows an empty space of about 10 cm. In other words, Bayer's big Chinese-Latin dictionary – as it exists today – is essentially a reference list to a *Hai Pian* dictionary.

What is a *Hai Pian* dictionary?

There are several Chinese dictionaries with titles that include the two characters *Hai* (ocean) and *Pian* (tablets of bamboo or wood for written records). We have seen Parrenin mentioning both the *Hai Pian* and the *Pian Hai* dictionaries in his letter to Bayer of 30 July 1734 (A8). These works differed from the standard dictionaries by not containing quotations from the literature. They were not highly regarded by the Chinese scholars, who complained about the great number of erroneous or non-existing characters to be found in them. Parrenin, in the letter mentioned, seems to endorse this opinion.

These dictionaries were well known in Europe in the seventeenth and eighteenth centuries. Andreas Müller lists two volumes of a *Hai Pian* in his first catalogue of Chinese books in the Electoral Library in Berlin (See Note 100 to Preface to the *Museum Sinicum*) and mentions this work in several of his works. There were one or more in the Royal Library in Paris at Bayer's time. Fourmont, in his *Linguae Sinicae Grammatica duplex* (1742, pp. 356-9) gives a detailed description of a work called *Hai Pian Zhao Zong*. It must be the same, he says, as the *Hai Pian* mentioned by the missionaries and by

Andreas Müller. It contains a dictionary in eleven volumes in which the characters are arranged according 'the nature of things' – beginning with a section on the heavens, the sun and the moon, etc. followed by sections about the year and the months, one on various instruments, ships, etc., one on the parts of the body, and so forth. The characters are not arranged under radicals as in the *Zi Hui* dictionary, and all in all, he says, it is more like an index or a catalogue of characters than a real dictionary.[70]

What was the *Hai Pian* which Bayer used?

He never specifies which kind it was or what edition. The dictionary is not among the Bayeriana in Glasgow. However, Mr. David Weston, librarian of the Special Collection of the Glasgow University Library, searching in vain for this dictionary in the collection, found a small but interesting piece called 'Two pages of a Chinese Dictionary'. These two pages – one sheet – is from a *Hai Pian* dictionary and it seems quite likely that they are from the copy which Bayer used when constructing his big Chinese-Latin dictionary. With this sheet in hand we may perhaps imagine how Bayer went about in making his dictionary.[71]

Traditional Chinese books are produced from sheets on which two consecutive pages are printed from one wood block. The narrow space between the two pages contains the title of the book and the leaf number, sometimes also the number of the chapter (*juan*). To make a book out of it, these sheets are folded along the space between the pages, forming double pages with the printed text on the outside. Then all these double pages are put in the right order and stitched together at the back. The title of the book is on each of the double pages to prevent the inadvertent inserting of pages from another work being produced at the same time. Hence, as Bayer wrote in his *Museum Sinicum*, 'one has to put one's hand in between the two pages to read the title' (see p. 128).

For Bayer who wanted to make his own dictionary from the characters of his *Hai Pian*, but arranged according to his own ideas, what would have been

---

70 Today only two volumes of this dictionary are to be found in the Bibliothèque nationale in Paris. There are also a few volumes of two other *Hai Pian* dictionaries, and a complete set of a *Pian Hai* edition in 20 volumes. (Courant: Nos. 4771-72, 4785, 4786 and 4787). – There is a 10 juan *Hai Pian* with 444 'radicals' arranged according to 38 initials in the Royal Library of Copenhagen (Kina 1300).

71 *Yin shi Hai pian* ('Pronunciation – Explanation – Haipian'). (Hunter Books, p. 396, No. 62.) – *Juan* 16, leaf 11. The pages measure 14 by 25 cm and contain 49, respectively 46 characters: the water radical with 3-4 extra strokes. – One or more pronunciations with their meanings are given, also some double words. Many of the characters are 'names of waters', the geographical position often taken from the old *Shuowen Jiezi* dictionary. In some cases only a pronunciation is given. There are no citations from the literature, but under *Jiang*, river, it is stated that the expressions 'three rivers', 'nine rivers', 'middle river' and 'northern river' (or Yangzi Jian) occur in the 'Tribute of Yu' section of the *Book of History*.

more natural than to cut the string that keeps the double pages together? Then the sheets would fall apart and he could rearrange them – or parts cut from them – to suit his own system. However, in the course of time, when such sheets and parts of sheets may have been lying around on tables and chairs in his room, it may have happened, as it happens to all of us, that one or more of them was mislaid and found its way into a bunch of papers where it did not belong.

In 1737, when packing his books and manuscripts to be sent ahead to Königsberg, he may have decided not to take all these pieces of paper with him, perhaps at that time he had despaired of ever realizing his gigantic plan. In Glasgow, a single sheet, having strayed into some other manuscript, may have emerged when the Bayeriana were first examined in the University Library, the librarians not suspecting how interesting it was for the history of Bayer's dictionary, just cataloguing it as 'Two pages of a Chinese Dictionary'.

All this is speculation, of course, but perhaps not too fanciful to explain why Bayer's *Hai Pian* is not among the Bayeriana and why there is one leaf of a *Hai Pian* dictionary in the collection.

Bayer's *Lexicon Sinicum* contains no information about the author's general ideas for constructing it. There is no preface or epilogue, nor do we find any section in the many volumes, explaining the method employed in compiling it 'from old Chinese lexica and other works'. However, from an examination of the 23 volumes preserved today it is possible to form an opinion of what he had in mind.

Probably he decided to use the *Hai Pian* as the basis for his own dictionary, partly because of its great number of characters – perhaps 'all the characters of the language'? – partly because of what seemed to him to be the 'senseless order' in which they had been arranged by the Chinese author. He, Bayer, could do better! His idea must have been to proceed from this great Chinese work, but to arrange the characters in a systematic way: firstly, by deciding on a number of radicals and arranging them according to the number of strokes; secondly, by placing derivates in separate sections according to the position of the radical in them. It seems that to some degree he had given up the complicated system he had invented for the dictionary in his *Museum Sinicum* – anyhow it had not been successful. Working now with the *Hai Pian,* and rearranging its characters as stated above, he was still producing *a system;* that was the important thing for him, now as before. This seems to be the only possible explanation for the scarce attention he pays to the pronunciation and the meaning of all these characters. He had his transcript of Parrenin's dictionary with its approximately 10,000 characters, arranged alphabetically, he could have taken many more transliterations and translations from it than he actually did. But this part of his project he seems to have regarded as of secondary importance, something to be done at some time in the future. We have to keep in mind that Bayer worked with this project from his late thirties until his death at the age of 44 years. Even in the eighteenth century, when the *average* lifespan was so much shorter than it is today, a healthy man of that age would, of course, be looking forward to and making plans for many years to come.

But why did he present a number of volumes at a meeting in the Academy in December 1734? His fellow academicians must have realized at a glance at the pages that this was not a finished manuscript of the dictionary, ready to be printed. However, there is a strange note in the minutes of the meeting on 2 December 1734: 'Korff insisted that everything should be done to have Bayer's Chinese dictionary printed as soon as possible'.[72] How can that be explained? Perhaps, in offering the volumes, Bayer explained that this was only to demonstrate his industriousness in the service of the Academy, adding that he had an extra copy of it at home and that he intended to fill in the many blanks in the course of time? We can only guess.

There is, however, a manuscript in the Glasgow University Library that seems to elucidate the history of Bayer's dictionary project.

It is a draft of a part of a Chinese-Latin dictionary, the character for *yan,* to speak – radical No. 149 in the 214 radical system – followed by 190 characters with two to fifteen extra strokes. All these characters are transliterated and the first 32 and a dozen, spread over the following pages, are translated, many of the entries carrying double words and a few phrases.

This looks like a draft belonging to a very early and less ambitious stage of Bayer's dictionary project, before he decided to put his faith in the *Hai Pian* dictionary. Here he seems to be doing what Parrenin imagined, and presumably what he would have liked him to do: extracting from his alphabetically arranged Chinese-Latin dictionary the characters belonging to a certain radical, in the present case the *yan* radical, arranging them according to the number of extra strokes, and adding his transliterations and translations.[73]

Bayer abandoned this relatively modest project and embarked on a very different one, a giant project that may at first sight seem foolhardy, perhaps almost insane for a man who knew as little Chinese as he did.

However, in the grammar chapter of the *Museum Sinicum* we have seen him excusing the imperfections of the dictionary included in that work, suggesting that 'if he had had the entire set of 80,000 characters at his disposal, and if he had been able to muster the strength required, he would have arrived at the true system of the Chinese characters'. Perhaps we should

---

72 This is quoted in Ju.Ch. Kopelevič's work on the first years of the St Petersburg Academy, the *Osnovanie Petersburgskoi Akademii Nauk* (1977), p. 148.
73 Bayer MS E. 13. – That Bayer was actually working here with Parrenin's 'Chinese-Latin Dictionary', with its admixtures of French and Spanish words appear from the fact that in two places we find French words among Bayer's translations.

imagine that during these many years, working for hundreds and hundreds of hours on his fantastic plan, he was actually trusting that some day some kind of illumination would come to him. Just by working on, patiently arranging 'all the characters of the language' in a 'philosophical way', from the simplest ones to the most complicated forms, the system itself, 'the noblest achievement of the human race', as Fourmont had said, would one day be revealed to him. Then he would be in possession of the key to it: *the true Clavis Sinica!*

However, let us return to the dictionary as it is preserved in the Archive of the Academy of Sciences in Leningrad and look at its contents.

It starts with the class of one-stroke radicals; they are the same nine 'simple strokes' we have heard so much about in the preceding chapters of the present book. Each of them is followed by a number of derivates, but here, in contrast to the *Museum Sinicum,* references are simply given to higher classes where they appear as radicals. On the first twenty pages there are a few references to 'Martini's Grammar' and to 'Mentzel'. There is also a long note on the character which is No. 8 in the dictionary of the *Museum Sinicum,* with some self-criticism. It is only when we come to the two-stroke radicals that the references to the *Hai Pian* begin to appear.

Bayer took his radicals from that work, and also the derivates, line by line. His opinion, that these radicals are 'real' radicals, nearly all of them, is obvious from a note about a 20-stroke character in volume XXVI: '*Hai Pian,* book 8, p. 15, line 7 regards it as a radical but that is wrong, for it has no derivates'.

As to the use of Parrenin's dictionary, his transliterations and translations appear here and there, but very rarely. Bayer concentrated on the derivates of a few characters: *yi,* one, *ren,* man, and *niao,* bird. Some of the comments found here are related to missionary problems. In Volume XIII the character *yi,* change, is followed by two pages about the *Yi Jing,* the *Book of Changes,* which occupied the minds of the missionaries. In Volume XIV, under the radical *huang,* majestic, Emperor, there is a double word Huang Di, 'The Supreme Emperor of Heaven, but according to others just the combination of celestial spirits (Parrenin)'. Bayer adds: 'This term is the cause of great controversy between the Jesuits and the other missionaries. Cf. Philippe Couplet in the Preface to the *Confucius Sinarum Philosophus.*'

In general, the policy of postponing the work with the transliterations and translations is obvious from the fact that a number of the most common Chinese characters, which Bayer knew by heart, their pronunciation as well as their meaning, occur only with the usual reference to the *Hai Pian* dictionary.

At the end of the Bayer's big dictionary there is a pleasant surprise for the patient examiner of the 23 volumes in the Archive of the Leningrad Academy of Sciences. When he arrives at Volume XXI and comes to *niao,* bird, he finds small drawings of 17 species of birds. A little later there are pictures of a mouse, a tortoise and of a Chinese dragon. Bayer states that he took them from his *Cao Gangmu,* the Chinese Classic on natural history and pharmacology. We have heard above how, in his letter to Bishop Benzelius of 1732, he enlarged upon the utility of inserting pictures of animals and plants in his Chinese-Latin dictionary, once it came to be printed . . .

12
FINALE

LAST WORDS

In 1737 Bayer had decided to leave Russia and to return to his native Königsberg. It is not known how he expected to manage there or what situation might be offered to him, but with his many erudite publications he could probably feel rather sure of being summoned by more than one German university. He had tendered his resignation and had been honourably discharged. He had sent his valuable books and manuscripts ahead by sea and was ready to leave with his family at the beginning of the following year.

Then he received a letter from Paul de Mauclair, one of the editors of the *Bibliothèque Germanique,* dated Stettin, 25 October 1737. Mauclair wrote:

> Honorable, most noble and most learned Professor!
> Just in case you do not see the French journals as early as we do here I have made the enclosed copy (from the *Journal des Sçavans*) for your information. If you want to defend yourself against Mr. Fourmont I offer to print your rejoinder, translated into French, in the *Bibliothèque Germanique.* However, as the *Meditationes Sinicae* is written in Latin, I take the liberty to advise you to answer in that language once you have received a copy of the book itself . . .[74]

Bayer had not seen the *Meditationes Sinicae,* but he knew that a copy of it was on its way to him. Choosing not to wait but to respond immediately to Fourmont's attack, he wrote a rejoinder in German and sent it off.

He was unable to react to the words with which Fourmont had introduced his critique of the *Museum Sinicum,* for they were omitted in the *Journal des Sçavans:*

> The learned Bayer, who speaks of me in the most friendly way and whose friendship I appreciate, and will always appreciate, will read, I am sure, my remarks about his book and take them in good part.

Of these remarks, formulated in a very rude and insulting way, we need only present the main parts, as summarized in the *Journal des Sçavans,* those which Bayer saw and to which he replied in his last words. What he read here were statements like these:

---

[74] Glasgow University Library, Bayer MS A 19. – Paul Emilius de Mauclair (approx. 1697-1742), pastor of the Reformed church in Stettin, member of the Societas Regia Scientiarum, one of the editors of the *Bibliotheque Germanique.*

'In the Chinese grammar which this German has given us he never speaks about how to read the characters (la méthode de lire les caractères)'.

'All the Chinese words are given only in Latin and without tone marks, thus horribly confusing the language (ce qui jette une horrible confusion dans cette langue).'

'A Chinese syllable can be accented in a number of ways, corresponding to the same number of characters (*sic*). Moreover, the same word, with the same accent (i.e. tone and aspiration) can have 20, 30, 50, 80 or even more different meanings, and consequently be expressed by a similar numbers of letters (characters). For example, the word *ki* can be written with 280 different characters. The lack of tone marks made the *Museum Sinicum* despicable in Peking, where it was brought by some missionaries.'

'Bayer's Chinese characters are miserably (pitoyablement) engraved and must have been printed from a very poor (chetif) manuscript.'

'Bayer speaks about what are called the 'keys' or 'tribunals' in Chinese grammar and knows how important they are for the proper construction of a dictionary. Why then does he not pay more attention to them in his own dictionary, which contains no trace of these grammatical arrangements?'

'Fourmont concludes by saying that M. Bayer has taken great pains, but the results of his efforts are nearly useless for his reader, for, in a sense, it is asking for the impossible to try to teach spoken Chinese without characters (*sic*) and written Chinese by means of such miserable characters.'[75]

This is not all but most of what Fourmont had to say about Bayer's *Museum Sinicum*. It is tempting to analyse this text, or rather the original one as it appears in the *Meditationes Sinicae* – what Fourmont said and especially what he did not say about it. However, we shall resist that temptation and just look at Bayer's reply. It was printed the following year in the *Bibliothèque Germanique* (Vol. XLIII, pp. 51-65) under the title 'Reflections de M. Bayer . . .sur le jugement peu favorable qu'on a porté sur ses ouvrages dans l'extrait des *Meditationes Sinicae* de M. Fourmont'. In a footnote the editor, speaking about 'the late Mr. Bayer', remarks that he did not get time to see Fourmont's book and only knew it from the review in the *Journal des Sçavans*. He also says that Bayer may have known, as the editor knows from a good source, that in earlier times Fourmont had expressed his respect for him. No wonder, he continues, that Bayer was puzzled when he saw the review.

The fact that Bayer's rejoinder in the *Bibliothèque Germanique* was a translation from his handwritten German text *may* account for some of the oddities of these fourteen pages. It is clear, however, that he was writing under great emotional strain but also that he was trying to repress his indignation and bitterness – successfully, nearly all the way.

Bayer starts by saying that he is puzzled: he cannot imagine that the excellent Fourmont should have said such things about him, but, on the other hand, he has no reason to doubt the veracity of the reporting journalist.

---

75 *Journal des Sçavans,* January and February, 1737, pp. 413-21 and 552-61.

His defence for omitting tone marks seems half-hearted and not quite clear, especially, perhaps, because at that time he was beginning to insist that his works should be printed with these 'accents' by the Academy printers.

He reminds the readers that the Peking Jesuits have given up the tone marks. The *Confucius Sinarum Philosophus,* edited in Paris by Couplet, and the works of Du Halde and Souciet appear without these marks. He also quotes the passage from Parrenin's letter to him of 1734 (Bayer writes 1735) about the uselessness of the tone marks, the passage he had included in his *Zi Hui* article, not yet printed. This seems beside the point, at least partly, because Parrenin is speaking about the near absence of tones in fluently-spoken Chinese.

To the accusation that he does not teach his reader how to read a Chinese character, he replies as follows:

> About five years ago, while working on my big dictionary, I thought that I had discovered a way to give rules for the pronunciation of the characters . . . but now I can assure the public that what Andreas Müller and Mr. Fourmont have promised them is in fact an impossible thing.

Here something seems to have gone wrong. The text says 'les regles certaines pour faire connaître la prononciation des caractères à leur seule vue', but that can hardly be what Bayer meant to say. It may be a slip of his pen or the translators misunderstanding of his words. It is true that the part of Chinese characters now called the 'phonetic' often indicates or suggests an approximate pronunciation, but that is not generally so. And anyhow there is nothing in Bayer's printed or unprinted works that deals with rules for pronouncing Chinese characters. Furthermore, neither Müller nor Fourmont, in the extract of his 1722 paper – the only piece of his that Bayer knew – ever mention such rules.

Bayer must have read Fourmont's words about 'la méthode de lire les caractères de cette langue' correctly, i.e. as referring to a method according to which one could understand the *meaning* of Chinese characters. This is what Müller and Fourmont thought they had found, a *Clavis Sinica,* and this is what Bayer had hoped to find all his life. However, as we have seen in the chapter dealing with the Peking correpondence, Parrenin's letters, especially the last one, had made it clear to him that there was no such thing as a *Clavis Sinica.* In all probability it is with Parrenin's words in his mind that he 'assures the public' that what Müller and Fourmont had promised – and what he himself had hinted at several times in his printed works – is 'an impossible thing'.

Bayer admits that his Chinese characters are not as fine as they ought to be. This is partly because he is using the written characters – the Running Hand –

not the forms seen in printed books, and partly it is the fault of the engraver. He has put some strokes too far from each other, to some he has not given the proper strength and precision, and sometimes he has forgotten important strokes. Moreover, he himself has also made mistakes.

Bayer says he cannot comment on the keys to which Fourmont refers before he has read his book.

> I agree that my dictionary in the *Museum Sinicum* is not a perfect one, as I said in my Preface, but it not totally devoid of keys. I can assure the readers that in the manuscript of my big dictionary I have arranged everything with even more care and precision than in the dictionaries of the Chinese.

The phrase about 'not totally devoid of keys' is a strange one, taking into consideration his discussions about the dictionary in his *Museum Sinicum* and its many 'roots'.

Finally, Fourmont's statement about his work being despised in Peking forced Bayer to disclose his relation with the learned China Jesuits. He says that it was he himself who sent his *Museum Sinicum* to them, and that they received it 'with marks of esteem that I know I do not deserve. They do not restrict themselves to simple compliments, but always send me their opinion about my work'. Referring to his correspondence with them in later years he says:

> They – the Peking Jesuits – are the ones who have urged me on to continue my Chinese studies, who have helped me with their advice and who have shown me ways I could not have found without them. If, after the *Museum Sinicum,* I have made some progress, I can say in truth that I owe it to the China Jesuits, and to them alone. How can it be said, then, that they despise me?

It is only in the very last lines that his self-control breaks down:

> The final part of the review is full of passion and confusion. To reply to that would be a waste of time and even beneath my dignity.

LAST DAYS

We have heard about the letter that Bayer drafted on 8 February 1738 to Count Ostermann, dealing with the help he had obtained from Peking for reading the text of the Dalai Lama's seal. In the last line of it he speaks about taking medicine (see p. 170).[76]

---

76 A letter from Bayer dated 11 January (old style?) is printed without comments in Cordier's 'Fragments d'une histoire . . .' pp. 223-4 (see Note 14). It has no addressee but it must be to

G. F. Müller says in his *Materiali* that Bayer fell ill on 11 February.[77] The day before he had written two letters to Paris, one to Nicolas Fréret of the Académie des inscriptions et belles-lettres, a colleague of Étienne Fourmont, the other to Étienne Souciet S. J., the Peking Jesuits' man in Paris. They are cast in the same mould; both are cries of distress and cries for help.[78]

In the letter to Fréret Bayer thanks him for a Chinese book, the *Bamboo Classic,* which he has sent him, announces his forthcoming studies of the *Zi Hui* dictionary and the *Spring and Autumn Annals* and reminds him of their mutual friends in Europe and Peking. He adds, naively or perhaps ironically in the actual situation, that they are working in the same field, a relation that is always conducive to friendship. Only then does he get to the purpose of his letter.

> Please give my thanks to Fourmont for the *Meditationes Sinicae,* which he has left (for me) with Delisle's sister. In the spring I hope to receive this valuable gift. I have just seen in the *Journal des Sçavans* what he writes about my *Museum Sinicum* in that book – contemptuously and harshly, but also obscurely and confusedly. I have reacted to it very moderately, my reply will appear in the *Bibliothèque Germanique.* In the meantime I want you to tell this learned man that my respect for him has not diminished for that reason. I admire true excellence and merit in an adversary and even in an enemy . . .

In his letter to Souciet he also speaks of other things before coming to the point. He has just read Du Halde's great four volume *Description géographique . . .de l'Empire de la Chine,* greatly enjoying that excellent new book. And Gaubil in Peking has offered to send him any supplementary information and explanation he might wish after reading the book. He asks what has happened to Prémare's *Notitia Linguae Sinicae* – Koegler had told him that it had been sent to Paris. Bayer also says that he owns 'your and Gaubil's four volume work, i.e. Souciet's *Observations mathématiques . . .* (1729-32). If a fifth volume is to appear, he wants to be informed about it, so that he can buy it at once – 'I cannot do without it'.

All this was a backdrop to the following:

> I am very much looking forward to obtaining a copy of Fourmont's *Meditationes Sinicae.* I was surprised to see what the *Journal des Sçavans* said about it. I have sent a brief and moderate reply to the *Bibliothèque Germanique.* But can't you see that by
>
> Delisle. Saying that he is in bed, Bayer asks Delisle to write to his sister in France and get her to send him the copy of the *Meditationes Sinicae* that Fourmont had deposited with her. A Königsberg merchant, whom Bayer knows, does business in Bordeaux and could bring it with him. Then he would have it in Königsberg in the spring.

77 *Materiali,* p. 466.
78 Glasgow University Library, Bayer MS C 23 and 24.

attacking me he actually aims at you and Father Du Halde and all the French Jesuits in Peking?[79]

Six days later, on 18 February Joseph-Nicolas Delisle, Bayer's great friend at the St Petersburg Academy, wrote a letter to the same Nicolas Fréret in Paris. He speaks about letters and gifts he has received from Father Gaubil in Peking, and then tells Fréret what has happened to Bayer:

> Recently Mr. de Mauclair, pastor in Stettin and one of the editors of the *Bibliothèque Germanique,* has sent Bayer, with whom he has a lively correspondence, an extract of one of the latest numbers of the *Journal des Sçavans.* In this number Bayer is severely attacked in a review of Fourmont's book. Mr. Bayer immediately sent a rejoinder, written in German, to Mr. de Mauclair, asking him to translate it into French and insert it in his *Bibliothèque Germanique.* He does not write or speak French although he is able to read it. Thereupon Mr. Bayer became ill and was unable to read his rejoinder and a letter he had written to you about the matter in the Academy. I was not present, and anyhow I would not have understood the German letter. It is Mr. Bayer who told me these things. I am sending you his letter . . .[80]

Bayer died three days later, on 21 February. G. F. Müller says on p. 466 of his *Materiali* that it was from an acute disease (eine hitzige Krankheit). We do not know the nature of this disease, but any experienced physician knows that the chances of surviving a violent and dangerous disease are lessened if it hits a person whose constitution is shattered by sorrow or despair.

A few days after the burial his widow handed over to the Academy a number of manuscripts ready to print, some autobiographical notes, and his voluminous correspondence with learned foreign persons. She asked to be given one year's salary, as had been given to the widow of another academician before. They gave her the salary for the rest of the year, 808 roubles and 45 kopeks.

---

79 Fourmont mentioned Bayer's letter to Fréret in his *Linguae Sinarum . . . Grammatica duplex . . .*, printed four years after Bayer's death, in 1742. He says that he had sent him a complimentary copy of his *Meditatione Sinicae . . .*, he liked him very much and wanted to be his friend forever. He had told him so, but Bayer felt that he had criticized him too severely and wrote to Fréret, complaining bitterly of his insults. 'I had thought at the time, and still think, that he would have preferred me to pass over in silence the grammar and the little dictionary he had published and had sent to me, but that was not possible. I therefore feel obliged to print here once more my comments on his work' (pp. XXV-XXVI). – Which he does, without mentioning Bayer's two large and much better informed articles about the *Zi Hui* dictionary and the *Spring and Autumn Annals,* printed in the *Commentarii* of the St Petersburg Academy, or his articles in the *Miscellanea Berolinensia,* of which he can hardly have been ignorant.

80 This letter is printed in Danielle Elisséeff-Poisle's Fréret biography, mentioned in Note 155 to the Preface.

The family returned to Königsberg in September; Bayer's father was still alive there. All that we know about the following years is that Bayer's widow lived for another 20 years in that city, and that the daughter, who owned a copy of the big Chinese-Latin dictionary, married an officer in Tettenborn.

A few months after the death of Bayer, in July 1738, a short, unsigned note appeared in the *Memoires de Trevoux*.

Theophile-Sigefroy Bayer, of the St Petersburg Academy of Science, died after January this year, for he wrote to Father Souciet as late as on 10 February. Some years ago he published his *Museum Sinicum*. Fourmont criticized it in his *Meditationes Sinicae*. Bayer who only knew about this from the *Journal des Sçavans*, replied with great modesty in the *Bibliothèque Germanique*. Bayer was a German. Czar Peter I had called him to St Petersburg when he founded his Academy. His articles, published in the *Mémoires* of this Academy, fully justify the choice of the Czar and show that Bayer excelled in more than one discipline. He was also a gentleman (honnête-homme) and as straightforward (droit) as he was learned.

This testimony may well have been written by Souciet himself. The only note about his demise, printed in the Jesuits' *Mémoires de Trevoux*, it gives a final touch to the story about Bayer and the Jesuits.[81]

---

81 *Mémoires de Trevoux*, July 1738, pp. 1510-11.

雍正二年新鐫

梅誕生先生原本

聯璧字彙

古吳坡文堂梓行

Fig. 15. Title page of Bayer's copy of the *Zi Hui* dictionary.

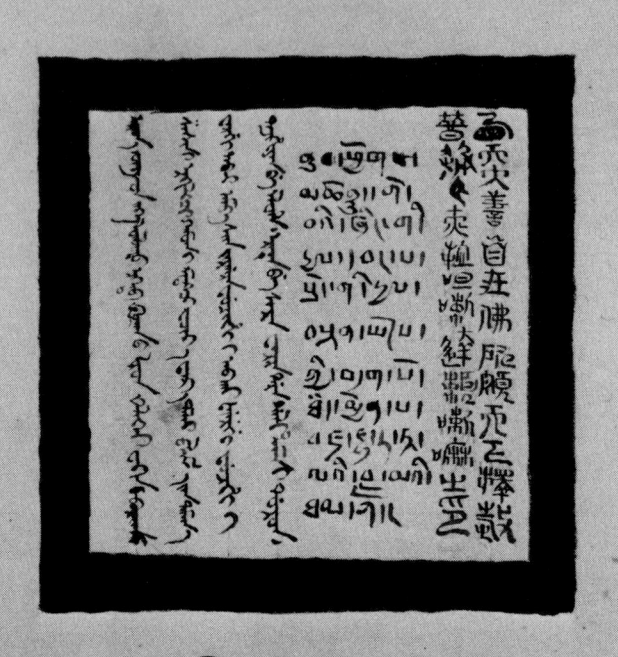

Sigillum magnum Dalai lamae, descriptum a me ex
authentica illius epistola it. 1734
Petropolin missa
Tota scripta erat litteris Schar
nigro colore, Sigillum ipsum rubrum. Invo-
luta telae sericae viridi.

Fig. 16. The Dalai Lama's seal (see p. 169).

篆字
chuen cu
antiqui Caracteres
adhuc in usu pro ins-
criptionibus, sigillis &c

楷字
kiai cu
Caracteres qui nunc sunt
quotidiani usus

篆字		楷字	
四 sse	一 y unum	四 sse	一 y unum
壁 py	窻 chuam	壁 py parietes siue muri	窻 chuam fenestra
圖 tu	風 fum	圖 tu pictura	風 fum ventus
書 xu	月 yue	書 xu Libri	月 yue Luna
消 siao	共 cum	消 siao terere	共 cum simul
白 pé	黃 hoam	白 pé albam	黃 hoam flavum
晝 cheu	昏 hoen	晝 cheu Diem	昏 hoen obscurum

lege a sinistra ad dextram
nota: pé cheu significant diem, hoam, hoen significant tempus
ante primam vigiliam noctis, hoc est hora nona uespertina. hoc posi-
ti.

Fig. 17. Parrenin's poem in seal and standard characters (see p. 163).

Lexicon Sinicum

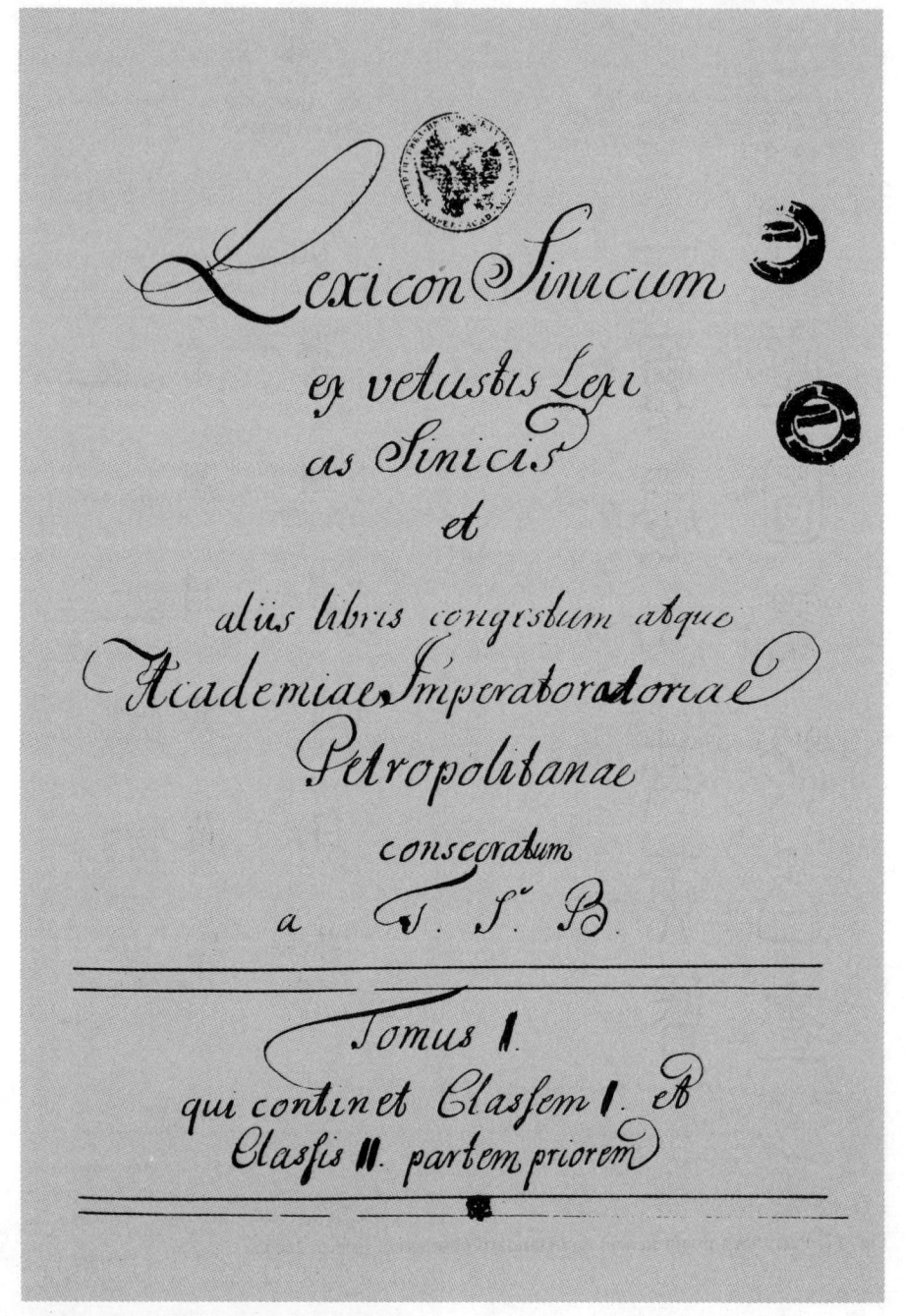

ex vetustis Lexi
cis Sinicis
et
aliis libris congestum atque
Academiae Imperatoratoriae
Petropolitanae
consecratum
a T. S. B.

Tomus I.
qui continet Classem I. et
Classis II. partem priorem

Fig. 18. Title page of Bayer's big dictionary.

Fig. 19. First page of Bayer's big dictionary.

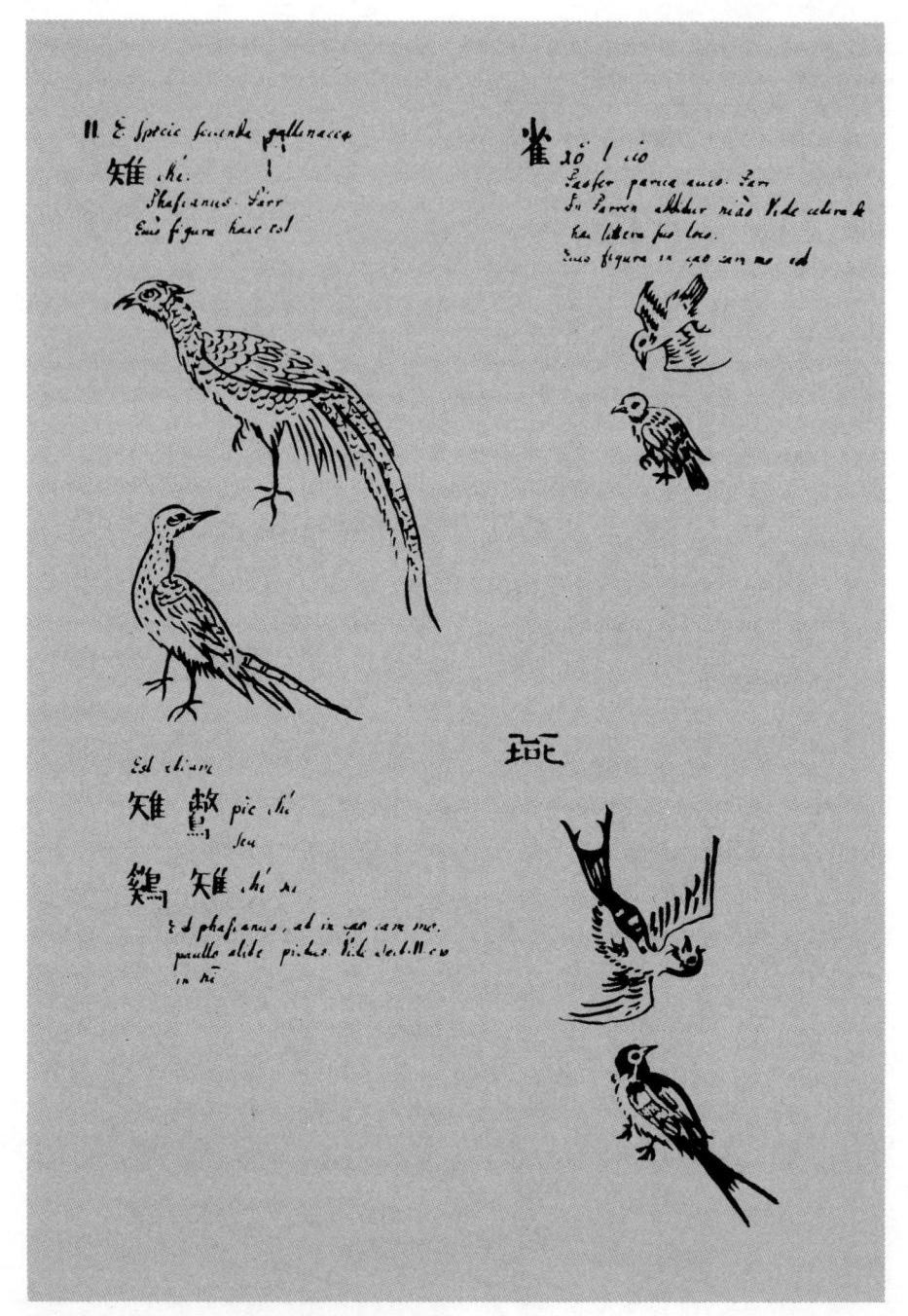

Fig. 20. Page from Bayer's big dictionary, the last volume.

EPILOGUE

In the last half of the eighteenth century the Jesuits in China pursued their production of works to be published in Europe. Most of them were printed after the suppression of the order in the magnificent *Mémoires concernant l'Histoire, les Sciences, les Arts, les Moeurs, les Usages etc. des Chinois*, 16 large volumes published at Paris between 1776 and 1814. There are several long articles about the Chinese language, enthusiastic as always and as always poor in exact information. Bayer's works are mentioned in one place, but only to be dismissed as 'this kind of erudition'.[82]

In Europe that period is singularly devoid of studies of the Chinese language. The mere existence of Bayer's *Museum Sinicum* and Fourmont's two books, the *Meditationes* and the *Grammatica duplex*, may have had a paralysing effect on potential learners. Since, obviously, these two great scholars had not been able to teach them how to speak or read Chinese, this language may have seemed simply to be out of reach for a European student.

Deguignes (1721-1800) and Deshauterayes (1724-95) belong to the history of sinology, but in fact they were general orientalists and historians. They probably knew very little Chinese and never wrote about it except in one paper where Deguignes takes the occasion to characterize the Chinese language as 'barbarous' and 'not fully formed and polished'.[83] They never mention Bayer's name.

However, we have heard that Bayer wrote to Bishop Benzelius in 1734 that his *Museum Sinicum* was nearly sold out shortly after its publication. Other readers, outside the circle of learned orientalists, must have read it out of curiosity or for pleasure. So let us close this book by quoting from one of them.

Among Boswell's 'Columns' for the *London Magazine*, the one in the February issue 1782 is entitled 'On Words'. The last paragraph of it runs as follows:

> If such superficial speculation upon words, as I have ventured to utter in this essay, can at all amuse, how must the mind be filled when we study a regular system of language. I am at present engaged in looking into a book of which I heard accidentally. It is entitled *Bayeri Museum Sinicum*, being a complete account of the Chinese language, printed at Petersburgh, in 1730; and it appears to me to display an aggregate of knowledge, ingenuity, and art, that is enough to make us contemplate such powers of mind with inexpressible veneration.[84]

82 Volume I, p. 278.
83 Deguignes' remarks appear on pp. 162-3 in vol. 36 of the *Mémoires de l'Academie des inscriptions et belles-lettres*, 1774.
84 I am grateful to Mr. Claus Magnussen, Librarian, Aarhus State and University Library, for having called my attention to these lines.

218   EPILOGUE

Here, finally, Bayer had found a sympathetic reader who understood what was the heart of the matter for him – the *system* of the Chinese language.

APPENDIX

BIBLIOGRAPHIES – MANUSCRIPTS – LETTERS

There are four *bibliographies* of Bayer's printed and unprinted works. The first one was published three years after his death in the article about his life and works, 'Mémoires historique sur la vie et les ouvrages de Mr. BAYER', based partially on a manuscript of his own. It lists 39 works and 11 to be printed, not including the huge 'Lexicon Sinicum'. (*Bibliothèque Germanique*, Vol. 50 (1741), pp. 99-113.) The second one appeared in G. Sharpe's 'Appendix de Lingua Sinica et Tartarica' to his edition of the *Syntagma Dissertationum quos olim Thomas Hyde separatim edidit . . .*, Oxford, 1767. Sharpe got it from an East Prussian man of science by name Johann Reinhold Forster, the father of the more famous traveller Johann Georg Adam Forster. Sharpe's correspondent seems to have known the Bayer family. This bibliography contains unpublished works not on Bayer's own list, including a 'Dissertatio de Christianis Sinicis et Tartaris'. The third one was inserted by G. F. Müller in his *Materials for the History of the Imperial Academy of Sciences*, pp. 467-70 – 'as far as possible a complete list of his works, the eternal monuments to the vast and profound erudition of that man'. – The last bibliography is that which is to be found in Franz Babinger's *Gottlieb Siegfried Bayer . . .*, Munich, 1915. It includes most of the works mentioned in the previous lists and also works in Russian and books and manuscripts in various archives.

In the Special Collections Department of the Glasgow University Library there is a large and important collection of *manuscripts* and *letters*, as well as Chinese books owned by Bayer. It includes more than 100 items, all the way from his first feeble attempts to construct a Chinese vocabulary when he was 19 years old, to the last years of his life and copies of letters he wrote few days before he died. This collection was bought after Bayer's death from his widow by Heinrich Walter Gerdes (1690-1742), pastor at the Lutheran Church in Trinity Lane in London, who had corresponded with Bayer (see p. 159). Some time between 1765 and 1780 it came to William Hunter (1718-83), the noted physiologist and obstetrician, who bequeathed all his various collections to Glasgow University. (Personal communication from Mr. David J. Weston, Assistant Librarian, the Special Collections Department, Glasgow University Library.) Some of the manuscripts are listed in Henri Cordier's *Bibliotheca Sinica*, Col. 1633-4 and 1650-3, but Mr. Weston is now preparing a complete catalogue of all material related to T.S. Bayer in the Glasgow University Library.

There are seven letters from Bayer to Johann Christoph Wolff (1683-1739), dealing with his Chinese studies, in the Staats- und Universitätsbibliothek Hamburg, Sup.Ep. 114 and 122.

Bayer's Lexicon Sinicum', 23 volumes in Folio, is kept in the Archive of the Akademia Nauk in Leningrad.

Important printed letters are to be found in the *Thesauri Epistolici Lacroziani Tomus I-III*, edited by I. L. Uhl, Leipzig 1742-6, and in the *Sylloge Nova Epistolarum varii Argumenti*, I-V, also edited by Uhl, Nuremberg 1760-9. Several important letters are printed in A. Erikson's edition of the *Letters to Erik Benzelius from learned Foreigners*, I-II, Göteborg, 1979.

BIBLIOGRAPHY

Aiton, A.J. and Shimao, W. 'Gorai Kinzo's Study of Leibniz and the I Ching Hexagrams', in *Annals of Science,* 38 (1981): 71-92.
Aleni, Guilio. *Tianzhu Jiangsheng Chuxiang Jingjie* ('Historia evangelica'). Nanking, 1637.
—— *Wan You Zhen Yuan* (The true origin of all things). Peking, 1628.
Arnauld, Antoine. *Oeuvres de Messire Antoine Arnauld.* Paris, 1780.
Assemani, Simonio. *Bibliotheca orientalis Clementino-Vaticana.* Rome, 1719-28.
Aubespine, Gabriel de. *Observationes de veteribus ecclesiae ritibus.* Paris, 1623.
Aymon, Jean. 'Observatio circa scientiam universalem Sinensium, in libro Confucii . . .', in *Acta Eruditorum,* 1713, pp. 46-8.

Babinger, Franz. *Gottlieb Siegfried Bayer (1694-1738). Ein Beitrag zur Geschichte der morgenländischen Studien im 18. Jahrhundert.* Munich, 1915.
Bayer, Theophilus Sigefridus. 'De Confucii libro Ch'un cieu', in *Commentarii Academiae Scientiarum Imperialis Petropolitanae,* VII, 1740, pp. 362-426.
—— *De Eclipsi Sinica liber singularis . . . accedunt praeceptionum de lingua sinica duo libri . . .* Königsberg, 1718.
—— 'De Ferdinandi Verbistii S.J. scriptis, praecipue vero de ejus Globo Terrestri sinico', in *Miscellanea Berolinensia,* VI, 1740, pp. 180-92.
—— *De Horis Sinicis et Cyclo horaria . . .* St Petersburg, 1735.
—— 'De Lexico Sinico Cu gvey', in *Commentarii,* VI, 1738, pp. 339-64.
—— 'De Re Numaria Sinorum', in *Miscellanea Berolinensia,* V, 1737, pp. 175-84.
—— *Museum Sinicum in quo Sinicae Linguae et Litteraturae ratio explicatur . . .* St Petersburg, 1730.
—— *Programma quo Bibliothecam Senatus Paleo-politani . . .* Königsberg, 1718.
—— *Vindiciae verborum Christi ἠλι, ἠλι, λαμα σαβαχϑανὶ quorundam oppositae.* Königsberg, 1718.
Bernard, Edward. *De Mensuris et Ponderibus antiquis libri tres.* Oxford, 1688.
Bold, John. 'John Webb: Composite Capitals and the Chinese Language', in *Oxford Art Journal,* 4 (1981): 9-17.
Bouvet, Joachim. *Portrait historique de l'Empereur de la Chine.* Paris, 1697.
Boym, Michael. 'Clavis medica ad Chinarum doctrinam de pulsibus', in *Miscellanea curiosa sive Ephemerides medico-physica Germanicae Academiae Naturae Curiosorum.* Nuremberg, 1686.
—— *Flora Sinensis . . .* Vienna, 1656.
Brockes, Barthold Heinrich. *Irdische Vergnügen in Gott,* I-IX. Hamburg, 1721-48.
Buglio, Louis, Magelhães, Gabriel de, and Verbiest, Ferdinand. *Innocentia Victrix,* Guangzhou, 1671.
Bülffinger, Georg Bernhard. *Specimen doctrinae Sinarum moralis et politica . . . accedit de litteratura Sinensi dissertatio extemporalis.* Frankfurt-on-Main, 1724.

Castell, Edmund. *Lexicon heptaglotton . . .* London, 1669.
Chamberlayne, John. *Oratio Dominica in diversas omnium fere gentium linguae versa . . .* Amsterdam, 1715.

Chan, Wing-tsit. *A Source Book in Chinese Philosophy.* Princeton, New Jersey, 1963.
Ch'en Shou-yi. 'John Webb: A forgotton Page in the early History of Sinology in Europe', in *The Chinese Social and Political Review (Peking)* 19 (1935): 295-330.
Cleyer, Andreas (Ed.) *Specimen medicinae sinicae . . .* Frankfurt, 1682.
Collani, Claudia von. 'Chinese Figurists in the Eyes of European Contemporaries', in *China Mission Studies (1550-1800) Bulletin,* IV, (1982): 12-23.
—— *Die Figuristen in der Chinamission.* Frankfurt-on-Main, 1981.
—— *P. Joachim Bouvet, S.J. – Sein Leben und sein Werke. Monumenta Serica Monograph Series XVII,* Nettetal 1985.
Confucius Sinarum Philosophus sive Scientia Sinensis latine exposita, studio et opera Prosperi Intorcetta, Christiani Herdtrich, Francisci Rougemont, Philippi Couplet, Patrum Societatis Jesu. Paris, 1687.
Cordier, Henri. *Bibliotheca Sinica.* Paris, 1904-08, with Supplement 1922.
—— 'Fragments d'une histoire des études chinoises au XVIIIe siecle', in *Centenaire de l'École des Langues orientales vivantes 1795-1895.* Paris, 1895.
Cosmas. *Christian Topography,* in Yule, Henry. *Cathay and the Way thither.* London, 1913-16.
Couplet, Philippe. *Catalogus S.J. qui post obitum Sti. Francisci Xaverii . . . im Imperio Sinarum Jesu Christi fidem propagarunt . . .* Paris, 1686.
Courant, Maurice. *Catalogue des livres chinois, coréens, japonais etc. de la Bibliothèque nationale.* Paris, 1902-12.
Cummings, J.S. *The Travels and Controversies of Friar Domingo Navarrete.* Cambridge, 1962.

D'Elia, Pasquale (Ed.). *Fonti Ricciane. Storia dell'introduzione del christianesimo in China.* Rome, 1942-9.
Deguignes, Chrétien Louis Joseph (Ed.). *Dictionnaire chinois, français et latin.* Paris, 1813.
Dehergne, Joseph. *Répertoire des Jésuites de Chine de 1552 à 1800.* Rome and Paris, 1973.
Demoment, Auguste. 'Le Père Dominique Parrenin', in *Mémoires de l'Académie des Sciences, Belles-Lettres et Arts de Besançon,* 175(1962-3): 225-43.
Des-Vignoles, Adolphe. *Chronologie de l'histoire sainte et des histoires étrangères . . .* Berlin, 1738.
Du Halde, Jean Baptiste. *Description géographique, historique, chronologique, politique de l'Empire chinoise et de la Tartarie chinoise.* Paris, 1735.
Duret, Claude. *Thresor de l'histoire des langues de cest univers . . .* Coligny, 1616.
Duyvendak, J.J.L. *Holland's Contribution to Chinese Studies,* London, 1950.

Elisséeff-Poisle, Danielle. *Nicolas Fréret (1688-1749) – Reflexions d'un humaniste du XVIIIe siècle sur la Chine.* Paris, 1978.
Erikson, Alvar (Ed.). *Letters to Erik Benzelius the Younger from Learned Foreigners.* Göteborg, 1979.
Feller, Joachim Friedrich. *Otium Hannoveranum sive miscellanea ex ore et schedis Leibnitii . . .* Leipzig, 1718.

Fourmont, Étienne. *Linguae Sinarum mandarinicae-hieroglyphicae grammatica duplex* . . . Paris, 1742.
—— *Meditationes Sinicae* . . . Paris, 1737.
(Fourmont, Étienne) 'Dissertation de M. de Fourmont sur la litterature chinoise' (review), in *Mémoires pour l'Histoire des Sciences et des Beaux Arts (Mémoires de Trevoux),* 1722, pp. 1574-80.
(——) 'Sur la litterature chinoise' (Secretary's report), in *Histoire de l'Académie royale des inscriptions et des belles-lettres,* Vol. V, 1729, pp. 312-19.
Franklin, Alfred. *Histoire de la Bibliothèque Mazarine.* Paris, 1901.
Fréret, Nicolas. 'Reflexion sur les principes generaux de l'art d'écrire et en particulier sur les fondements de l'écriture chinoise', in *Histoire de l'Académie royale des inscriptions et belles-lettres,* Vol. VI, 1729, pp. 609-35.
—— 'De la poesie des chinois', ibid. III, 1717, pp. 289-91.
(Fréret, Nicolas) 'Sur la langue chinoise' (Secretary's report), ibid. Vol. V, 1729, pp. 303-12.

(Gaubil) Simon, Renée (Ed.). *Le P. Antoine Gaubil, S.J.: Correspondance de Pekin 1722-59.* Geneva, 1970.
Gause, Fritz. *Die Geschichte der Stadt Königsberg.* Cologne and Graz, 1965-71.
Gernet, Jacques. *Chine et christianisme. Action et réaction.* Paris, 1982.
Gesner, Konrad von. *Mithridates de differentiis Linguis.* Zürich, 1555.
Godwin, Joscelyn. *Athanasius Kircher – a Renaissance Man and the Quest for lost Knowledge.* London, 1979.
Goncalves, J.A. *Diccionario China-Portuguez.* Macao, 1833.
Gonzales, Juan de Mendoça. *Historia de las cosas mas notables, ritos y costumbres, del gran Reyno dela China* . . . Rome, 1585.
Greaves, John. *Epochae celebriores astronomicis, historicis, chronologices Chataiorum* . . . *ex traditione Ulug Beigi* . . . London, 1650.
—— *Binae tabulae geographicae, una Nessir Eddini Persae, altera Ulug Beigi Tatari* . . . London, 1652.

Haupt, Johan Thomas. *Neue und volständige Auslegung* . . . *des Ye-Kim.* Rostock and Wismar, 1753.
Hayton the Armenian. *Flos Historiarum Partium Orientis.* The part concerning China is printed in Yule, Henry: *Cathay and the Way thither.* London, 1913-16.
Herbelot de Molainville de, Barthélemy. *Bibliothèque orientale* . . . Paris, 1697.
Hottinger, Johann Heinrich. *Etymologicum orientale sive lexicon harmonicum heptaglotton* . . . Frankfurt, 1661.
Hummel, Arthur W. *Eminent Chinese of the Ch'ing Period.* Washington, 1943.
Hyde, Thomas. *Mandragorias, seu Historia Shahiludi.* Oxford, 1694.
—— *Historia religionis veterum Persarum* . . . Oxford, 1700.

Intorcetta, Prospero. *Historica relatio de ortu et progressu fidei ortodoxa in Regno Chinensi per missionarios Societatis Jesu.* Regensburg, 1672.
—— (Ed.). *Sapientia Sinica.* Jiangchang, 1662.
—— (Ed.). *Sinarum Scientia Politico-Moralis.* Canton and Goa. 1667.

Kaempfer, Engelbrecht. *Amoenitatum exoticarum politico-physico-medicarum fasciculi V*. . . Lemgo, 1712.
Kirch, Christfried. 'Brevis disquisitio de eclipsi Solis, quae a Sinensibus anno 7 Quang Vuti notata est . . .' in *Miscellanea Berolinensis*, Continuatio I, 1723, pp. 133-9.
Kircher, Athanasius. *China monumentis qua sacris qua profanis illustrata* . . . Rome, 1667.
—— *Oedipus Aegyptiacus* . . . Rome, 1652-4.
—— *Prodromus Coptus sive Aegyptiacus* . . . Rome, 1636.
Kirchère, Athanase. *La Chine* . . . *illustrée* . . . *avec un dictionaire chinois et français* . . . Amsterdam, 1670.
Klaproth, Julius. *Verzeichniss der chinesischen und mandchurischen Büchern und Handschriften der kgl. Bibliothek zu Berlin*. Paris, 1822.
Kopelevič, Ju.Ch. *Osnovanie Petersburgskoi Akademii Nauk*. Leningrad, 1977.
—— and Juskevič, A.P. *Christian Goldbach 1690-1764*. Moskow, 1983.
Kraft, Eva. '*Andreas Cleyer*', in *Festschrift zum 86. Deutschen Ärztetag*, Kassel 1983, pp. 25-40.
—— 'Christian Mentzel's chinesische Geschenke für Kaiser Leopod I', in *Schloss Charlottenburg-Berlin-Preussen, Festschrift für Margarete Kühn*. Munich, 1975.
—— 'Die chinesische Büchersammlung des Grossen Kurfürsten und seines Nachfolgers', in *China und Europa,* the catalogue of the Berlin exhibition, 1973, pp. 18-25.
—— 'Ein Koffler Autograph', ibid., pp. 26-9.
—— 'Frühe chinesische Studien in Berlin', in *Medizin-historische Journal,* 11 (1976): 92-128.

Lach, Donald F. *Asia in the Making of Europe*. Chicago and London, 1965-77.
Lacroze, Mathurin Veyssiere de. *Histoire du christianisme des Indes*. The Hague, 1724.
—— *Vindiciae veterum scriptorum contra L. Harduinum, S.J.P.* Rotterdam, 1708.
—— *Lexicon Aegyptiaco-Latinum* . . . Oxford, 1775.
Lambech, Peter. *Commentarii de Augustissima Bibliotheca Caesarea Vindobonensi*. Vienna, 1665-79.
Lange, Lorenz. *Journal de la résidence du Sieur Lange, agent de sa Majesté Imperiale de la Grande Russie à la cour de la Chine dans les années 1721 et 1722*. Leiden, 1726.
Lanier, Lucien. *Etude historique sur les relations de la France et du royaume de Siam de 1662 à 1703*. Versailles, 1883.
Le Chou-King, un des livres sacrés des chinois . . . traduit par le feu P. Gaubil . . . Paris, 1770.
Le Comte, Louis. *Nouveaux mémoires sur l'état présent de la Chine*. Paris, 1696.
Legge, James. *The Chinese Classics*, I-VII. Hongkong and London, 1861-72.
Leibniz, Gottfried Wilhelm. 'Annotatio de quibusdam ludis: inprimis de ludo quodam sinico', in *Miscellanea Berolinensia* I, 1710, pp. 22-6.
—— 'Brevis designatio meditationum de originibus gentium, ductis potissimum ex indicio linguarum', ibid. I, 1710, pp. 1-16.
—— *Collectanea etymologica* (Ed. I.G. Eccard). Hanover, 1717.
—— *Dissertatio de Arte Combinatoria*. Leipzig, 1666.

—— 'Explication de l'arithmétique binaire . . . (qui) donne le sens des anciennes figures chinoises de Fohy', in *Mémoires de l'Académie royale des Sciences,* 1703, pp. 85-9.

—— 'Lettre sur la philosophie chinoise à Mons. de Remond', in Kortholt's edition of *Epistola ad diversos,* Vol. II, 1735, pp. 413-94.

—— *Opera philosophica* (Ed. J.E. Erdmann) Halle, 1840.

G.G.L. (Ed.) (Leibniz) *Novissima sinica historiam nostri temporis illustratura* . . . s.l., 1697 and 1699.

(Leibniz) 'Erklärung der Arithmeticae binariae, welche vor 3000 Jahren bey den Chinesern im Gebrauch gewesen, und bisher bey ihnen selbst vorlohren, neulich bey uns wieder funden worden', in *Curieuse Bibliothec,* 1705, pp. 81-112.

(Leibniz) Kortholt, Christian (Ed.). *Viri illustris Godofridi Guilielmi Leibnitii Epistola ad diversos* . . . I-IV. Leipzig, 1734-42.

Le Moyne, Etienne. *Varia Sacra, seu Sylloge variorum opusculorum graecorum* . . . Leiden, 1685.

Les deux cousines (Yu jiao li), translated by Abel Rémusat, Paris, 1822 and again by Stanislas Julien, 1864.

Levšin, B.V. (Ed.). *Avtografy učenych v Arkive Akademii Nauk SSSR* Moskow, 1978.

Leyser, Polycarp. *Apparatus literarius . . . ex omnis generis eruditione depromens studio societatis Colligentium,* I-II. Wittenberg, 1717-18.

Li Zhuomin. *Li's Chinese Dictionary (Li Zhi Zhongguo Wen Zidian).* Hongkong, 1980.

Longobardi, Niccolo. *Traité sur quelques points de la religion des chinois.* Paris 1701. Reprinted in Kortholt's edition of Leibniz's letters, Vol. II, 1735, 165-266.

Loose, Hans Dieter. *Berthold Heinrich Brockes (1680-1747) – Dichter und Ratsherr im Hamburg.* Hamburg, 1980.

Lundbæk, Knud. 'Chief Grand Secretary Chang Chü-cheng and the early China Jesuits', in *China Mission Studies (1550-1800) Bulletin,* III (1981): 2-11.

—— 'Dr. Mentzels kinesiske Børnebog', in *Danmark-Kina,* December 1982.

—— 'Imaginary Ancient Chinese Characters', in *China Mission Studies (1550-1800) Bulletin,* V (1983):

—— 'Notes sur l'image du Neo-Confucianisme dans la littérature européenne du XVIIe a la fin du XIXe siècle', in *Actes du IIIe Colloque international de Sinologie.* Paris, 1983.

—— 'The first Translation from a Confucian Classic in Europe', in *China Mission Studies (1550-1800) Bulletin,* I (1979): 1-11.

—— 'The Image of Neo-Confucianism in *Confucius Sinarum Philosophus*', in *Journal of the History of Ideas,* 44 (1982): 19-30.

—— 'Une grammaire espagnole de la langue chinoise au XVIIIe siecle', in *Actes du IIe Colloque de Sinologie,* Paris, 1980.

Magaillans, Gabriel de. *Nouvelle relation de la Chine.* Paris, 1688.

Mailla, Joseph Anne Marie de Moyriac de. *Histoire générale de la Chine.* Paris, 1777-85.

Maizeaux, Pierre des. *Recueil de diverses pieces sur la philisophie . . . par Messieurs Leibniz, Clarke, Newton, etc.* Amsterdam, 1720.

Marcianus. *Periplus of the Outer Sea,* in Yule, Henry: *Cathay and the Way thither.* London, 1913-16.
Martini, Martino. *De Bello tartarico Historia.* Antwerp, 1654.
—— *Novus Atlas Sinensis.* Amsterdam, 1655.
—— *Sinicae Historiae Decas prima.* Munich, 1658.
(Martini, Martino?) 'Historiae Sinicae Decas secunda', in Thévenot's *Voyages.*
Masson, Philippe. 'Dissertation critique ou l'on tâche de faire voir, par quelques exemples, l'utilité qu'on peut retirer de la langue chinoise pour l'intelligence de divers mots et passages difficiles de l'Ancien Testament' Vol. II, pp. 96-153. Continued with slightly varying titles in Vol. III, pp. 29-106, and Vol. IV, pp. 29-69, in *Histoire critique de la Republique des Lettres tant anciennes que modernes.* Utrecht/Amsterdam, 1712-18.
Ma Yong. 'Martino Martini, pioneer of modern sinology', in *Lishi Yanjiu* No. 6(1980): 153-68 (in Chinese).
'Mémoire historique sur la vie et les ouvrages de Mr. Bayer', in *Bibliotheque Germanique,* Vol. 50, 1741, pp. 99-113.
Mémoires concernant l'Histoire, les Sciences, les Arts, les Moeurs, les Usages etc. des Chinois. Paris 1776-1814.
Meniski, François Mesgnien. *Linguarum orientalium turcicae, arabicae, persicae Institutiones . . .* Vienna, 1680.
Mentzel, Christian. 'De radice Chinensium Gin-Sen', in *Miscellanea curiosa sive Ephemerides med.phys. Germ. Acad. Caes. Leopold. Nat. cur . . .* Dec.II, Annus V (1686), pp. 73-9.
—— *Kurtze Chinesische Chronologia oder Zeit-Register Aller Chinesischen Kaiser . . . auch mit zween Chinesischen erklärten Tafeln . . . bezogen aus der Chineser Kinderlehre Siao Ul Hio oder Lun genande . . .* Berlin, 1696.
—— *Sylloge minutiarum Lexici Latino-Sinico-Characteristici . . .* Nuremberg, 1685.
Montfaucon, Bernard de. *Collectio nova patrum et scriptorum graecorum.* Paris, 1706.
Montucci, Antonio. *Urh-Chih-Tsze-Tëen-Se-Yin-Pe-Keaou.* London, 1817.
Moule, A.C. *Christians in China before the year 1550.* London, 1950.
Müller, Andreas. *Abdallae Beidavaei Historia Sinensis.* Berlin, 1678.
—— *Alpha kai Omega – Alphabeta ac Notae diversarum Linguarum . . .* Berlin, 1703.
—— *Anderer Theil des Catalogi der Sinesischen Bücher bey der Churfürstlichen Brandenburgischen Bibliothec.* Berlin, 1683.
—— *Andreae Mulleri Greiffenhagii Unschuld gegen die heftigen Beschuldigungen . . .* Stettin, 1683.
—— *Basilicon Sinense.* Berlin, 1679.
—— *Besser Unterricht von der Sinenser Schrift und Druck . . .* Berlin, 1680.
—— *Catalogus Librorum Sinicorum Bibliothecae Electoralis Brandenburgicae.* Berlin, before 1683.
—— *Deutsche Übersetzung und Erklärung des zur Probe seines Sinesischen Schlüssels gnädigst fürgelegten Textes und Thematis aus den Sinesischen Jahrbüchern . . .* Berlin, 1683.
—— *Excerpta manuscripti cujusdam Turci, quod ad cognitione Dei et hominis ipsius a quodam Azizo Nesephaeo Tartaro scriptum est . . .* Berlin, 1665.
—— *Geographia mosaica generalis ex Genesios capite decimo.* Berlin, 1689.

—— *Hebdomas Observationum de Rebus Sinicis*. Berlin, 1674.
—— *Imperii Sinensis Nomenclator geographicus*. Berlin, 1680.
—— *Marci Pauli Veneti . . . de Regionibus Orientalibus Libri III . . . itemque . . . de Catajo . . .Disquisitio*. Berlin, 1671.
—— *Monumenti Sinici, quod anno Domini MDCXXV terris in ipsa China erutum . . . lectio seu phrasis, versio seu metaphrasis, translatio seu paraphrasis*. Berlin, 1672.
—— *Oratio Dominica Sinice cumque versione et notis itemque Oeconomia Bibliothecae Sinicae*. Berlin, 1676.
—— *Specimen Lexici Mandarinici . . . uno exemplo syllabae XIM commonstratum . . .* Berlin, 1684.
—— *Speciminum Sinicorum . . . Decimae de Decimis . . .* Berlin, 1685.
—— *Symbolae Syriacae sive Epistolae duo Syriacae amoebaeae . . .* Berlin, 1673.
(Müller, Andreas) Ludeken, Thomas (pseudonym). *Oratio orationum . . . versiones praeter authenticam fere centum . . .* Berlin, 1680.
Müller, August. 'Eröffnungsrede' (Andreas Müller), in *Zeitschrift d. Deutschen Morgenländishcen Gesellschaft*, 35 (1881): III-XVI.
Müller, Gerhard Friedrich. '*Chinesische Gesandten Ceremonielle . . .*' in *Sammlung Russischer Geschichte*, I, pp. 34-74, St Petersburg 1732.
—— 'De scriptis Tanguticis . . .', in *Commentarii Academiae Scientiarum Imperialis Petropolitanae*, Vol. X, 1742.
—— *Materiali dlja istorii Imperatorskoi Akademii Nauk*, Vol. 6, 1725-43. St Petersburg, 1890 (in German).
Mungello, David E. 'Die Quellen für das Chinabild Leibnizens', in Studia Leibnitiana, Band XIV/2 (1982), pp. 233-43.
—— *Leibniz and Confucianism – the Search for Accord*. Honolulu, 1977.
—— *Curious Land:* Jesuit Accomodation and the Origin of Sinology. Stuttgart, 1985.
—— 'The first complete translation of the Confucian Four Books in the West', in *International Symposium on Chinese-Western Cultural Interchange in Commemoration of the 400th Anniversary of the Arrival of Matteo Ricci in China*. Taipei 1985, pp. 515-41.
—— 'The Jesuits' use of Chang Chü-cheng's commentary in their translation of the Confucian Four Books (1687)', in *China Mission Studies (1550-1800) Bulletin*, III, (1981): 12-22.
—— 'The reconciliation of Neo-Confucianism with Christianity in the writings of Joseph de Prémare, S.J.', in *Philosophy East and West*, 26 (1976): 389-410.

Navarrete, Domingo Fernandez. *Tratados historicos, politicos, y religiosos de la Monarchia de China . . .* Madrid, 1676.
Needham, Joseph. *Science and Civilisation in China*, Vol. I-V (10 volumes), Cambridge, 1954-83.
Needham, Joseph and Lu Gwei-djen. *Celestial Lancets. A History and Rationale of Acupuncture and Moxa*. Cambridge, 1980.
Nessel, Daniel de. *Catalogus sive recensio specialis omnium codicum manuscriptorum graecorum nec non orientalium . . .* Vienna and Nuremberg, 1690.
Noël, François. *Observationes mathematicae et physicae in India et China facta . . .* Prague, 1710.

—— *Sinensis Imperii Libri Classici Sex* . . . Prague, 1711.

Ošanin, I.M. *Kitaisko-Russkii Slovar* (Chinese-Russian Dictionary). Moscow, 1952.

Paravey, le Chevalier de. 'Des patriarches anterieurs à Ty-Ko ou Noë . . .', in *Annales de philosophie chrétienne,* Vol. XVI, 1837, pp. 115-34.
Pfeiffer, August. *Introductio ad Orientem* . . . Wittenberg, 1671.
Pfister, Louis. *Notices biographiques et bibliographiques sur les Jésuites de l'ancienne mission de Chine 1552-1773.* Shanghai, 1932.
Pinot, Virgile. *Documents inédits relatif à la connaissance de la Chine en France de 1685 à 1740.* Paris, 1932.
—— *La Chine et la formation de l'esprit philosophique en France.* Paris, 1932.
Plano Carpini, Johannes. *Liber Tartarum.* See Rubrouck.
Polo, Marco. *Travels.* English edition by Yule, Henry: *the Book of Ser Marco Polo* . . . London, 1871/1909.
Possevino, Antonio. *Bibliotheca selecta qua agitur de Ratione Studiorum* . . . Rome, 1593.
(Prémare) 'Lettre inédite du P. Prémare sur le monothéisme des chinois', in *Annales de philosophie chrétienne,* III (5. serie), 1861, pp. 128-51.
—— *Notitia Linguae Sinicae.* Malacca, 1831.
—— *Vestiges de principeaux dogmes chrétiens tirés des anciens livres chinois.* Paris, 1878.

Rawski, Evelyn S. *Education and popular Literacy in Ch'ing China.* Ann Arbor, 1979.
Really, Conor. *Athanasius Kircher – Master of a Hundred Arts.* Rome and Wiesbaden, 1974.
Reeland, Adriaan. *Dissertationum miscellarium partes tres.* Utrecht, 1706-7.
Rehbinder, C.M.V. *Ätten Rehbinder genom åtta sekler.* Stockholm, 1925.
Remond de Montmort, Pierre. *Essay d'analyse sur les jeux de hazard.* Paris, 1713.
Rémusat, Abel. *Élémens de la grammaire chinoise.* Paris, 1822.
—— *Mélanges asiatiques* . . . Paris, 1825-6.
—— *Nouveaux mélanges asiatiques.* Paris, 1829.
Renaudot, Eusèbe. *Anciennes relations des Indes et la Chine, de deux voyageurs mahométans* . . . Paris, 1718.
—— *Historia Patriarcharum Alexandrinorum Jacobitorum* . . . Paris, 1713.
Ricci, Matteo. *Tianzhu Shiye (The true meaning of the Lord of Heaven).* Peking, 1603.
Roccha (Rocca), Angelo. *Bibliotheca Apostolica Vaticana* . . . Rome, 1591.
Roy, Olivier. *Leibniz et la Chine.* Paris, 1972.
Rubrouck, William of. *Travels.* English edition by Rockhill, William W.: *The Journey of William of Rubruck with two accounts of an earlier Journey of John Pian de Carpini.* London, 1900.
Rudbeck, Olaus sen. *Atland eller Manheim.* Uppsala, 1675.
Rudbeck, Olaus jun. *Specimen usus linguae gothicae* . . . Uppsala, 1717.
—— *Thesaurus linguarum Asiae et Europae harmonicus* . . . Uppsala, 1716.
Rule, Paul A. *K'ung-Tzu or Confucius? The Jesuits Interpretation of Confucianism.* Unpublished Ph.D. Dissertation, Canberra University, Australia, 1972.

Sainte Marie, Antoine de. *Traité sur quelques points importants de la mission de la Chine.* Paris, 1701. Reprinted in Kortholt's edition of Leibniz's letters, Vol. II, 1735, pp. 267-412.
Saumaise (Salmacius), Claude. *Plinianae exercitationes in Solini Polyhistoria.* Paris, 1629.
Scaliger, Joseph Justus. *Opus novum de Emendatione Temporum,* Paris, 1583.
Semedo, Alvaro. *Imperio de la China . . .* Madrid, 1642.
Sharpe, Gregory. *Syntagma dissertationum quos olim Thomas Hyde separatim edidit . . .* with an *Appendix de Linguae Sinensi* by G.S. Oxford, 1767.
Simon, Walter. 'The China illustrata Romanisations', in Egerod, Søren and Glahn, Else (Ed.) *Studia Serica Bernhard Karlgren dedicata.* Copenhagen, 1959.
Souciet, Etienne. *Observations mathématiques, astronomiques, géographiques, chronologiques, et physiques, tirées des anciens livres chinois; ou faites nouvellement aux Indes et à la Chine par les Pères de la Compagnie de Jésus.* Paris, 1729-32.
Spizelius, Theophilus. *De Re litteraria Sinensium Commentarius . . .* Leiden, 1660.
Sutton, Geoffrey Howard. 'Neun Briefe von Barthold Heinrich Brockes an unbekannte Empfänger', in Hans-Dieter Loose's book on Brockes, see under Loose.

Tautz, Kurt. *Die Bibliothecare der Churfürstlichen Bibliothek zu Cölln an der Spree.* Leipzig, 1925.
Texeira, Pedro. *Relaciones de Pedro Texeira . . .* s.1, 1610.
Tentzel, Wilhelm Ernst. *Curieuse Bibliotec.* Frankfurt and Leipzig, 1704-6.
(Tentzel, Wilhelm Ernst) *Monatliche Unterredungen einiger guten Freunden.* Leipzig, 1689-98.
Thévenot, Melchisédech. *Relations de divers voyages curieux.* Paris, 1663-72.
—— *Veterum Mathematicorum Athenaei . . .* Paris, 1693.
Thomassin, Louis. *Glossarium universale Hebraicum . . .* Paris, 1697.
Trigault, Nicolas. *De Christiana Expeditione apud Sinas suscepta ab Societate Jesu.* Augsburg, 1615.

Uhl, I.L. (Ed.). *Sylloge nova Epistolarum varii argumenti I-XI.* Nuremberg, 1760-69
—— *Thesauri Epistolici Lacroziani Tomus I-III.* Leipzig 1742-6.

Vasil'ev, V.P. *Graphic System of Chinese Characters: An Attempt at the first Chinese-Russian Dictionary* (in Russian). St Petersburg, 1867.
Visdelou, A. and Galand, C. (Ed.). *Supplément à la Bibliotheque Orientale de M. D'Herbelot.* Paris, 1780.
Vossius, Isaac. *Variarum Observationum Liber.* London, 1685.

Waldeck, G.F. 'Le P. Philippe Couplet, Malininois, S.J.' in *Analectes pour servir à l'histoire ecclastiaque de la Belgique,* Vol. IX, 1872, pp. 5-31.
Walton, Brian. *Biblia Sacra Polyglotta . . .* London, 1653-57.
—— *Biblicus apparatus chronologico-topographico-philologicus . . .* Zürich, 1673.
Webb, John. *A historical Essay endeavouring a Probability that the Language of the Empire of China is the primitive Language.* London, 1669.

Wienau, R. 'Sylloge minutiarum Lexici Latino-Sinico-Characteristici', in *Acta historica Leopoldina,* No. 9, 1975, pp. 463-72.
Wiesinger, Liselotte and Kraft, Eva. 'Die chinesische Bibliothek des Grossen Kurfürsten und ihre Bibliothekare', in *China und Europa,* the catalogue of the Berlin Exhibition, 1973, pp. 166-73.
Wilkins, John. *Essay towards a real character and a philosophical language.* London, 1668.
Witek, John W. *Controversial ideas in China and in Europe: A biography of Jean-François Foucquet* (1665-1741). Rome, 1982.
Witsen, Nicolaas. *Nord en Oost Tartaryen . . .* Amsterdam, 1692 and 1705.
Wolff, Christian. *De Sapientia Sinensium Oratio . . .* Trevoux, 1724.

Yang Guanxian. *Pi Sie Lun (Bie xie lun).* Peking, 1659.

Zacher, Hans J. *Die Hauptschriften zur Dyadik von G.W. Leibniz.* Frankfurt-on-Main, 1973.

GLOSSARY OF CHINESE TERMS

Ba Gua Fangwei 八卦方位

Ben Cao Gangmu 本草綱目

Bi 壁

Cao Zi 草字

Chun Qiu 春秋

Cong Gu 從古

Da Qin 大秦

Da Xue 大學

De 德

Dui Zi 對子

'Fa Lam Çi Ya' 法郎切 濟亞

Fanqie 反切

Fangwei 方圍

Feng Huang 鳳凰

'Foe Lam Çy Ya' 拂郎 祭補 亞

Gang Jian Bu 綱鑑補

Gong 公

Gu 故

Guanhua	官話
Gui Hai Hui	癸亥晦
Hai Pian	海篇
Huang di	皇帝
Jian Zi	檢字
Juan	卷
Kai Shu	楷書
Kang Xi Zidian	康熙字典
'Keu'	口
'Kium'	刀
Kong Shi Zhuan	孔氏傳
Kong Shi Zu Ting Guang Ji	孔氏祖庭廣記
'Kua Keu Kuai? (Li) Po Chim Ye'	咼：口戾不正也
Kui Bi Yi Jing	奎壁易經
Kun	坤
Kun Yu Quan Tu	坤輿全圖
Li Si	李斯
Lishi Zongwen Zidian	李氏中文字典
Liushisi Gua Fangwei	六十四卦方圍
Liu Yeqiu	劉葉秋

GLOSSARY

Mantou	饅頭
Mei Yingzuo	梅膺祚
Ming	螟
Mulu	目錄
Nan	男
Niao	鳥
'Niu' (Nü Gua)	女媧
Pian Hai	篇海
Pin Zi Jian	品字箋
Qian	乾
Qilin	麒麟, 麐
Ren	人亻
Sha	殺
Shang	上
Sheng	聖 (聖)
Sheng Jiao Xin Zheng	聖教信證
Shuowen Jiezi	說文解字
Songban	宋版
Sui Bi Shu	遂筆書
Tai Ji	太極

Tian Shen Hui Ke	天神會課象
Tianzhu Jiang Sheng Chu Xiang Jing Jie	天主降生出象經解
Tianzhu Shi Yi	天主實義
Tong Lun	通論
Wan Li	萬曆
Wan You Zhen Yuan	萬有真原
Wen Lin Sha Jin Wan Bao Quan Shu	文林沙錦萬寶全書
Wu Zhu	五銖
Xiao Er Lun	小兒論
Xiao Xue	小學
Xing Li Da Quan Shu	性理大全書
Xu Yuanmeng	徐元夢
Yan	言
Yang	羊
Yesu Hui	耶穌會
Yi Jing	易經
Yi Tu Jie	易圖解

Yin	印			
Yin Duo Ze	殷	鐸	澤	
Yin Shi Hai Pian	音	釋	海	篇
Yu	羽			
Yu Jiao Li	玉	嬌	梨	
Yun Bi	運		筆	
Za Zi	雜		字	
Zhang Juzheng	張	居	正	
Zheng Zi	正		字	
Zheng Zi Tong	正	字	通	
Zhi Shan	至		善	
Zhou	周			
Zhou Yi	周		易	
Zi Hui	字		彙	
Zi Zhi Tong Jian (Gangmu)	資	治	通	鑑 (綱目)
Zhongguo Zidian Shi Lüe	中	國	字	典 史 略
Zhong Wen Da Cidian	中	文	大	辭 典
Zuo Zhuan	左			

INDEX

Abaga, 40
Aiton, A.J., 84
Al-Baidawi, 40, 63, 71, 136
Al-Banakati, 40n.
Albrecht, Michael, 161n.
Alfaro, Pietro de, 44
Alieni, Giulio, 66, 128n.
Analects, 48n., 49n., 50n., 132
Anaxagoras, 136
Anaximander, 136
Antonio of Florence, 41
Arghun, 41n.
Arnauld, Antoine, 48
Ars combinatoria, 6, 102, 124, 172
Asisus Nesephaeus, 62
Assedeus, Solomon, 92
Assemani, Guiseppe, 90-1
Aubespine, Gabriel de, 91
Avanzo, Francesco, 45
Aymon, Jean, 50-1

Babinger, Franz, 1, 12n., 189, 219
Barhebraeus, Georgius, 42
Barnimus, Hagius, 68
Bartsch, Gottfried, 4, 5, 11, 68, 70, 72
Bartsch, Heinrich,, 14
Bayer, T.S., Chinese studies:
  Books: *De Eclipsi Sinica Liber singularis* 14, 15, 20, 31-8, 74n., 78n., 93n., 133n., 140, 162n., 177.
  – *De Horis Sinicis* 21, 114, 166-8, 171-3. – *Museum Sinicum* 3, 4, 5, 11, 20-1, 35n., 38, 39-140, 151, 154-7, 160n., 167, 171, 177-9, 181, 183, 189n., 190, 191n., 198, 201-2, 204-10
  Articles: On Chinese coins 185-6 – On Fourmont's criticism 205-7 – On his Peking correspondence 185 – On the Spring and Autumn Annals 160, 179-84 – On the works of Ferdinand Verbiest, S.J. 186-7 – On the *Zi Hui* dictionary 174-9 – The Big Chinese-Latin Dictionary 120, 188-203
Beckmann, Johannes Cristoph, 71

Benzelius, 7, 93n., 182, 188, 189, 217, 220
Bernoulli, Nicolas and David, 17
Bignon, Jean Paul, 67n., 87-8
Biron, Ernst Johann, 171, 173
Blæsing, David, 73
Blumentrost, Lorenz, 16, 18
Bold, J., 58n.
Book of Changes, 114, 154n., 168, 171-3, 194
Boswell, James, 218
Bouvet, Joachim, S.J., 84,˙ 108, 113
Boym, Michael, S.J., 56
Brancati, Francois, S.J., 162n.
Brockes, Barthold Heinrich, 21n.
Brucker, Johann Jacob, 184
Bülffinger, Georg Bernhard, 4, 17, 89, 104-9, 194
Buglio, Lodovico, S.J., 35n.

Carius, 188
Cassini, Giandominico, 74, 89
Castell, Edmund, 61, 62n.
Chamberlayn, John, 99, 160
Chang Chü-cheng, 51n.
Ch'en Shou-yi, 58n.
Chun Qiu, see *Spring and Autumn Annals*
Cicero, 72n.
Ciphers, roman, 112-13
Chalier, Valentin, S.J., 165n.
China . . . illustrata . . . , 56, 62-3, 86, 99, 112, 134
Clarke, Samuel, 61, 62n.
Clavis sinica, Andreas Müller's, 62, 66, 68, 69, 72, 74-5, 106
Clavis sinica, Christian Mentzel's, 79, 110-11, 120
Cleyer, Andreas, 58, 70, 78, 111
Collani, Claudia von, 139n.
Commentarii Academiae Scientiarum Imperialis Petropolitanae, 18, 20, 156, 160, 165, 174-84
Confucius Sinarum Philosophus, 32, 35, 48-51, 80, 81n., 114, 128, 131-3, 160, 180, 181n., 202

— China Jesuits signing approbation, 49
Cordier, Henri, 1, 84, 159 n., 188, 207 n.
Cosmas Indicopleustes, 39, 91
Couplet, Philippe, 32, 35-6, 47 n., 49, 58, 74-5, 79, 84, 94, 96, 110, 158, 162, 166, 169, 180, 194, 202
Crysorroas, 57
Cummings, J.S., 48 n., 49 n.

Dalai Lama, 169-70, 194, 207
Danet, Pierre, 165 n., 196
De Bello tartarico Historia, 52 n.
De Christiana Expeditione apud Sinos, 47 n.
De Pei, 168
Deguignes, Joseph, 135 n., 217
Deguignes, C.L.J., 125 n.
d'Elia, Pasquale, S.J., 34 n., 158 n.
Delisle, Joseph Nicolas, 17, 19 n., 67, 88-9, 95, 208 n., 209
Demoment, Auguste, 155 n.
Deshauterayes, see Le Roux de Deshauterayes
Des-Vignoles, Alphonse, 85 n., 159, 161, 171
Diaz, Francesco, 109
Diaz Vocabulary, 14, 15, 32, 37, 94, 109, 125 n., 126-7, 189, 196
Diogenes Laertes, 136
Dionysios the Areopagite, 73
Doctrine of the Mean, 48 n., 49 n., 50 n., 110, 132 n.
Dominico, 99 n.
Dorn, B., 188, 197
Du Halde, Jean Baptiste, S.J., 158, 169, 208
Duyvendak, J.J.L., 53 n.
Duret, Claude, 45 n.

Edelheer, Jacques, 53
Egerod, Søren, 57 n., 126 n., 129 n.
Elisséeff-Poisle, Danielle, 87 n., 88 n., 209
Epicharmus, 60
Erastothenes, 73
Erikson, A., 220
Euler, Leonard, 17

Falcon (Salcon), Nicolas, 41
Feller, Joachim Friedrich, 103 n.
Feng Yin-jing, 164 n.
Figurism, 138-9
Forster, Johann Reinhold, 219
Four Books, 48 n., 51 n., 80, 132 n., 160, 181
Fourmont, Étienne, 1, 80 n., 88-9, 91, 93 n., 96, 98, 104-6, 118, 120 n., 121, 127, 129 n., 155 n., 159, 178, 194, 198, 204-10
Fourmont, Michel, 88, 98
Fréret, Nicolas, 88, 105, 129 n., 208-9
Friedrich III, 11
Friedrich Wilhelm, the Great Elector, 11, 62, 69, 72
Friedrich Wilhelm I, 11, 70, 83-4
Fu Muen Gi, 39
Fu Xi, legendary Chinese emperor, 112, 114, 172

Gabiani, Giandominico, S.J., 47 n., 74
Gaiatheddin Muhammad Cobenda (Uljaitu), 42
Galland, C., 90 n.
Gaubil, Antoine, S.J., 154-70, 181, 208
Gause, F., 14
Genghis Khan, 42, 164
Gerdes, Heinrich Walter, 160, 219
Gernet, Jacques, 35 n.
Gesner, Johan Mathias, 151
Gesner, Konrad von, 45
Ghazan, 40
Glahn, Else, 57 n.
Godwin, Joscelyn, 62 n.
Goldbach, Christian, 17, 18 n., 21 n., 57 n.
Golius, Jacobus (Gohl), 52, 63, 94, 96-7, 99, 105, 140
Gollet, Jean Alexis, S.J., 139 n.
Goncalves, J.A., 125 n.
Gonzales, Juan Mendoza de, 44-5, 55, 71, 136
Gram, Hans, 151 n.
Great Learning, 15 n., 35, 48, 49 n., 50 n., 55 n., 110, 132 n., 133 n., 134
Greaves, John, 40 n., 53-4
Greaves, Thomas, 61, 62 n.

Grebnitz, Elias, 71-72
Grelon, Adrien, S.J., 47n., 74
Grimaldi, Filippo, S.J., 75, 81, 84
Guang Wu, 31

Hai Pian (dictionary), 151, 163, 171, 189, 191-2, 198-202
Haupt, Johan Thomas, 114n.
Hayton the Monk, 41
Hayton, Armenian king, 41
Henning, Marcus, 45
Herbelot, Barthélemy, 90
Herdtrich, Christian, S.J., 49, 80n.
Hermann, Jacob, 17
Hervouet, Yves, 195n.
Hesiod, 136
Hevelius, Johannes, 67, 95
Hexagrams, order of, 114, 172-3
Hinckelmann, Abraham, 60
Historia Osrhoënae . . ., 20
Historia Regni Graecorum Bactriani . . ., 20
Hottinger, Johan Heinrich, 3
Huang, Arcadius, 87-8, 104, 129n., 178
Hulagu, 39
Hunter, William, 219
Hyde, Thomas, 61, 62n., 80-1, 84, 92, 96, 111, 126, 140, 219

Innocentia victrix, 34, 35n.
Intorcetta, Prosper, S.J., 34n., 48, 50, 131

Jablonsky, Paul Ernst, 15
Jariges, Philip Joseph, 196n.
Julien, Stanislaf, 129n.
Juškevič, A.P., 18n., 57n., 87n.

Kaempfer, Engelbrecht, 85
Kang Xi, 34, 87n., 121, 128n.
Kang Xi dictionary, 121, 125n., 169
Keyserling, Baron, 19, 157
Kirch, Christfried, 79, 159, 161, 189
Kircher, Athanasius, 49, 50, 55-6, 62, 76n., 69, 86, 112-3, 128, 130, 134, 136, 138
Klaproth, Julius, 152n.
Klotz, Christian Adolph, 7

Kochanski, Adam Adamandus, S.J., 69, 72
Koegler, Ignatius, S.J., 139n., 154-70
Kopelevič, Ju. Ch., 18n., 57n., 87n., 201n.
Korff, I.A., 201
Kraft, Eva, 71n., 77n., 132n.
Kranz, Johannes, 75
Kublai Khan, 40, 42
Kurtze Chinesische Chronologia . . ., 81n., 134, 137

Lacroze, Mathurin Veyssière de, 13, 13n., 14, 15, 31-2, 34, 67n., 85, 89n., 91-2, 93n., 98n., 103, 133n., 134n., 156n., 164, 175n., 188, 196, 220
Lactantius Firmanus, 136
Lambeck, Peter, 34n., 86n., 131-2
Lange, Lorenz, 100, 167
Lanier, Lucien, 50
Le Comte, Louis, 47n., 126
Le Gobien, Charles, 47n.
Le Moyne, Étienne, 53
Le Roux Deshauterayes, M.A.A., 183n., 217
Legaspi, Miguel Lopez, 44
Legge, James, 132n., 181n., 182-3
Leibniz, Gottfried Wilhelm, 6, 66n., 68-9, 75, 82-4, 90n., 92, 97, 102-4, 108, 113, 114, 124n., 158n., 180n., 194
Leonissa, Giovanni Nicolai de, 192n.
Leutmann, J.G., 185-6
Leyser, Polycarp, 32, 37, 38, 85-6
L'Hôpital, Marquis de, 104
Li Shi, 193
Li Shi-zhen, 190n.
Li Shi Zhongwen Zidian (dictionary), 126n.
Lionne, Arthus de, 87n.
Longobardi (Longobardo), Niccolo, 34, 55, 158, 164-5, 180n.
Loose, Hans Dieter, 21n.
Lotter, Johann Georg, 120, 166
Loyola, Martin Ignatius de, 44
Lu Gwei-Djen, 58n.
Lucaris, Cirillo, 51
Ludeken, Thomas, 68
Ludolff, Hiob, 14, 75, 77n., 89n., 103n.

Lundbæk, Knud, 46 n., 57 n., 127 n., 158 n.

Ma Yong, 52 n.
Magelhãs (Magaillans), Gabriel, 35 n., 47 n.
Magliabechi, Antonio, 90
Magnussen, Claus, 217 n.
Maigrot, Charles, 86, 87 n., 158, 161, 164
Mailla, J.A.M. Moriac de, 32 n.
Mairan, Jean Jacques Dortous de, 193 n.
Maizeaux, Pierre de, 104 n.
Mangu Khan, 39
Marcianus of Heraclea, 39
Marin, Jeronimo, 44
Martini, Martino, 36, 47 n., 52-5, 63, 71, 94, 110, 112, 120-1, 136, 156 n., 180, 202
Mascow, Johann Jacob, 86
Masson, Philippe, 59, 105
Mauclair, Paul Emilius de, 187, 204, 209
Maurus, Johannes S., 63
Mei Jing-zi, 125 n.
Mendoza, see Gonzales de Mendoza
Meniski, François Mesgnien, 69
Mentzel, Christian, 11, 13, 32, 35-7, 50 n., 58, 60, 66 n., 77-83, 85-6, 92, 96, 103, 109-11, 115 n., 117, 120, 125 n., 132 n., 134-5, 153, 160, 194, 202
Michael Chen Fuzong, 80
Minorelli, 158, 161
Montesquieu, Charles, 184
Montcornet, Balthazar, 70 n.
Montfaucon, Bernard de, 91
Montmort, Nicolas Remond de, 103, 113 n., 180 n.
Montmort, Pierre Remond de, 104 n.
Montucci, Antonio, 109 n., 125 n.
Mortimer, Cromwell, 187 n.
Moule, A.C., 56 n.
Müller, Andreas, 4, 11, 33, 36, 40 n., 54, 55 n., 60-77, 85 n., 86, 92, 95, 99 n., 103, 105-6, 111, 113 n., 114, 130, 177, 187, 199, 206
Müller, August, 61 n.
Müller, Gerhard Friedrich, 17, 18, 152, 188-90, 208-9, 219

Mungello, David E., 35 n., 51 n., 84 n., 114 n., 139 n.

Nasir-al-Din, 39, 53-4
Navarette, Domingo, 33-4, 48, 157, 158 n., 165, 180
Needham, Joseph, 58 n., 171 n., 186 n.
Nessel, Daniel de, 86
Nestorian Stele, 41, 55-7, 62, 64-5, 75, 77, 90 n., 156-7, 165
Nicholson, William, 60
Nicudar, 42
Noah, 136-7
Noël, François, 51, 67, 96, 140, 157
Notitiae Linguae Sinicae, see Prémare
Nouveaux mémoires sur l'état present de la Chine, 48 n.
Nouvelle relation de la Chine, 47 n.
Novissima sinica, 83 n., 74, 90 n.
Novus Atlas Sinensis, 52 n., 94 n.
Nü Gua, 118, 136-7, 177
Nunnus, 61

Ogdai, 39
Ogegin, 179
Opitz, Martin, 70
Origen, 73
Ošanin, I.M., 126 n.
Ostermann, Andrei Ivanovich, 20, 151, 157, 167, 169-70, 185, 190, 195, 207
Ovid, 136

Pada of Creutzenstein, Leopold Maximilian von, 152, 166 n., 189
Parrenin, Dominique, S.J., 20, 151, 154-70, 179, 185, 189-90, 191-6, 198, 201 n., 206
Pasqualin, Paolo Guiseppe, 87
Paulli, Simon, 76 n.
Pauthier, Guillaume, 138 n.
Pauw, 184
Pereira, André, S.J., 139, 154-70
Pereira, Diego, 43
Pfeiffer, August, 64-5
Phlegon of Tralles, 73
Pian Hai (dictionary), 163, 193, 198
Picques, Louis, 36, 79-80, 94, 111
Pinot, Virgile, 138 n.

Plano Carpini, Johannes, 41
Plautus, 99 n.
Polo, Marco, 40-1, 63-4, 91
Polyglot Bibles, 3, 61, 62 n.
Porrath, Anna Kathrina, 12
Possevino, Antonio, 46 n.
Potoçki, Jean, 152 n.
Prémare, Joseph, S. J.
  His Figurism 138
  On Mythology 35 n.
  His *Notitia Linguae Sinicae* 127, 129 n., 155 n., 156, 179 n., 208
Prester John, 164
Programma quo Bibliotheca . . ., 14 n.
Prokopowitsch, Theophanes, 5, 93, 96

Qian Long, 168
Qin Shi Huang Di, 180, 193

Rada, Martin de, 44
Raguzinskij-Vladislavich, Sawa, 20, 100 n., 151, 154, 190
Rashid-al-Din, 40 n.
Rawski, Evelyn S., 135 n.
Really, Conor, 62 n.
Reeland, Adrian, 98, 105
Rehbinder, Henrik Johan, 161 n.
Relations de divers voyages curieux, 50 n., 57 n., 67 n.
Rémusat, Abel, 1, 80 n., 128 n., 129 n., 183
Renaudot, Eusèbe, 89-90, 105
Rhubarb (Rheum officinale), 45
Ribera, Bernado, 94, 129
Ricci, Matteo, S. J., 33 n., 34, 46 n., 75, 157, 169
  His Tianzhu Shiyi 34 n., 162, 164
Rocca, Angelo, 45
Rodriguez, Juan, 127
Rostgaard, Frederik, 47 n.
Rougemont, François de, 47 n., 49
Roy, Olivier, 158 n.
Rubrouck, William of, 40
Rudbeck, Olaus, 59
Ruggieri, Michele, 45-6, 132 n., 169
Rule, Paul A., 138 n.
Rumpf, Georg Everhard, 76 n., 78

Sainte Marie, Antoine de, 180 n.
Sartorius, Johannes, 13
Saumaise, Claude (Salmacius), 51-3
Scaliger, Joseph Justus, 45, 53
Schall, Adam, S. J., 57
Schreiber, Michael, 72
Schumacher, Johann Daniel, 18, 19
Semedo, Alvaro, 46-7, 55, 62 n., 106, 115
Seraphim, A., 189
Shao Yong, 114 n., 172 n.
Sharpe, Gregory, 81, 188, 219
Shuo wen jiezi (dictionary), 125 n., 177, 199 n.
Sima Guang, 31, 35, 36
Simon, Renée, 154 n.
Simon, Walter, 57 n.
Sinicae Historiae Decas prima, 52 n.
SINOTRONIC CS 4000, 126 n.
Slaviček, Karl, S. J., 154-70
Sloane, Hans, 187 n.
Souciet, Étienne, S. J., 89, 158, 159 n., 181, 208, 210
Spinola, Francesco, S. J., 80
Spizelius, Theophilus, 55
Spring and Autumn Annals, 156 n., 159 n., 160, 179-84
Starck, Sebastian Gottfried, 61, 68
Sutton, Geoffrey Howard, 21 n.
Sylloge minutiarum lexici . . ., 77, 117

Teixera, Pedro, 52
Tentzel, Emil Wilhelm, 37, 61 n., 65, 70, 72 n., 75, 113
Terence, 63
Tertullian, 91
Thales, 136, 169
Theocritus, 5
Thévenot, Melchisédech, 50 n., 57 n., 67, 69, 79, 90, 120, 131
Thomassin, Louis, 59
Thousand Character Book, 99
Tibetan idol, 161
Tratados historicos . . ., 33, 48 n., 158
Trigault, Nicolas, 47 n., 55, 84

Uhl, I. L., 188, 196, 220

Uljaitu, 42
Ulugh Beg, 53-54
Ussher, James, 137n.

Vasil'ev, V.P., 126n.
Velasco, Luis de, 44
Verbiest, Ferdinand, S.J., 140, 157, 160, 166, 167n., 185-7
Villanueva, José, 127
Vincent of Beauvais, 41
Vindiciae Verborum Christi . . ., 13n.
Visdelou, Claude de, 87, 90n.
Voss, Isaac, 58, 90

Waldeck, C.F., 49n.
Wallenroth Library, 12
Walton, Brion, 61, 62n.
Wan Bao, see *Wen lin . . .*
Wang Shu-he, 58
Webb, John, 58, 168
Wenlin Shaqin Wanbao Quanshu, 57n.
Weston, David J., 199, 219
Wienau, R., 77n., 78n.
Wilkins, John, 4, 61, 106
Witek, John W., 139n.
Witsen, Nicolas, 66-7
Wolff, Abraham, 13, 92

Wolff, Christian, 16, 107n., 160, 169
Wolff, Johann Christian Christoph, 6, 19n., 31n., 166n., 190-1, 219

Xavier, Francesco, S.J., 43, 126
Xiao Er Lun, 82, 134-40
Xingli Daquan shu, 50n., 180n.
Xu Yuan-meng, 195n.

Yang Guang-xian, 33-4n.
Yates, Frances A., 138n.
Yong Le, 50n.
Yong Zheng, 153n., 186
Yu Jiao Li, 129n.

Za Zi, 81n., 135n.
Zacher, Hans J., 114n.
Zeno, Apostolo, 87
Zheng Zi Tong (dictionary), 82, 83n., 111, 119, 174, 178, 195n.
Zhong Wen Da Cidian (encyclopaedia), 176n.
Zhu Xi, 31n.
Zi Hui (dictionary), 82, 110n., 111, 117, 125n., 151, 160, 163, 174-9, 181, , 185, 189, 191-4, 198-9, 208,
Zishi Tongjian, 31n., 35